Contents

List of figures and tables

Figures

Tables

About the authors

Claudia Megele is the Head of Service for Quality Assurance and Principal Social Worker at Wiltshire Council, and a fellow of National Institute of Health Research (NIHR). Claudia is a practitioner, researcher and digital scholar with over 20 years of experience across academia, research and practice. She is a leader in holistic safeguarding (i.e. safeguarding both online and offline), digital professionalism and digital citizenship and ethics, as well as psychosocial and relationship-based practice. Her work includes over a decade of social media research, practice and leadership. Her research is specifically focused on psychosocial understanding of digital and social media and their impact on identity, safeguarding, relationships, professionalism and wellbeing.

Peter Buzzi is an international consultant with extensive experience in innovation and large transformation projects in Japan, Europe, the UK and the US.

SAFEGUARDING CHILDREN AND YOUNG PEOPLE ONLINE

A guide for social workers

Claudia Megele, with Peter Buzzi

First published in Great Britain in 2018 by

Policy Press
University of Bristol
1-9 Old Park Hill
Bristol
BS2 8BB
UK
t: +44 (0)117 954 5940
pp-info@bristol.ac.uk
www.policypress.co.uk

North America office:
Policy Press
c/o The University of Chicago Press
1427 East 60th Street
Chicago, IL 60637, USA
t: +1 773 702 7700
f: +1 773-702-9756
sales@press.uchicago.edu
www.press.uchicago.edu

British Library Cataloguing in Publication Data
A catalogue record for this book is available from the British Library

Library of Congress Cataloging-in-Publication Data
A catalog record for this book has been requested

ISBN 978-1-4473-3182-7 paperback
ISBN 978-1-4473-3184-1 ePub
ISBN 978-1-4473-3185-8 Mobi
ISBN 978-1-4473-3183-4 ePdf

Cover design by Policy Press
Front cover image istock
Printed and bound in Great Britain by CMP, Poole
Policy Press uses environmentally responsible print partners

Foreword

The internet is an extraordinary force for good but it is not designed with children in mind. Now more than ever, the internet offers children unlimited opportunities to learn, to explore and to engage with others and this critical part of their lives will only continue to grow. With this rapid progression however, more parents and carers are feeling increasingly out of their depth and unsure about the impact this digital engagement is having on the lives of children.

Increasingly children inhabit a world dominated by near constant social engagement through digital means. They are growing up in a world of 'selfies' and 'likes' where they wield the power to communicate globally. Given children's extensive online engagement, more needs to be done to prepare them for the risks that they might face online and to ensure that the digital space in which they interact is as supportive as possible.

Offline, adults aim not just to educate their children as they grow up, but to help them develop resilience and the ability to interact critically with the world; recognising that without these 'softer' skills, they cannot grow up as enabled agents and citizens to lead healthy, rewarding and productive lives. Given the impact and importance of digital technologies in everyday life, the same level of care, attention and importance should be given to children's online education and digital resilience. This book enables anyone working with children to do so while ensuring children and young people's safety and wellbeing both online and offline.

This book is unique in its approach as it encourages parents, carers, social workers and other safeguarding professionals as well as all adults working with children or involved in safeguarding them, to consider online risks in a critical and systematic manner and in the context of enhancing children's digital media knowledge and skills and digital citizenship. Too many approaches have previously favoured restrictive measures that either limit children's digital opportunities and growth or aim to prevent them from accessing the internet or a smartphone. It is important to recognise that these approaches are inadequate and often when these methods are employed, children continue their risk-taking behaviour without adult supervision exposing them to added risks while the opportunity for positive digital engagement and learning is lost. Rather than safeguarding young people, this disadvantages them as they experience less digital engagement, poorer digital literacy and therefore increased vulnerability to online risks.

This is perhaps most acute for looked after children whose social workers, foster parents or carers are often daunted by the prospect of online risks and digital safeguarding – when social media seems unlimited, how do you prevent inappropriate contact? This book addresses that critical question among others and provides a way of understanding and thinking about risk that enhances a child's digital rights and citizenship while still mitigating online risks.

As Children's Commissioner, I often hear about the 'digital deficit' that looked after children experience. Whether because they lack the technology or because they are simply not allowed internet access in the same way that their peers enjoy, their digital engagement seems to be limited. In today's world, denying children and young people access to the internet or digital technologies means isolating them from infinite resources, opportunities, and learning that are essential for their healthy development and resilience in a digital society. This not only increases their vulnerability but also their sense of isolation. This book addresses these challenges and provides a framework for understanding the dimensions and significance of children's online identities and behaviours while ensuring their safety and healthy development. Ultimately this book helpfully contributes to a wider narrative that we need to address. That is, how do we provide children with the support and equip them with the resilience, the information and the power they need to engage creatively and positively with the digital world?

While exploring children's online lives, our research has found that most teenagers lack basic digital literacy knowledge and do not know how to report their concerns on social media sites - or won't because they believe nothing will be done.

Teenagers are regularly agreeing to terms and conditions they could never be expected to understand, meaning they are waiving their right to privacy and allowing the content they post to be sold, without realising they are doing so. We also know that it isn't uncommon for teenagers to send naked pictures of themselves to each other or to come across hateful messages or pornographic material while browsing.

These risks could be prevented, in part, and better handled through improved digital literacy education. I recommended that digital citizenship should be taught from the age of four to fourteen with a voluntary extension for older children who would show the way to get the best out of the internet. It would include what it means to be a responsible citizen online, how to protect your rights online, how to respect others' rights online, and how to both engage and disengage with the online world. Therefore, I am pleased to see the robust digital citizenship programme proposed in this book. I also want to see greater transparency from social media companies. I want them to rewrite their terms and conditions and to take responsibility for how well they deal with concerns and complaints from their younger users. I would also like to see an independent digital ombudsman who would mediate between children and social media over the removal of content thereby providing some much needed online support. What we need is a positive and enabling approach to effective safeguarding while enhancing children's digital resilience, understanding and citizenship, and this book enables parents and professionals to do just that.

Anne Longfield
Children's Commissioner for England

"This is a much needed book which should be essential reading for young people and adults alike. If it stimulates a wider and easier discussion between them it will have served a very useful purpose. The rapid changes in the means of communication have resulted in many of us having to work hard to keep up. In fact it often feels like a game of catch-up. A colleague teased me that I probably use less than 5 per cent of the computing power of the smartphone in my hand! On reflection I had to conclude he was right. We adults have to accept that it is to the young that we look for help. The opportunities for good are quite remarkable, indeed, unlimited. But, sadly, those same powers can be misused and bring with them both dangers and harm. Therefore we must do all we can to ensure that young people are equipped to have all the benefits and are able to have healthy online engagements and enhance their digital citizenship, but are also able to avoid the dangers, risks and harm that may be associated with them. Children's safety and well-being are just too important to be put at risk by the misuse of technology or lack of informed support and guidance.

In this book the authors have helpfully created a systematic structure and approach to thinking about online risks which makes the subject so much more accessible and practical. The discussions and case examples demonstrate the complexities and intricacies of the online world and offer helpful advice for protecting children and young people while supporting them in their digital journey. This book is both informative and timely. I commend it most warmly and hope it will be very well used."

The Rt. Hon. The Lord Herbert Laming

"I warmly welcome this overdue, vital and measured guide to the safeguarding of children online. It provides comprehensive and practical guidance for the safeguarding of children and provides invaluable but pragmatic guidance to child protection staff, to parents, to teachers and to other professionals working with children. This book will make life considerably easier for adults who want to help children to navigate through online risks, while allowing them to gain the vast educational, cultural and entertainment benefits which the internet provides."

Professor Sir Martin Narey, Advisor to UK Government on Children's Social Care and former CEO of The Prisons and Probation Service in England and Wales

Introduction

This book is the fruition of our research, observations and experience over seven years, and we hope it contributes to greater appreciation and an evidence-informed understanding and assessment of online risks, protective factors and resilience for the effective and holistic safeguarding of children and young people.

Digital and social media technologies are an integral part of children's identities, experiences and development, and digital citizenship plays an increasingly important role in people's lives and is a critical component and a distinguishing factor that shapes children's identities and their future opportunities and life outcomes. Therefore, evidence-informed and comprehensive assessment of children's online identities, engagement and capabilities should be an essential and fundamental part of the holistic safeguarding of children and young people.

Notwithstanding these significant changes and developments, no books in social work currently address online risks and online safeguarding challenges and opportunities. Furthermore, there are no systematic and holistic models or approaches that can support practitioners in safeguarding children and young people online. Therefore, this book is aimed at filling that literature gap, and offering a holistic model that provides a systematic analysis and structured approach for assessing online risks, protective factors and resilience as well as examining online identities, behaviours, interactions and posts.

Traditionally the online safeguarding of children has been led by law enforcement and education, with the role of social work primarily focused on providing offline support. Therefore, this book equips social workers and all safeguarding practitioners with an evidence-informed understanding of online risks and resilience to enable them to take leadership in assessing online risks and the holistic safeguarding of children and young people while supporting their healthy and holistic development, including the development of their digital capabilities, digital citizenship and digital resilience.

The dichotomous thinking about human versus machine, online versus offline or virtual versus physical worlds fails to adequately describe the contemporary world (Haraway, 1991), and to recognise the seamless and liminal (simultaneously online and offline) experiences of children and young people. Hence, there is a need for a framework that offers a holistic view of children's safeguarding by considering their development, identities, behaviours, interactions and experiences, and by taking into account how 'human agents routinely produce both themselves and their machines as part human and part machine' (Downey et al, 1995, p 267). Indeed, digital citizenship and digital resilience are inextricably weaved into children's lives, and are fundamental and indispensable dimensions of children's lives and healthy and positive development (both online and offline, and both digital and physical). Furthermore, the rapidly changing context, forms and content of digital and social media technologies entail continuous and evolving risks, challenges and opportunities. Given this dynamic and fast-moving landscape and the multiplicity and diversity of online risks, it is essential to cultivate and enhance children and young people's digital resilience as a protective factor against inappropriate or adverse online exposure and experiences.

In this context, reactive approaches to safeguarding children that focus on children's offline experiences and consider their online engagement as a source of risk and an auxiliary activity at best, or an unnecessary and problematic activity at worse, are inadequate, and a negation of the liminal experiences of children and their fundamental importance for children's healthy development. Indeed, failure to adopt a holistic approach to children's lives and wellbeing is tantamount to neglect and inadequate care, professional failure and lack of due diligence. Hence, assessments and safeguarding should not only integrate online and offline risks, they should also support and enhance the development of children's digital capabilities, digital citizenship and digital resilience. Restrictive approaches should be used as a last resort and instead, assessments and safeguarding should be growth-oriented and promote choice, increase future possibilities and opportunities for children and young people, and enhance their life outcomes.

Therefore, drawing on relevant theory, research and the concept of sociomateriality and the liminal nature of human experience, in this book we offer a holistic model and structured approach to understanding and assessing online risks, protective factors and resilience and the safeguarding of children and young people both online and offline.

This book has the following objectives:

- To offer an introduction to online risks and online safeguarding.
- To offer a critical, evidence-informed, structured approach and analysis of online risks, protective factors and resilience and to examining online identities/profiles, behaviours, interactions and posts.
- To offer a critical, structured and systematic approach to understanding children's experiences and their inclusion in assessments and the safeguarding of children and young people online as well as the integration of this methodology into the assessment triangle for a holistic approach to assessments and safeguarding.
- To equip safeguarding practitioners with a critical and evidence-informed understanding of online risks, protective factors and resilience.

Given the importance of online digital identities and digital citizenship, and to meet the above objectives, we suggest that the online experiences of children can be thought of as the fourth dimension of the assessment triangle. Furthermore, drawing on relevant theory, research and practitioners' wisdom, we offer the 10 C's psycho-socio-ecological model as a systemic, critical and systematic framework for the assessment of online risks, protective factors and resilience, and their integration into the assessment triangle for the holistic safeguarding of children and young people both online and offline.

Below is a brief overview of the different chapters in this book:

Chapter 1 briefly considers the fast evolving and vastly diverse digital and social media landscape and some of its implications for practice and safeguarding. It introduces the concepts of digital footprint, digital childhood and cyborg childhood, digital professionalism, digital knowledge, skills and capabilities, the ENABLE model and smart learning wheel, and the principles of smart learning in the age of smart technologies.

Chapter 2 briefly examines online identity and introduces the identity prism for a holistic view and analysis of online identities.

This is followed by a discussion of digital citizenship, online boundaries and an overview of the differences between online and offline environments. The chapter concludes by introducing the Relational Boundary Scale (RBS) (Megele and Buzzi, 2018a) for a structured and analytic approach to understanding and assessing personal and professional relationships and boundaries.

Chapter 3 sets the foundation for the rest of the book. It begins with a discussion of risks, protective factors and resilience, and introduces the 10 C's risk typologies followed by a presentation of the 10 C's psycho-socio-ecological model as a framework for comprehensive yet situated and contextually relevant assessment of risks and safeguarding; this framework can also be used for examining online identities/profiles, behaviours, interactions, posts and other artefacts, or for creating online digital profiles on social networking sites (SNSs). We suggest that the 10 C's risk and potential typologies can be thought of as the fourth dimension of the assessment triangle, with the overall analysis of these risk typologies to be mapped and transposed on to and situated within the context of the psycho-socio-ecological model. In this manner, the 10 C's psycho-socio-ecological model provides a comprehensive, structured and dynamic understanding and critical analysis of risks and resilience, and a practical framework for assessments and holistic safeguarding of children and young people.

Chapter 4 discusses play and online media as a developmental space, and after a brief discussion of gamification, it presents a theoretical framework followed by a model for systematic and critical analysis of online/video games and their associated risks for children and young people. It then offers a brief example of dark play, concluding with a list of safeguarding considerations in relation to online/video games.

Chapter 5 is composed of two parts. The first begins with a brief discussion of 'internet addiction', followed by relevant safeguarding considerations. The second part focuses on challenges of safeguarding in relation to online gambling. The chapter concludes with a discussion of cognitive restructuring technique and some suggested considerations relating to restoring boundaries and balancing online–offline engagements.

Chapter 6 discusses sexting and its implications and challenges for social work and social care practice and safeguarding. It also presents a case example and offers a list of questions to offer a practical framework for use of the 10 C's psycho-socio-ecological model in practice, and for the holistic assessment of risks, protective factors and resilience.

Chapter 7 begins with a landmark case that resulted in a change of legislation in the UK. This is followed by a discussion presenting the stages of grooming and child sexual abuse, and a case example applying the 10 C's psycho-socio-ecological model. The chapter concludes with a brief review of emotions and behaviours associated with child sexual abuse.

Chapter 8 begins with a definition of cyberbullying and the differences between online and offline bullying. It then explores the role of the bystander and the influence of the online environment on bystander behaviour. This is followed by a brief note about the effects of cyberbullying and a review of some relevant legislation. The chapter concludes with detailed analysis of a case example using the 10 C's psycho-socio-ecological model.

Chapter 9 offers an introduction to cybercrime and some of its challenges. This is followed by a discussion of cyber-harm, the anti-social and pro-harm community, aggression in online romantic relationships and cyber-stalking, and gang aggression and violence. The chapter then presents a case example involving gang violence, and concludes with a reflection about the role of youth justice.

Chapter 10 offers an overview of online radicalisation followed by a case example. The example is analysed and unpacked using the 10 C's psycho-socio-ecological model. The chapter concludes with some practice reflections in relation to radicalisation.

Chapter 11 concludes by offering a glimpse and brief overview of the more significant current technological trends and developments and their impact on social work, health and social care.

The first three chapters of the book set the foundation for the book, while Chapters 4 to 10 offer specific case examples of some of the more significant and frequent challenges in safeguarding children and young people.

Online safeguarding is a vast and developing area of practice and research, and this is the first book that offers a comprehensive risk typology and practice model for assessment of online risk and practical safeguarding of children and young people. However, digital and social media technologies present complexities and significant opportunities and challenges. Aware of the diversity of online experiences and the nuanced and complex challenges associated with online safeguarding, we have tried to avoid simplistic and reductionist answers to complex problems. Therefore, this book does not offer a procedural guide to online safeguarding; instead it offers a model and set of tools and principles that can apply across different situations. Furthermore, in spirit of defending complexity, rather than providing 'guidelines', this book offers 'mindlines' (mindful suggestions and principles to keep in mind) for practice.

We hope you enjoy reading this book, and that it can help practitioners and parents/carers better appreciate the experiences and challenges faced by children and young people while supporting and safeguarding their developmental journey and healthy digital citizenship.

1

Digital lives and cyborg childhood

Tallulah Mary Scarlett Wilson was 15 years old when she jumped in front of a train and killed herself. The *Regulation 28: Prevention of Future Deaths report* (Chief Coroner of England & Wales, 2014), sent to the Secretary of State at the time, indicates:

> The jury found that, as a result of Tallulah's dissatisfaction with her friendship group, she created an online persona.
>
> She posted about self harm and suicide. She included photographs that she said were of herself following cutting.
>
> Her consultant psychiatrist gave evidence that, with hindsight, it seems that when her Tumblr account was deleted (following her mother's discovery of the damaging nature of her posts), Tallulah may have felt herself to be in some way deleted. Thousands of people had read her posts and she had gained great satisfaction from that. So on the one hand, her internet use may have had a negative impact; and yet on the other hand, preventing her internet use may have had a negative impact.
>
> The jury included the following in the narrative determination.
>
> This case has highlighted the importance of online life for young people. We all have a responsibility to gain a better understanding of this, which needs to be achieved through appropriate dialogue. This is a particular challenge for health professionals and educators.
>
> **Coroner's concerns**
> During the course of the inquest, the evidence revealed matters giving rise to concern. In my opinion, there is a risk that future deaths will occur unless action is

taken. In the circumstances, it is my statutory duty to report to you.

The **Matters of Concern** are as follows.

Although Tallulah was treated by a number of healthcare professionals, and her mother was extremely concerned about her wellbeing, no person who gave evidence felt that, at the time they were looking after Tallulah, they had a good enough understanding of the evolving way that the internet is used by young people, most particularly in terms of the online life that is quite separate from, but sometimes seems to be used to try to validate, the rest of life. (pp 1–2)

Unfortunately, the tragic story of Tallulah is not an isolated case and demonstrates that lack of due attention and understanding of the practice implications of technology may result in inadequate safeguarding, leading to tragic outcomes.

In contrast, the story of Bethany Mota who, after experiencing significant cyberbullying, was able to develop her social presence and identity through her YouTube channel demonstrates that with appropriate support, guidance and opportunity, young people can find validation and positive reward through their online engagement which can enable them to overcome even significant challenges such as cyberbullying (NBC News, 28 April 2015). Experiences such as those of Tallulah and Bethany demonstrate that positive and healthy online engagement is a question of quality of engagement within a psycho-socio-ecological context and that such engagements are often closely linked with children and young people's sense of self and identity, and offer potential for both positive growth and harm.

The spread, frequency, intensity and tragic consequences of cyberbullying, cyber-aggression and other forms of cyber-abuse and cyber-offending are an increasing and evolving safeguarding challenge. And as highlighted by the above examples, a lack of understanding of the various risks and their ramifications can have significant implications. However, given the vast and diverse range of technologies and their rapid evolution, many parents and practitioners feel they do not have the necessary knowledge and experience to be able to guide and advise the children and young people.

Therefore, it is important that parenting classes include digital literacy and digital citizenship education and that parents' digital literacy and knowledge and skills in relation to digital citizenship are considered and assessed as an integral part of parental capacity. Furthermore, practitioners should have clear guidance and training about e-professionalism/digital professionalism and online safeguarding and, as discussed later in Chapter 3, assessments and safeguarding should be holistic and should integrate both online and offline safeguarding. While this has been acknowledged in the Knowledge and Skills Statement for newly qualified social workers, we suggest that new digital knowledge, skills and capabilities, digital citizenship, e-professionalism/digital professionalism and online safeguarding also be included in the Professional Capabilities Framework as well as Knowledge and Skills Statement for social workers at all levels of experience.

Digital access and engagement, digital risks and resilience, digital literacy and digital citizenship have become the new sources of inequality in society affecting children and influencing their potential development and future opportunities. Therefore, it is essential that assessments include careful consideration of the child's digital access and engagement, knowledge of digital risks, digital resilience, digital identity and digital citizenship as an integral part of the holistic safeguarding of children and young people. Questions around public and private, audience, privacy, confidentiality, self-disclosure, digital permanence and deleting information, digital footprint and others should be conversation starters in practice, to assess and enhance children's digital access, digital resilience, digital literacy, digital identity and digital citizenship.

Although this book is the first dedicated to e-safeguarding in social work, it is part of a trilogy of books on online safeguarding that encompasses e-safeguarding children and young people, adults, and those experiencing mental health difficulties. The primary objective of this book is to offer a holistic and effective model and methodology for the assessment of online risks, their ramifications and their integration into the assessment triangle for evidence-based and holistic safeguarding of children and young people.

Children and young people's biopsychosocial developments are accompanied by increasing self-awareness, and in adolescence this includes a desire for autonomy and social belonging. Hence, as part of their developmental journey, through shared symbolisms, norms and behaviours, young people define themselves in relation to their peers and environment and as distinct from their parents. So in adolescence young people may attribute particularly high value to appearance (looks, style, grooming, etc), social symbols (clothing, mobile phone and technological gadgets, etc) and popularity (belonging and social acceptance). These factors, combined with peer pressure and the need for social acceptance, amplified by the effect of digital and social media technologies, create a constant competition for attention, and an increasingly challenging developmental landscape for young people where the 'wrong' appearance, missing social symbols or lack of adherence to group norms may result in harsh labelling, social exclusion or bullying.

Notwithstanding these challenges, social media offers unlimited positive and transformative potential for children and young people, and can help mitigate the risks of adverse outcomes.

Examples of helpful technology

Daniel is 16 and is able to contact his social worker via WhatsApp. This means that he can reach her even when he has no credit on his phone.

Johnson is 20 years old. He experiences psychosis and post-traumatic stress, and hears voices. However, his experience has improved as his use of avatar therapy has helped him develop a greater sense of control over the voices he hears.

Adolescents' risk-taking behaviour offers the potential for their learning, discovery and growth, but can also become a source of vulnerability as it exposes them to increased risks online. Furthermore, the transitional and identity challenges of adolescents may result in strengths (for example, capacity for change) and vulnerabilities (for example, more impulsive or emotional decision-making), which may be exacerbated by psychosocial challenges. For example, Ybarra and Mitchell (2004) demonstrate that the presence of psychosocial challenges can significantly increase the likelihood of bullying and harassing others – about one in three (32 per cent) of online perpetrators compared to one in ten (10 per cent) of non-perpetrators reported frequent substance abuse, and this increased the likelihood of online aggression against others by four times. Furthermore, research suggests that many young people seem to lack the ability to determine when to withhold personal information, even when they have received such training (boyd, 2008), and when to stop communication with strangers once identities have been revealed (Mesch and Talmud, 2010).

The challenges of e-safeguarding vary widely, and many digital and social media risks and potential negative outcomes have been normalised in society, their effects etched and relegated to the 'collective unconsciousness' that further complicates safeguarding practice. For example, there seems to be widespread diffusion of responsibility and complacency regarding terms and conditions and privacy. Although many social networking sites (SNS) regularly upgrade, update and change their software applications, and although many times this affects their users' privacy settings, most people neither recheck their privacy settings nor read the terms and conditions and the privacy policies for the different websites, SNS or social media platforms they use, not even when advised about changes in these policies – hence our reference to 'collective unconsciousness' as opposed to 'collective consciousness'. In a sense, we have grown used to 'the situation', and tend to assume that since so many others are using the same SNS it should be okay – this is an example of how risks are normalised in society and people's everyday experiences.

An example of compulsive technology

Sarah is 14 and lives in London. She was cycling frantically to get to her local library, and when she got there, she logged on to a computer and emailed her online friend, Jackie, in New York, 'begging' her for a 'BIG favour'. Sarah's parents had confiscated her phone for two weeks, and so she was emailing her username and password for Snapchat to Jackie, and needed Jackie to log in to her Snapchat account every day for the next two weeks to post random pictures and messages back and forth between Sarah and her friends. The subject or content of the message didn't matter. All that mattered was that it would keep the live stream of messages between Sarah and her friends, known as Snapstreak, alive; Snapstreaks 'die' if friends don't snap back and forth for 24 hours. Jackie is a Snapchat user herself – running a dozen Snapstreaks, she checks her phone about every 10 to 15 minutes. To keep the Snapstreaks going and when she at school and in a class, she just snaps a photo of the ceiling or the wall. Thanks to Jackie's help, Sarah's Snapstreak has been running for the past 210 days. Both Sarah and Jackie feel guilty if they don't respond immediately to their friends' snaps as they "don't want to leave them hanging".

This sort of excessive, and obsessive, behaviour binds many young people today, and is part of the reason why Snapchat is the 'darling' of social media at the moment. Indeed, this type of behaviour is the reason behind the business success of Snapchat, where it is valued at about US$20 billion, while Twitter, with a similar number of users, is valued at about US$3 billion.

Snapchat uses gamification techniques to generate user engagement. For example, long Snapstreaks are rewarded with coloured hearts and other emojis on users' profiles, and a number next to the emoji shows the number of days they have been Snapstreaking continuously. Indeed, the entire design of Snapchat and its functionalities are based on a combination of psychology, augmented reality and gamification techniques. Even the relationship between users is gamified by assigning various badges that classify the relationship. Most Snapchat posts disappear in 1 to 10 seconds, although Snap stories last for 24 hours, and Snapstreaks stay alive as long as they are regularly updated. It is not difficult to understand the reason for Snapchat's popularity among young people. For young people developing their social identity and seeking social belonging, Snapchat offers a combination of digital belonging, the fun of augmented reality, gamified social status and recognition, and digital catharsis. Snapchat users have long bought a myth about the ephemerality of messages and hence, the 'lack of consequentiality'.

However, the question is, what does the young person gain by compulsively snapping photos every few minutes to keep a Snapstreak alive? What is the significance of a Snapstreak badge beside a username, aside from indicating a compulsive snapping habit? It is, indeed, difficult to see the value of vacuous online postings as they neither represent valuable content nor a moment of interest or significance, and nor do they represent a relational bond between the snapping friends beyond the bond of Snapstreaking together. Indeed, in a market-oriented attentional economy, it is the eyeballs and clicks that generate dollars and cents, or pounds and pennies, and hence, in this case, 'addiction' is defined as business success and drives valuations.

This highlights the larger socioeconomic context that generates and intensifies risks and safeguarding challenges in society. This represents the dilemma and disconnect between a market economy obsessed with the triangle of efficiency, productivity and profit, without ever having to answer efficiency, productivity and profit for who, and quid bonum.

The Snapchat ecology (see Chapter 3) generates various risks of adverse outcomes for young people, and features such as Snapcash have increased such risks. Snapcash is a fast and free way of sending money between friends. The following scenarios are two examples of how Snapchat could be used by sexual predators.

Example from Snapchat

Old Snapchat scenario (before Snapcash)
- User A receives a snap from User X.
- User A replies with a snap of their own, still not knowing who they're sending pictures or videos to, or why.
- A mutual attraction develops and they exchange personal details.
- Eventually User X convinces User A to send some nude snaps.
- User X is now in possession of child pornography and has broken the law.

New Snapchat scenario (after the launch of Snapcash)
- User A receives a snap from User X.
- User A replies with a snap of their own, still not knowing who they're sending pictures or videos to, or why.
- A mutual attraction develops and they exchange personal details.
- Eventually User X asks User A to send some nude snaps.

- User A refuses.
- User X offers to send User A money via Snapcash.
- User A reluctantly agrees, sends nude snaps and receives money from User X for producing what is, in effect, child pornography.

Digital and cyborg childhood

Opportunities and challenges

Steven is a three-year-old boy from a middle-class English family. Shortly before his first birthday, his mother began showing him animated children's songs on her iPad. Steven was excited about the music and the images, and as soon as he could talk, he began singing, as he could, some of the songs his mother played for him. When Steven was about two, his mother bought him his own iPad and introduced him to a computer-based animated language teaching app. Initially he could not manipulate the screen, and so his mother handled the controls. However, he quickly learned what to do, and began manipulating the screen by himself, and soon learned how to play games on his iPad. His mother was pleased by his progress, and to enhance his cognitive abilities and eye-hand coordination, she introduced him to some simple games to learn about animals, play the piano and so on. Steven quickly learned about the games and his mother was delighted with his progress, developing his digital literacy and preparing himself for the digital world. However, as things progressed his mother became more concerned as he became more and more attached to his iPad and video games. Now, Steven is just over three. He is restless and inseparable from his iPad. Every night he sleeps with his iPad by his side and every morning when he wakes up, he picks his iPad up, logs in to games sites and plays games all day. He is no longer interested in going outdoors or reading nursery rhymes, colouring or scribbling on paper.

Children and young people move between online and offline spaces and experiences in a seamless manner, and it is essential that they are able to engage and enhance their digital literacy and digital citizenship in the same manner that they develop their knowledge of themselves and the world around them. Indeed, children's experiences can be better defined as liminal experiences that take place in an in-between 'potential space' (Megele, 2015) that is neither fully online nor fully offline; it is rather a hybrid of both online/virtual and offline/physical/corporeal experiences (Buzzi and Megele, 2011a). 'Digital childhood' refers to children experiences of living and growing in an increasingly digital world. However, as we have elaborated elsewhere (see Buzzi and Megele, 2011a), Merleau-Ponty's assertion '... that visceral body whose capacity for language and society is the foundation of all other institutions ...' (O'Neill, 1989, p 3, quoted in Buzzi and Megele, 2011a), and the methodology of semiotic phenomenology (Lanigan, 1992, quoted in Buzzi and Megele, 2011a) offer us a theoretical framework to capture the reflexive expressions and (re)presentations of the liminality of human subjectivity, straddling both offline/physical and online/virtual realms. This theorisation encompasses and goes beyond digital childhood and the cyborg ontology, and allows us to define cyborg childhood and cyborg identity as '... the way that human agents routinely produce both themselves and their machines as part human and part machine' (Downey et al, 1995, p 267); representing an inseparability and a merging and fusing of human and machine. Therefore, considerations of assessment, safeguarding, identity, risks, needs, protective factors and resilience should be positioned within this general and holistic framework, and be carried within the context of such liminality, including both online and offline aspects of identities, risks, needs, protection and resilience. Furthermore, children's notion of risk, protection and resilience and safeguarding concerns and priorities may differ significantly from adults' or practitioners' concerns. Therefore, it is important that the definition, identification and assessment of risks, needs, protective factors and resilience are carried out co-productively and in a developmentally appropriate manner together with children and young people.

Digital footprint

Digital and social media technologies are an integral part of young people's identities and experiences. However, online posting and use of digital and social media technologies create a digital trace that remains in time and generates a digital footprint or trail that can be searched and retrieved at any time in the future. Such a trace can influence and shape online identities, reputations as well as future opportunities and possibilities, and can be used by employers, regulators, people who access services, friends and colleagues, criminals and fraudsters, or others for various purposes, ranging from checking a person's suitability for employment to cyberbullying, identity theft and other criminal purposes.

Our private attitudes and expressions have become much more visible and public today than they ever before. Once posted online, behaviours, actions, conversations, interactions and ideas that would have gone unnoticed, undisputed and forgotten in the past find relative permanence (Megele, 2014a, 2014b) and become searchable and retraceable to their original creator/producer. This poses ethical and safeguarding challenges for both practitioners and young people. Many employers and employment agencies use online searches and applicants' digital footprints to check their backgrounds and to evaluate their suitability. Furthermore, recent fitness to practice hearings in the UK indicate that regulators use online information and postings in their judgments and decision-making. Digital footprint also has significant implications for children's identity, rights to privacy and digital citizenship. A study conducted by the Parent Zone, on behalf of Nominet and involving 2,000 parents, showed that on average parents share/post 973 photos of their children online before the child's fifth birthday; an average of 195 photos per year and rising to 208 photos per year for children below the age of 16 (Nominet, 2015). The study also shows that 17% of these parents had never checked their Facebook privacy settings and almost half (46%) had only checked their privacy setting once or twice, and although 70% of parents used smartphones for taking and posting photos online, fewer than half (49%) were aware that location data could be stored with the photo. Also, 39% of parents on Facebook and 17% of parents on Instagram thought that they had the sole rights to images posted online. However, the terms and conditions of most SNS, including Facebook and Instagram, state that they have the right to use uploaded images to promote their services without explicitly asking permission of the user who uploaded the photo. These figures are concerning, as children's photos can be misused by sexual predators (*The Telegraph*,

13 January 2015) and may be used in grooming and to target children. Therefore, what is needed is a more nuanced and critical understanding and approach to question of privacy and decisions relating to online posting of information and images.

E-professionalism/digital professionalism and our changing relationship with technology

As social technologies – both in terms of devices (for example laptops, pads, smartphones, etc) as well as media and services – are increasingly embedded in everyday life and experiences, they change the way we use and relate to technology. Indeed, 'our tools are not just external props and aids ... they are deep and integral parts of the problem-solving systems we now identify as human intelligence' (Clark, 2006) (Google is a good example of such tools).

This new way of being and relating to technology goes beyond use of digital and involves a seamless merging of human and technology that expands our capabilities and offers unlimited opportunities, risks and challenges. However, our changing relationship with technology also highlights the need for e-professionalism, or digital professionalism.

Although the principles of digital professionalism are similar to those of traditional/face-to-face professionalism, digital professionalism requires practitioners to extend and apply the profession's ethics and values in a meaningful and contextually relevant manner in digital context. However, this does not mean that digital professionalism is simply an extension of existing concepts of face-to-face professionalism. Digital professionalism also involves the ability to identify and effectively manage new risks and opportunities and to use the affordances of digital and social technologies to enhance practice and its outcomes. Therefore, digital professionalism can be thought of as the intersection between the face-to-face professional ethics, values and principles with the roles, risks, affordances and challenges of digital and social media technologies and in the context of the changing and shifting social, cultural and political landscape within which professionals operate and professionalism is achieved (see Figure 1.1).

Figure 1.1: Components of digital professionalism

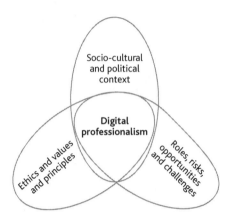

Source: Megele and Buzzi (2018d)

Although professional values do not change significantly online versus offline, there are significant differences between online and offline communications, behaviours and environments; we will explore these differences in Chapter 2. Drawing on the work of Jenkins et al (2006), there is a range of knowledge, skills and capabilities that underpin e-professionalism/digital professionalism. Figure 1.2 presents an overview of the knowledge and skills required for digital professionals, while Figure 1.3 offers an overview of the digital capabilities required for digital professionalism.

Figure 1.2: Knowledge and skills for digital citizenship and digital professionalism

Figure 1.3: Digital capabilities for digital professionalism

Digital Capabilities for Digital Professionalism

- Simulate: interpret & construct models of the world (e.g. problems, solutions, processes).
- Identify & manage online risks and opportunities and make respectful, purposeful & meaningful choices.
- Curate & evaluate the reliability and credibility of information & sources.
- Multitasking: capability to scan the environment and shift focus onto salient information and details.
- Transmedia appropriation: follow gather information across multiple media & remix media & content to produce meaningful information.
- Coproduction: collaborate to achieve common goals and to coproduce shared solutions and outcomes;
- Negotiate one's journey across diverse communities and media & recognise & appreciate multiple perspectives & diverse values & norms.
- Networking: connect, share & relate to others to develop one's social capital in a meaningful manner;
- Pool knowledge & experiences & tap into collective intelligence to inform, complement and enhance one's thinking, knowledge and behaviour
- Use & relate to technology as an extension of self to enhance own experience knowledge, thinking and decision making.
- Ethical recognition: to assess varying circumstances & to respond in an appropriate, ethical, proportionate and professional manner.

ENABLE: the principles of smart learning in the age of smart technologies

Jenkins et al (2006) argue that through affiliation (formal and informal membership of online communities), self-expression (producing new creative forms of content), collaborative problem-solving (working in groups and teams and using media – Wikis, alternative reality, etc, to develop new knowledge) and circulation (sharing and flow of data, content and information), children and young people take part in a participatory culture, and this serves as a new distinguishing and critical success factor separating those who 'succeed' from those who are being 'left behind' as they enter school and the workplace. Such a context poses at least four important challenges:

- *Participation gap:* unequal access to digital opportunities, experiences, skills and knowledge exacerbates existing inequalities in society that influence children and young people in preparing themselves for full and effective participation in an increasingly digital world.

- *Transparency problem*: being born and raised digital may challenge young people in learning to see and recognise the ways media influence and shape the world and the perceptions of the world.
- *Ethical challenge*: the shifting, overlapping and dissolving online boundaries and digital convergence between content, context, contact and conduct pose ethical challenges in defining the different domains of life, and generate risks and ontological uncertainties in relation to individual identity and development.
- *Challenge of digital citizenship*: the evolving notions, nature and forms of knowledge, learning and development, professionalism, relationships and socialisation influence practice as well as children and young people's identities and their preparation and future possibilities for a healthy, effective and rewarding social participation and citizenship.

Given the importance of continuous learning and professional development, practitioners can use the principles of smart learning to tap into the power of smart and social technologies for their CPD. Figure 1.4 presents the ENABLE smart learning wheel, which encapsulates the principles of smart learning, while Figure 1.5 offers an example of the application of the ENABLE smart learning principles.

Figure 1.4: ENABLE smart learning wheel

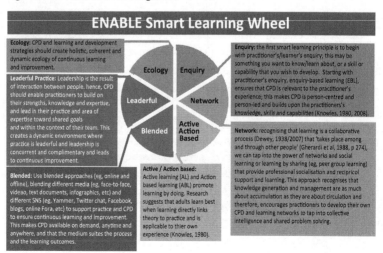

Figure 1.5: An application of the ENABLE smart learning techniques

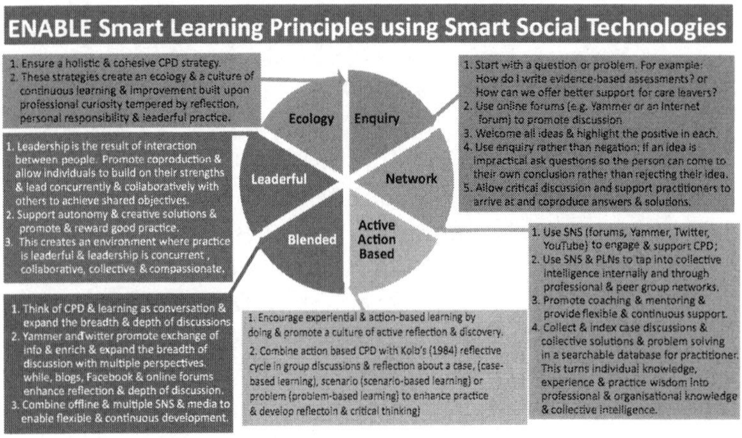

ENABLE Smart Learning Principles using Smart Social Technologies

In this sense, the ENABLE (Enquiry and Networked Active Blended Leaderful Ecology) model offers a dynamic and flexible approach to 'smart' learning in the age of 'smart' and social technologies. Therefore, the components of ENABLE pedagogy include:

- *Enquiry-based learning* is learner-centred and begins with learners' curiosity and enquiry, offering situation-focused open-ended and flexible learning that is relevant to learners' experiences and needs. It can be used to develop learners' skills, analysis and critical thinking and reflective capabilities.
- *Networked learning* leverages social learning and co-production, and taps into learners' zone-of-proximal development to scaffold their knowledge and capabilities (Vygotsky, 1978; Megele, 2014a, 2014b).
- *Active and action-based learning* engages learners in experiential learning and Kolb's (1984) cycle of concrete experience, reflective observation, abstract conceptualisation and active experimentation, developing higher thinking and deep/higher learning.
- *Blended learning* allows for a blending of approaches (for example, combining enquiry and active learning), systems (for example, different SNS), environments (online/virtual and offline/face-

to-face) and modes of learning (formal, informal, non-formal) in a complementary manner, to offer holistic and effective learning and to enhance learners' experience.

- *Leaderful learning and leaderful practice* recognises that leadership is relationally defined and is a distributed, social and dynamic phenomenon constructed in interaction and collaboration with others, therefore encouraging concurrent leadership. This conceives of leadership as a journey and as a continuous process of becoming rather than a destination or individual quality.

- *Evidence-informed and co-productive ecology:* the above combination of approaches should form an integrated and integrative evidence-informed and co-productive leaderful ecology (Megele, 2014a, Megele and Buzzi, 2018a), offering continuous learning, improvement and development.

The ENABLE model has been used in academia, charities and local authorities to implement dynamic and effective CPD programmes,, and can be used at all levels of learning to develop professionals' digital citizenship and digital professionalism.

A mindline about language and its impact

Humans are storytellers, and as we read, speak, interact and communicate we draw a picture of ourselves and of others and of our perception of 'reality'. Indeed, the rhetorical routine of conversations constructs particular versions of 'truth', circumstances and experiences, and guides our thoughts, emotions and behaviour, shaping our experiences, possibilities and hence, our 'destiny'. As McLuhan (1964) suggests the medium is the message, and the way we communicate and the choice of medium transforms the very essence and meaning of the message.

Therefore, as we speak about digital and social media technologies and their applications and impact, we express our experience of it, and in expressing our experience, we shape it by positioning ourselves in relation to that experience, its meaning, significance and significations. In effect, by speaking about our experiences we not only communicate our experiences, we also transform and shape them by defining their nature and by positioning ourselves in relation to the psychosocial appendices, dilemmas and intricacies associated with those experiences. In this sense, talk, conversation and communication can be treated as social actions that explore, frame and shape the interplay between people, sociocultural practices and institutional and social structures and dynamics. Therefore, talking about safeguarding conditions and shapes its meaning, significance, concerns and practices in society.

There are inherent risks with digital convergence and the widely integrated digital and social media technologies. However, as offline vulnerabilities and potentials are projected and amplified in online spaces, behaviours, posts and practices, and as these permeate diverse domains and increasing aspects and moments of everyday lives, they present a new hybrid and liminal 'reality' that shapes the contemporary human experience. This underlines the significant responsibilities, opportunities and challenges faced by safeguarding practitioners who have to navigate and manage increasingly complex, multilayered and evolving challenges in safeguarding children and young people, both online and offline.

Speaking of language and its impact, although some social work authors have used Prensky's (2001) notion of 'digital natives' and 'digital immigrants', these are contested terminologies (Selwyn, 2009) that construct a digital divide between young people and older adults treating each as monolithic groups, and depicting young people as technologically equipped, adept and tech-savvy; this is stigmatising for adults, and discounts the experience of young people who don't have access to technology. Hence, we encourage practitioners to adopt a more critical perspective in relation to digital knowledge and skills, and digital citizenship. Therefore, this book offers an integrated model for a critical and evidence-informed understanding and an analytic and structured approach to identification and assessment of risks, protective factors and resilience for the holistic assessment and safeguarding of children and young people.

The next chapter examines digital citizenship and boundaries, the differences between online and offline environments, and their implications for safeguarding practice.

2

Online identity, digital citizenship and boundaries

Online identity

Gilroy (1997, p 301) suggests 'We live in a world where identity matters', while Hall (1996, p 2) argues that, in recent years, we have seen 'a veritable discursive explosion' around the concept of identity, which reflects its centrality to the question of agency and politics, including identity politics. Indeed, advances in technology have added new dimensions to identity, and have made the concept of identity ever more diverse and complex.

But what is identity? What would you say if someone asked you who you are? Would you just give your name? Or would you say what you do? 'I am a ....' Or where you live or come from? 'We are actually neighbours ....' 'I live in ....' etc. These and other indications are different ways we identify, describe and relate to ourselves and others, and may be considered as dimensions of our identity or as part of our identity narrative. But what is identity? What do we mean by 'self' or 'being ourselves'?

Selves in post/late modernity are set within a growing array of life options (Giddens, 1991), and digital and social media technologies, from different SNSs to Bitmojis, offer infinite ways we can present and make sense of identity. We offer a more comprehensive discussion of identity elsewhere (see Megele and Buzzi, 2018b), but although a detailed discussion of identity is beyond the scope of this text, a brief examination of identity can help us highlight some of the important differences between online and offline domains and behaviours and their associated risks and significance. Therefore, let us briefly examine the notions of narrative, performative and dialogical identity, as the combination of these theorisations of identity can help us better understand the contemporary dimensions of identity, and the impact and influence of digital and social media technologies on its creation, maintenance, representations and development.

Narrative identity

Identity can be understood as narratives, stories that people tell themselves and others about themselves and others, stories about who they are and are not, and how they would/should be (Martin, 1995). This allows for a decentring of self that treats 'oneself as another' (that is, telling ourselves about ourselves), and is the essence of reflective identity providing the 'narrative component of the comprehension of self' (Ricoeur, 1992, p 201, quoted in Megele and Buzzi, 2018b).

SNSs and blogs, vlogs, tweets, snapchats, Facebook posts, comments, likes, Yaks and more, offer unlimited possibilities for telling ourselves and others stories about ourselves and others. In this sense, it serves as a mirror offering a projection of self to self and others, and providing the 'narrative component of the comprehension of self'. Hence, cyberspace offers a unlimited potential for reflection, learning and self-development.

Performative identity

Goffman's (1959) seminal work, *The presentation of self in everyday life*, offers a dramaturgical analysis of social life as a theatrical performance (people performing roles), while Turner (1979, p 72) states that 'Man is homo performans ... in the sense that man is a self-performing animal and his performances are, in a way, reflexive: in performing he reveals himself to himself.' Indeed, Butler (1988) argues that the creation of selves is an embodied performance that is processual, wherein individuals are always 'on the stage' and 'within the terms of the performance' (1988, p 526), yet as script can be read and enacted in different ways, identity performance can lead to different reflections and interpretations (Megele and Buzzi, 2018c). Hence, while social life is about playing social roles and all performances are citations or enacted ways of doing (for example, gender, race, class, ethnicity, age, profession, skills, abilities, etc), selves are liminal and negotiated in and through a process of becoming rather than a fixed entity, and therefore, conceptualising identity as performance does not mean that it is 'false'; it is rather because identity is done through performance.

Thinking of identity as performance, and considering that social media offer a virtually unlimited audience and that identity performances are particularly powerful in the presence of an audience (Megele, 2014b) helps us understand how social media can encourage exaggerated behaviour and magnify risks and vulnerabilities online.

Dialogical identity

An important aspect of theatre performance is dialogue. Indeed, everyday conversations, communications and interaction can be conceived as dialogue. In Bakhtin's (1984) words:

> … to be, means to be for the other and through him, for oneself. Man has no internal sovereign territory, he is always on the boundary; looking within himself he looks in the eyes of the other or through the eyes of the other. I cannot do without the other; I cannot become myself without the other; I must find myself in the other; finding the other in me in mutual reflection and perception. (Bakhtin, 1984, pp 311-12)

Hence, relational self and dialogical identity are interactional, fluid and continuously becoming (constructed and defined in interaction with others), and are both reflective and constitutive (Megele, 2015; Megele and Buzzi, 2018c). This also highlights the significance of boundaries as the locus of self and its definition and formation (that is, boundaries define self). Given that interactions inevitably involve difference and power imbalance, dialogical identity helps us appreciate difference and explore intersectional power relations including gender, age, race, religion, ethnicity, culture, etc. Furthermore, dialogical identity highlights the importance of dialogue and voice, underlining the value and significance of mutual recognition, co-production, validation and validating experiences.

Prism of identity

Turkle (1995) reflects on the meaning of identity in the age of cyber-technology, and suggests that 'identity' should be considered as a third dimension of the analysis of public–private. Although technology, the internet and the context of our lives have significantly changed since the 1990s, the question of identity and identity (re) construction/maintenance remain important areas of reflection and research. Therefore, given the diverse, multidimensional and complex nature of identity in the digital age, we suggest that the combination of narrative, performative and dialogical approaches to identity forms an analytic yet pragmatic prism (see Figure 2.1) that offers a critical lens for a more holistic, relevant and dynamic understanding of online digital identities (Buzzi and Megele, 2011b; Megele and Buzzi, 2018c). This approach to identity is embedded in the 10 C's psycho-socio-ecological model for the holistic assessment and safeguarding of children and young people (this model is introduced in the next chapter).

Figure 2.1: Identity prism (see Megele and Buzzi, 2018c)

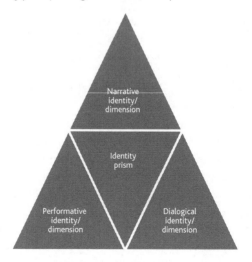

Digital citizenship

Initially digital citizenship was equated to internet access and was therefore focused on increasing the number of digital citizens (Mossberger et al, 2008). However, online identities create cyber-relationships, cyber-communities and cyber-sociality, and present both opportunities and challenges for individual growth and development as well as creative and holistic support and services, and co-productive e-governance including digital rights and responsibilities, as reflected in the notion of 'digital citizenship'. While artificial intelligence (AI) and other innovations further transform and exponentially increase the dimensions, opportunities and challenges associated with digital citizenship. Therefore, today, the notion of digital citizenship includes behavioural, attitudinal and other dimensions, including the rights and responsibilities aspects of citizenship. In other words, digital citizenship goes beyond access, and encompasses individuals' rights, responsibilities, safety, security and wellbeing, and involves the ability to make appropriate use of technology and to make safe, responsible and respectful choices online.

The latest report in the UK by the Growing Up Digital Taskforce of the Office of the Children's Commissioner (2017) acknowledges the importance of digital citizenship and highlights the need for digital citizenship education for children. It calls for three government interventions (see foreword):

1. the creation of digital citizenship programme, to be compulsory in every school from ages 4-14;
2. implementation of the intent of the General Data Protection Regulation, by introducing simplified Terms and Conditions for digital services offered to children; and
3. a new Children's Digital Ombudsman to mediate between under 18s and social media companies.

These are essential to cultivate and protect digital citizenship among children and young people. Indeed, we suggest that such a digital citizenship education/programme should include the following components (see also Figure 1.2):

- digital safety and security
- privacy and digital boundaries
- digital communication and relationships
- digital footprint
- self–image and identity
- reputation management
- digital and information literacy
- cyber–aggression and cyber–abuse (including cyberbullying)
- proactive citizenship and understanding the role of the bystander
- digital rights and responsibilities
- creative credit and copyright.

Promoting good digital citizenship helps promote respectful choices and behaviour online. Proactive digital citizenship includes civic digital participation and co-production, and is foundational for civil rights, equality and democracy. Furthermore, it can serve as a pre-emptive and proactive approach for addressing cyber-abuse and cyber-aggression. For example, while there are doubts about raising awareness as an effective prevention strategy for cyberbullying, there is increasing evidence and focus on influencing social norms and enhancing the role of the bystander to reduce bullying (Jones et al, 2011). This is an example of the importance of the role of bystander as a proactive digital citizen in addressing cyber-abuse and cyber-aggression, and promoting effective social norms that cultivate a healthy and dynamic digital citizenship.

Although schools should be responsible for the delivery of citizenship programmes and children's learning, they will need parental collaboration in promoting effective digital citizenship. However, although parents often express concern about their children's use of the internet and online activity, many parents feel that they do not have sufficient skills, knowledge and familiarity with technology to be able to guide their children. Therefore, as part of their parental and community engagement and programmes, schools and childcare centres should offer parental workshops that address digital citizenship topics and enhance parental skills in this area.

Practitioners and educators can use the 10 C's psycho-socio-ecological model (see the next chapter) together with the earlier mentioned components of digital citizenship education/programme to explore and enhance children and young people's digital knowledge and skills and digital citizenship.

This also highlights the role of local authorities including early intervention as well as safeguarding practitioners, especially when the local authority has parental responsibility or when parents need help in supporting their children's digital citizenship. In such cases, practitioners should be able to help complement parental skills and to explain, educate and support children with their digital citizenship skills – which means that practitioners should be well versed in this area. Employers must therefore ensure that practitioners have the appropriate training, knowledge, skills and understanding in relation to digital citizenship, including online risk assessment and safeguarding to ensure holistic support and safeguarding of children and young people.

Online boundaries

From borders between nations on a world map that represent territorial boundaries, which are at times reinforced by physical boundaries such as check points or passport control, to interpersonal boundaries defined in relationships between people, boundaries are often understood as points of demarcation or separation. However, as we have explored elsewhere (see Buzzi and Megele, 2011b), in a network society, boundaries can no longer be thought of simply as a spatial reality. Therefore, drawing on Bakhtin (1984), we define boundaries as points of encounter (rather than separation) and as thresholds (rather than barriers) that define, protect and enhance the integrity of identities, organisms, systems and subsystems (Megele and Buzzi, 2018c).

Digital and social media technologies have resulted in increasing dilution and fusion of boundaries, and a convergence of connections, content, contact and context offer significant opportunities and challenges for individuals, society and safeguarding. Contemporary human experience encompasses both online/virtual and offline/physical dimensions, and therefore self and human subjectivity are constituted and constructed at the boundary between self and the other, and are liminal (always becoming), straddling both online and offline dimensions, and always including a residual part of both.

Although such understanding of boundary helps us appreciate the dimensions and implications of online posts and behaviours, it also exposes a number of important challenges. Therefore, in the remainder of this chapter we explore some of the differences between online and offline environments and the implications, challenges and opportunities associated with them. We conclude by presenting the Relational Boundary Scale (RBS) as a tool for thinking about and assessing personal and professional relationships and boundaries.

Notion of place and digital embodiment

The notion of place in cyberspace is represented in multiple forms. While cyberspace and most social media platforms transcend physical geographies and spatial boundaries, others, such as Yik Yak, are bound by a dynamic notion of place and operate within a given radius from one's physical location (geolocation). While cyberspace offers a boundless world, there are various ways people can search and connect with their local communities based on geographic proximity.

Yik Yak: an example of place and digital embodiment

In a world of increasingly boundless world communication, Yik Yak is a popular social network that connects people in their local area and based on geographic proximity, generating a sense of local community. In fact, its motto is 'Find Your Herd', suggesting that 'Yik Yak helps you feel at home within your local community.' While other social media such as FourSquare help people to find entertainment, restaurants, shopping or services based on their location, Yik Yak also allows its users to announce their location to their network and to find people from their network who may be close by.

Although there are many positive uses for these and other social media platforms, they can also be used in harmful ways and ways that were not originally intended, such as for bullying. To combat this, Yik Yak has disabled yaks (Yik Yak posts) near middle schools and high schools.

32

When a user chooses to broadcast their location or a photo or a description in relation to a given place/venue, they are recreating that place and space through that picture or narrative while reflexively constructing their own digital identity by positioning themselves in that space and time. Although some may perceive cyberspace as virtual and therefore a 'bodiless realm', such practices inscribe and position the body within digital, physical and sociocultural space, and are reflective of the practice of digital embodiment. Other practices of embodiment in cyberspace include choice of online avatars or profile image or virtual or animated bodies. Such acts of embodiment have important implications for individual identity and safeguarding.

Audience and framing

Goffman (1959, p 72) insightfully states: 'All the world is not, of course, a stage, but the crucial ways in which it isn't are not easy to specify', and Megele (2014b) argues that identity negotiations are particularly powerful in the presence of an audience, and each social media posting, comment or conversation 'is produced in relation to, and for an audience' (p 48) be it an actual, hypothesised, implied or imagined audience. Even what may seem 'non-directed' or 'chaotic communication' on social media 'does not negate the foundational element inherent in all communication, that all communications are directed at some form of audience' (Megele, 2014b, p 48).

To explain framing of identities or identity management online, Megele draws on Heidegger's (1977) notion of enframing, and explains that enframing is a mode of representing self and the world, limiting the range of possibilities and 'allowable' experiences to promote a preferred version/representation of the world. Enframing 'is aimed at constraining or rewriting, or even prescribing, how the world is to be perceived. Nonetheless, we can never be free from enframing, although it filters our world' (Heidegger, 1977). This is the essence of online identity and reputation as well as identity and reputation management, and explains the importance and significance of online postings for children and young people as well as professionals.

Furthermore, Goffman's assertion refers to the performative aspect of the identity prism as described earlier. Indeed, each online posting or artefact is produced in relation to and for an audience. This audience may be actual, immediate and visible, with well-defined expectations, or it may be imagined or virtual or hypothesised, and constructed by the actor/speaker. In offline/ face-to-face interactions the audience is usually well defined, and the message is tailored for that specific audience within the context of the conversations, and guided by physical cues (Goffman, 1956). However, the lack of physical boundaries means that online interactions and posts have much greater visibility, and therefore, either explicitly and consciously or implicitly and unconsciously, are addressed to broad audiences, most of whom may be invisible or assumed (people who may be lurking, watching or reading a posting now or in the future). Megele (2014b) argues that identity negotiations/performances are particularly powerful in the presence of an audience, and so the perception of an ever-present audience magnifies the impact and dimensions of online postings. Furthermore, the lack of boundaries implies that different audiences (for example, friends and family as well as colleagues, one's boss, clients, etc) see the same posting. This transforms the notion of identity and poses important ethical challenges for both children and professionals, although we should note that some social media platforms such as Facebook allow the user to create separate audiences who will then only see postings within a given virtual space. Therefore, all communication and online postings 'are directed at some form of audience', and most are 'being sent to diverse, ambiguous, and/or imagined audiences' (Megele, 2014b, p 48).

Transformation of professionalism and the need for authenticity

Traditionally the distinction between personal and professional roles was interlinked and conceptualised as a function of physical space and location. Indeed, the separation of workplace from home provided a clear distinction between public and private spheres, with two distinct audiences and expected behaviours. Hence, professional identity was comprised of professional performance (behaviour) in the workplace and within the public sphere which was composed of employers, colleagues, clients, and so on, while private relationships and behaviour were contained within the private sphere of home life, with its own audience composed of family and friends, etc. However, this notion of identity bound by location and physical boundaries has been challenged and destabilised by the increasing penetration of digital technologies in every sphere of life, and because SNS have no physical boundaries that delineate audiences and corresponding performances/behaviours. These changes are indicative and a consequence of wider patterns of shifting, blurring and overlapping public and private boundaries in people's lives, and are made possible through the 'instrumentalisation of subjectivity'. Foucault (1978) argues that individuals are subject to discourse, and users of digital technologies are in effect subjects under construction by others (Romano, 1999). Hence, through instrumentalisation of subjectivity digital users are shaped by and try to shape themselves and their identity and to navigate and negotiate the online sphere and the fusion of online boundaries.

Consistency of behaviour, utterances, self-presentations and adherence to a social script (performance) is the essence of the authenticity of identities. Indeed, we can say that identities are formed with respect to a given audience and offer a promise of authenticity to that audience. However, in online interactions, individuals often find themselves in a network of relationships that transcend the context of interaction. This results in convergence of content, context and contact and adds a layer of complexity and a new dimension to online identities, posts and interactions. As social media allow for the creation and maintenance of multiple identities, to avoid overlap or conflict between identities (for example, between personal and professional identities), individuals may choose to maintain different identities to represent their different roles; although such a solution minimises overlap between different audiences, it has its own challenges and adds its own complexity. Online anonymity and the possibility for such multiple identities may then lead individuals to present 'idealised', 'desired' or 'imagined' selves rather than an authentic image of self in the present. Such discrepancies have significant implications for practice and professional conduct and safeguarding.

If we consider the challenging and complex nature of children's developmental journey and the many difficulties that young people face, their ability to disagree and even animatedly challenge others in productive ways is clearly crucial for their success and healthy development as well as the maintenance of a democratic and civil society. However, the ability to disagree productively is closely interlinked with one's resilience, authenticity and capacity for critical reflection. Indeed, for Heidegger (1962), authenticity is the fruit of critical reflection on one's situation and the extent to which various factors (family, culture, experience, etc) shape that situation. Authenticity requires the individual to take responsibility for their own identity, expressions and behaviours (Heidegger, 1962), and how that is reconciled within the community, society and as a form of speech (Arendt, 2000). The lack of authenticity and reflection and the inability to disagree productively can lead to misunderstanding and heighten online conflicts.

Online boundaries and paradigm shift in privacy

One of the most important, and often overlooked, differences between the online and offline environment is the paradigm shift in privacy. Whereas traditional communication was based on the concept of privacy, the foundational paradigm in social media technologies is the very fact that they are social and not private. Traditionally, individual behaviours, interactions and communications with others or one's environment were limited in reach and visibility. More importantly, individual-generated or organisationally generated data, information and artefacts were private and it was the individual or organisation that then decided whether and how to share that data, information or artefact. For example, messages, ideas, poems, stories or recording one's thoughts or experiences, whether scribbled on a piece of paper or captured in a diary or a recording device, were private to their creator who could then decide whether and how to share that information. However, if the same information is posted on social media (on a blog or Facebook page or tweet, etc), it would immediately be public and accessible to varying extents by others. Hence, there is a fundamental difference and ethical tension between social media technologies constructed around information sharing and dissolving boundaries, where every experience, interaction and artefact is 'social' and 'public' by default, vis-à-vis social work and safeguarding practice constructed around privacy and the confidentiality of interactions and information and the maintenance of professional boundaries, where every experience, interaction and artefact is private or confidential by default. This poses an important challenge and has significant implications, from aesthetical and ethical as well as psychosocial, personal, professional and practice perspectives.

Online disinhibition effect

At times one may say or do things online that they would not do offline and face-to-face. This is attributed to the 'online disinhibition effect'. The online disinhibition effect was first discussed by John Suler (2004) and may work in two directions. It can result in the disclosure of emotions, fears or desires, anxieties, personal information or secrets by the individual. It may also result in individuals behaving more expansively or overreaching or in unusual acts of kindness, generosity, etc. These types of behaviour are referred to as 'benign disinhibition' (Suler, 2004). However, online disinhibition can also result in harsh criticism, conflict, threats, production or use of pornography, sexting, harassment, bullying or other aggressive behaviours. This is referred to as 'toxic disinhibition' (Suler, 2004).

Looking at the individual in context, some of the types and aspects of benign disinhibition can be understood as attempts to reconcile interpersonal, intrapsychic or developmental issues and challenges, and to develop self by experimenting with one's emotions within a new context (Suler, 2004), or by engaging in 'identity management' and experimenting with new identities or with experiential dimensions of one's identity (Suler, 2002) to achieve 'self-actualisation'. While benign disinhibition may facilitate 'working through' one's emotional or identity challenges and achieving self-actualisation, toxic disinhibition involves an acting out and externalising of difficulties or negative emotions, and may represent a 'blind catharsis' (Suler, 1999); that is, a fruitless acting out of needs without any personal growth, see Snapstreak example in Chapter 1.

Suler (2004, p 321) notes that, 'As in all conceptual dichotomies, the distinction between benign and toxic disinhibition will be complex or ambiguous in some cases.' For example, engagement in a twitter chat such as @MHChat may be therapeutic for some people

(Suler, 1999; Megele, 2015; Megele and Buzzi, 2018b), while in a different context people may reveal emotions and personal stories or information or an aggressive attitude that may evoke feelings of vulnerability or shame. Indeed, given the wide variety of online subcultures, the meaning/interpretation and significance of an uttering or behaviour, depending on context, may vary significantly (Suler, 2004). In practice, difference, cultural relativity and psychosocial complexities may lead to misunderstanding and toxic disinhibition (Megele, 2015; Megele and Buzzi, 2018b, 2018d).

Suler (2004) posits that there are six underlying dynamics that result in online disinhibition effect, namely, dissociative anonymity, invisibility, asynchronicity, solipsistic introjection, dissociative imagination and minimisation of status and authority. Although at times one or two of these factors are sufficient, in most cases the interaction between three of these influences one's emotional and psychological barriers in a more complex and amplified manner (Suler, 2004).

The ever-present nature of social media and cyberspace, combined with the effects of solipsistic introjections and dissociative imagination, can generate a form of 'solipsistic presence' and 'virtual sociality' that is experienced as constant, continuous and all-permeating. This amplifies the impact of online experiences and hence, cyber-abuse can be experienced as unrelenting and all-invasive.

Furthermore, the disinhibition effect can facilitate self-disclosure, which can have therapeutic purposes. It can also facilitate online relationships and friendships. However, it can also give rise to false intimacy and unintended expectations that may result in frustration, anxiety and a breakdown in relationships. Cultural relativity and diversity can add a further layer of complexity to online relationships and the interpretation of online behaviour.

Dissociative anonymity

Technologically savvy, motivated users may be able to detect a computer's IP (Internet Protocol) address, but for the most part, others only know what a person tells them. If so desired, one can hide or alter part or all of one's identity. As the word 'anonymous' implies, people can have no name, or at least not their real name.

However, online anonymity refers to one's perception of being unidentifiable online. Indeed, by fashioning an online persona and profile through a personal webpage and choice of username (including fictitious or pseudo names), the creation of online profiles (choice of profile image and description, etc), and others, one can create and project a self and way of being that is similar or quite different from one's offline persona, age, background, personality, physical appearance, and even gender, lifestyle and lived experiences. Hence, cyberspace offers the opportunity to create and experiment with different online identities, and this has an important impact on young people and can be both supportive and challenging for their development. However, the possibility of creating identifies far from one's offline identity dilute the connection between the individual and their behaviour, creating a sense that one can dissociate self from their online behaviour and avoid the obligation of owning one's behaviour and its consequences. As we will see later in this book, the perception of anonymity and the online disinhibition effect have significant implications for online behaviour including various types of transgressions, aggressions, abuse, fraud, crime and offending behaviour.

It should be noted that the concept of anonymity is relative and more of a perception than reality. At any given time, each computer is uniquely identified by an IP address, and given that by law in many countries internet service providers (ISPs) archive users' browsing history, technically savvy and motivated individuals can detect computers' IP addresses and so trace postings and interactions to their source. Hence, although most users only know what others tell them online, there is no such thing as absolute anonymity. Indeed, the closest thing to untraceability is through the use of what is called Tor, or The Onion Router, which directs its user's internet traffic through a network of several thousand relays (computers that receive the message and pass it on, and by so doing change its IP address), in effect concealing the original user's location and usage (the user's technical identity) from detection or network surveillance, monitoring or traffic analysis. Notwithstanding the technical reality of the internet, the perception and experience of online anonymity relative to face-to-face interactions results in dissociative anonymity; for example, many sexual offenders, after their capture, admit that the perception of online anonymity gave them a buzz (European Online Grooming Project, 2012). Online anonymity can reduce self-awareness and result in deindividuation, which can, in turn, lower the person's ability for self-regulation, empathy and perspective taking (Suler, 2004).

The effect of online audience vis-à-vis anonymity

As a mindline it may be helpful to remember that there is a complex interaction between online anonymity and audience effect that does not allow the direct application of offline observations to online experiences. For example, applying the bystander intervention model in online social media settings, it becomes apparent that although social media offers increased visibility to online posts including cyber-aggression, cyber-abuse and cyberbullying, due to the dissociative anonymity and deindividuation effect of online media (Suler, 2004), this increased visibility does not necessarily lead to a positive intervention on the part of cyberbullying witnesses/bystanders. We will further elaborate on this point in the chapter on cyberbullying.

Invisibility

In many text-driven online environments people cannot see each other. For example, when people participate in forums, read or comment on a blog or website, tweet, re-tweet, 'like' or post on a Facebook page, they cannot see others in person; indeed, with the possible exception of webmasters and technologically savvy individuals, they cannot even know if there is anyone else present in that space who is reading or commenting about the same posting or blog. This physical invisibility online gives people the courage to try out new ideas or behaviours and to behave in ways that are different from their offline behaviour.

Although invisibility overlaps with dissociative anonymity (both help conceal one's identity), they are not the same thing (for example, people in an online chat may know a great deal about each other but still cannot see or hear each other, and this increases the disinhibition effect). Invisibility compounds and magnifies both the perception and effect of dissociative anonymity and online disinhibition (Suler, 2004; Megele, 2014b).

Asynchronicity

While most face-to-face interactions occur in real time and require an immediate response, most online interactions are asynchronous (that is, it is accepted that one may not receive an immediate response from a counterpart). For example, emails, online comments or other similar postings may take minutes, hours, days or even months before a reply is received. Not having to cope with someone's immediate reaction reduces cognitive demand for the individual, and has a disinhibiting effect (Megele, 2014b).

Solipsistic introjection

Absence of face-to-face cues combined with text communication can alter the perception of the interaction and self-boundaries, and this can generate a sensation of being merged with the mind of others online. Reading others' messages can be experienced as a voice inside one's head, generating a psychological presence for the other as if that other was assimilated or introjected into self and had become part of one's psyche. This can alter the perception of self-boundary and interpersonal dynamics, and can influence the sense of proximity, intimacy and relationships (Suler, 2004; Megele and Buzzi, 2018b, 2018d).

Even if one doesn't know the other (their voice or face, etc), consciously or unconsciously, in one's mind, a voice, face and physical appearance, and even thoughts, attitudes and behaviour/behavioural patterns can be assigned to them.

Dissociative imagination

The facilitation of dissociating from self and solipsistic introjection leading to creation of imaginary identities in one's mind lead, in essence, to dissociative imagination, which further magnifies the online disinhibition effect. Consciously or unconsciously, this can lead to experiencing an elaborate parallel dimension that includes and extends one's online experiences, characters and interactions, enriched and intensified by dissociative imagination in a parallel or 'second life' world that may be integrated or dissociated to varying degrees from one's offline/face-to-face world, identity and experiences.

Cocoon effect

Digital and social technologies enable individuals to tailor their social network by choosing who they wish to connect with and the type of information and postings they wish to see and interact with. However, connecting only with like-minded individuals and organisations based on one's own ideas, beliefs, preferences and agenda can create an echo chamber effect where one's ideas and beliefs are reinforced by our social network and vice versa. This limits an individual's exposure and experience and can generate a cocoon effect that can distort the individual's perception and exacerbate and heighten extreme views with little space for discussion or appreciation and tolerance for differing views and beliefs.

Minimisation of status and authority

Cyberspace has a levelling effect in the sense that usually one's power, status and authority offline seems to be irrelevant or of little impact online, and this creates a sort of equality as users tend to start interactions as equals (Suler, 2004). Offline, authority figures' power and status are expressed and observed through dress, possessions, trappings of their environment, body language, and so on. However, the absence of such power and status symbols in textual interactions and the online environment diminishes their impact. Indeed, even if people are aware of the offline power and status of a given individual, their authority is less visible and so has less influence on their persona and interactions online than offline. In most online interactions people tend to begin from a relatively equal position, and although one's offline identity may support their online influence to varying extent, what determines one's online social capital and influence relative to others is a combination of image management, medium-specific communication skills (for example, writing skills for sites such as Twitter or blogs, image creation/manipulation for sites such as Flickr or Instagram, etc), online presence and persistence, quality and power of ideas, social and networking skills and technical know-how.

In face-to-face interactions people are aware of others' presence and authority, and fear of embarrassment, disapproval or punishment moderates and regulates their interactions. Online in an environment that feels like a peer relationship and a diminished sense/perception of others' authority, interactions even with authorities are more disinhibited as people are more willing to speak out and to misbehave (Suler, 2004).

Furthermore, the internet was aimed at sharing ideas among peers, and was developed and operates with no central control. Indeed, its lack of regulation and freedom of expression, ideas and sharing have been and remain the source of its unlimited growth and potential for creativity. In this sense, the Internet promotes innovation, exploration and testing of ideas and independent-mindedness that minimises authority. Nonetheless, in the same manner that the presence of the police in a neighbourhood can serve as a deterrent to crime, the presence of the police/authorities online combined with effective digital citizenship can contribute to reducing incidences of cyber-abuse and cyber-aggression, including cyberbullying.

A new language and thought process

Cyberspace and each social media platform produce a new way of self-expression, communication and relating to self and others. We have elaborated on this challenge elsewhere (see Megele, 2014b, 2015, and Megele and Buzzi, 2018c, 2018d), and a detailed discussion of these changes and their implications is beyond the scope of this book. However, a brief reflection about this point is important for effective safeguarding. If we examine and compare a random selection of online profiles, behaviours, interactions and posts from different social media platforms (Facebook, Twitter, Snapchat, Instagram, YouTube, etc), we can identify clear differences in the type of engagement, content, self-expression, interactions and so on. This is a reflection of McLuhan's (1964) well-known assertion that 'the medium is the message', and goes beyond the simple format and representation of the content (image versus text, video, etc). Furthermore, different types of interaction and engagement, even on the same social media platform, can generate very different experiences, risks and ways of communicating and relating with self and others, and may require a different set of skills and cognitive abilities; given that language influences our communication, thoughts, behaviour, relationships and reflective capacity, this has significant implications (Megele, 2015). The Snapstreak story from Chapter 1 is an example of such an influence resulting in excessive, obsessive and addictive behaviour. In 'Theorizing Twitter chat' Megele (2014b) explores this difference in language and some of its implications in more detail.

Relational Boundary Scale (RBS)

The above-mentioned differences between online and offline dimensions and communications have an important impact on personal and professional relationships and boundaries. Therefore, the Relational Boundary Scale (RBS) offers a tool for learning about and assessing personal and professional relationships and boundaries.

From a systemic perspective, we can think of relationships in terms of boundaries that vary on a continuum, from diffused/enmeshed to balanced and then rigid boundaries (see Figure 2.2). Rigid boundaries reflect transactional relationships that are disengaged and lack warmth and empathy, and limit people and systems' adaptability, while diffused boundaries reflect transactional relationships that are enmeshed, and may lead to chaos and lack of security (Minuchin, 1974). Clear and healthy boundaries lie at the mid-point between rigid and diffused boundaries, and represent a balanced combination of the two. Such a classification of relationships and boundaries is used in systemic family therapy, and we can assign a score of 1, 2 or 3 to diffused, balanced and rigid boundaries respectively, to create a scaling mechanism for a practical approach to scoring and classifying relationships and boundaries.

Figure 2.2: Continuum of boundaries

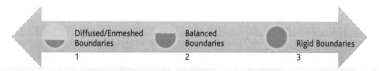

Diffused/Enmeshed Boundaries — 1

Balanced Boundaries — 2

Rigid Boundaries — 3

A discussion of complexity theory and the epistemological ramifications of a scaling mechanism are beyond the scope of this chapter, but considering the complexity and fluidity of identities, boundaries and relationships, and to offer a more nuanced representation and scaling mechanisms for assessing boundaries and relationships, we created the RBS, which offers a 10-point scale and allows for gradations of diffused, balanced and rigid boundaries (Megele and Buzzi, 2018a). The RBS scores run from 1, reflecting the virtual absence of boundary or an excessively diffused/enmeshed boundary resulting in a significant overlap of identities, boundaries, relationships or systems, to 9, representing a very rigid boundary, resulting in excessive exclusion, isolation or neglect (see Table 2.1).

Table 2.1: The Relational Boundary Scale (RBS)

Score	Description	Category
-1	Contradictory and conflicting combination of rigid and diffused/enmeshed boundaries with no balanced component (used for overall rating only)	Conflicting or contradictory
1	Virtual absence of boundary or excessively diffused/enmeshed boundary resulting in overlap of identities	Range of diffused/enmeshed boundaries
2	Diffused/enmeshed boundary	
3	Diffused/enmeshed boundary with some firm aspects	
4	Balanced boundary with some enmeshed characteristics	Range of balanced boundaries
5	Balanced boundary	
6	Balanced boundary with some rigid characteristics	
7	Rigid boundary with some balanced characteristics	Range of rigid boundaries
8	Rigid boundary	
9	Very rigid boundary resulting in exclusion and neglect	

A score of −1 was added to the RBS to represent transactional relationships that are characterised by a conflicting and contradictory combination of rigid and diffused boundaries at the two extremities of the scale. The RBS offers a structured and systematic approach to assessing professional boundaries in practice, and based on a given code of ethics. It should be noted that the application of RBS for assessment of relationships and boundaries should be based on, and in relation to, a clear professional code of ethics or code of conduct. When examining professional boundaries using the RBS, the two ends of the scale (that is, scores of 1, 2 or 8 and 9, as well as a score of −1) represent situations that are extreme; such situations usually result in breach or violation of the professional code of ethics. The RBS can also be used for teaching and learning about boundaries as it challenges learners to condense their analysis and understanding of boundaries and relationships in the context of a situation or case study, scenario, interaction or practice situation into a single number on the scale and then to reflectively support their choice/score.

In one research project (Megele and Buzzi, 2018a), the RBS was used to assess and enhance the participants' understanding of professional boundaries both offline and online. Participants were asked to critically analyse various vignettes of practice examples, online interactions and posts, and to use the RBS to assess the practitioners' ability to maintain appropriate professional boundaries based on the British Association of Social Workers' (BASW) code of ethics. All the participants subsequently participated in an online group discussion, to discuss their analysis for each practice situation, case scenario, online post or behaviour. Their feedback indicates that the RBS offered a structured and systematic approach to analysing each situation and case scenario, and enhanced participants' critical analysis and understanding of online and offline behaviours, boundaries and relationships. The RBS can be applied to both online and offline situations and case scenarios and, therefore, can be used for exploring, assessing, learning and teaching the challenges and nuanced complexities of personal and professional boundaries and relationships, both online or offline.

3

The 10 C's psycho-socio-ecological model for holistic safeguarding

This chapter sets the foundation for the rest of the book. We begin with a brief discussion of risk, risk of harm, protective factors and resilience culminating in a definition of holistic safeguarding. This is followed by a discussion of online risks, and a presentation of the 10 C's risk and resilience typologies and the 10 C's psycho-socio-ecological model, for a structured and holistic assessment of online risks and their integration into the assessment triangle, and to offer a systematic and comprehensive approach to the safeguarding of children and young people, and their families and carers. The terminology and the model introduced in this chapter is used throughout the book for analysing various types of online risks and challenges.

Exploring risks, harm, protective factors and resilience

Although the term 'risk' has often been used negatively and as synonymous to danger or harm, technically speaking risk is a probability of a given outcome, either positive or negative, based on a given set of conditions. In other words, risk is a marker that is correlated with, and in statistically based case scenarios, causes, a given outcome. Therefore, throughout this book we use the term 'risk' to reflect the probability of both positive and negative outcomes. Where we use the term 'protective factor' in combination with 'risk', this is simply to emphasise the role of protective factors and they are not intended as opposites.

The relationship between risk and outcome may be a direct/positive correlation (an increase in risk increases the outcome – for example, increased internet use increases the possibility of the child being exposed to age-inappropriate content), or an inverse/negative correlation (an increase in risk decreases the outcome – for example, increased bullying, leading to decreased social participation). It is worth mentioning that both harm and protection are outcomes, and when situated in a given context can present as risk of harm (RoH) or a protective factor (PF) respectively. It is important to note that risks are always relative to the person-in-context (that is, risks are in relation to a given person in a given context), and that often children's concerns and notion of risk are different from adults'. Therefore, any identification or assessment of risks, needs, protective factors or resilience should be done in co-production with children and young people and their families.

Like risk of harm, protective factors reflect the probability of a given outcome. In other words, protective factors are risk factors that are correlated with a positive/desirable outcome. Although risk of harm and protective factors are often conceptualised as opposites, they are more a question of degree of presence or absence of a given factor on a continuum. Protective factors modify or compensate for risk of harm either by mitigating and directly reducing risk itself (reducing the probability of a given negative/undesirable outcome) or by mitigating its outcome (reducing the strength of a negative/undesirable outcome) or by enhancing one's resilience and reparative capacity (Rutter, 1987). For example, although parental supervision does not reduce or eliminate the presence of sexual predators/offenders online, it prevents children accessing harmful websites, thus reducing the likelihood of the child being exposed to predators/offenders. It also enables quicker identification of inappropriate or predatory behaviour, and more resilient coping and response in case of such exposure/contact.

Consideration and management of risks are central in human and helping sciences including social work, social care, health and related professions. However, risks are usually a question of contextually defined thresholds rather than an absolute or fixed state. Often, risk of harm and protective factors represent two ends of a continuum, and harm and protection should therefore be viewed as thresholds. In other words, it is the outcome and measure of a given risk variable that makes it a risk of harm or a protective factor, and this highlights the importance of strength-based approaches that enhance protection and resilience. For example, the quality of the relationship between parents/carers and children is an important factor in children's lives and development. However, there is no 'perfect parenting'; instead, what is needed is 'good enough' parenting, meaning calibrating the relationship between good parenting (protective factor) and poor parenting (risk of harm) so that it becomes 'good enough' parenting. In other words, if we think of parenting on a continuum between poor parenting and good parenting, social work and safeguarding interventions should aim to move the relationship away from poor parenting toward good parenting until achieving the threshold of 'good enough' parenting; below that threshold the quality of parenting would be considered a risk of harm while anything above it will increasingly be considered a protective factor. We should note that although we can think about and visualise risk of harm and protective factors on a continuum (see Figure 3.1), the relationship between risk of harm and protective factors is often complex and non-linear. Furthermore, it is worth mentioning that the threshold for good enough parenting is presented as a thick bar rather than a line to emphasise that such thresholds reflect a range of alternatives and possibilities rather than a fixed and clear line.

From a safeguarding perspective, it is essential that practitioners develop a holistic understanding of risk, harm and protection as dynamic, relative, multidimensional, complex and situated phenomena. Risk of harm and protective factors are:

- *dynamic*, as they evolve in nature, content, impact, timeline, frequency and intensity
- *relative*, as they relate to specific variables and components, both in terms of intensity and how they are measured (a factor posing risk of harm can change and can even become a protective factor and vice versa if its relationship with its components is altered)

Figure 3.1: The risk continuum and the continuum of harm and protection

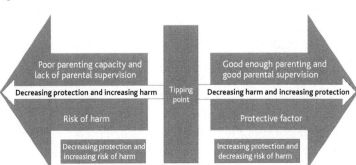

- *multidimensional*, as they usually result from an interplay of multiple factors
- *complex*, as harm and protection are products of multiple interlinked factors that often involve a complex set of relations and forward-and-backward feedback loops
- *situated*, as risks and their impact are relevant to and occur within a given context, and their outcome (harm or protection) is defined and shaped in relation to that context (see Figure 3.1).

Notwithstanding universal needs and risks, from a safeguarding perspective, any consideration or account of risks, needs, harm, protection or protective factors should be contextual. Indeed, even universal risks should be considered and expressed in a contextually relevant manner.

Risks of harm and protective factors can be specific (correlated with a specific outcome – for example, blocking a social media account is specific to not wanting any communication from that account), non-specific (correlated with multiple or a range of outcomes – for example, cyberbullying is correlated with a number of negative outcomes) or cumulative (the result of recurring risk, or of an interplay between multiple risks, or both – for example, repeated child sexual abuse or experiencing mental health difficulties and substance misuse). Cumulative risks often cause significant and complex long-term risks that may create systemic challenges. Therefore, from a safeguarding perspective, it is important to carefully consider the effects of cumulative risks including the intersection of risks and sociodemographic factors such as gender, race, ethnicity, culture and religion.

Risk is often thought of as an event, however, it is essential to consider the evolving nature of risk, harm and protection and their correlates within a given context and over time. This moves beyond an understanding of risk as an event, and considers the probability of an event and its impacts over time and within the individual's lived experience and psycho-socio-ecological context. Such an approach to risk is essential for effective safeguarding and to accurately identify and assess risks, needs, rights and resilience. For example, the death of a parent is a high-impact traumatic event in a child's life, and poses significant risks for the child's psychological and emotional wellbeing. However, the dynamic, relative, multidimensional, complex and situated nature of this risk is evidenced in terms of additional risks (for example, loss of income, social exclusion, lacking a role model, loss and grief leading to depression and mental health difficulties, and so on) that can influence, modify and complicate the impact of this event and result in ramification of risk with further significant implications for the child's development. Ramifications of risks and protective factors are part of the process of the evolution of risks and protective factors over time. It is important to note that risk is defined and assessed in relation to a given outcome within a given context, and although life is not a zero-sum game, at times one's loss may result in another's gain (a negative outcome for one person may be a positive outcome for another – for example, being burgled is a loss/negative outcome for the person but represents a financial gain for the burglar).

There are many types of risks, and a host of risks and positive and negative outcomes are embedded in the human life course, and social media have extended such risks and outcomes from pre-birth to post-death; such risks can influence life course outcomes. However, the individual's reaction and their vulnerabilities and resilience combined with the reaction of other people within the individual's psycho-socio-ecological sphere can either mitigate or compound the impact of negative events in the person's life. For example, people who experience mental health difficulties may react to a negative event in ways that intensify the negative impact of such events in their lives. This can then be exacerbated by society's lack of understanding and an unsupportive, inappropriate and intolerant reaction that further compounds the negative effects of such events.

Any assessment of risk should include careful consideration of the risk as well as evolution and ramification of the risk and its context and correlates over time. Hence, risks and outcomes and their ramifications must be captured in assessments with specific and proportionate interventions to mitigate and change the balance between risk of harm and protective factors.

Indeed, safeguarding practice is aimed at influencing the relationship between risks and their outcomes. Hence, effective safeguarding can be defined as a holistic, proportionate and purposeful intervention that modifies the evolution and combination of risks over time and in relation to the individual's psycho-socio-ecological context, to produce positive outcomes that support and optimise healthy growth and enhance the individual's choice, freedom, autonomy and potential while mitigating negative outcomes.

Finally, the term 'resilience' is a dynamic construct that refers to the ability to bounce back from, adapt and respond resourcefully to adversity and extraordinary circumstances to achieve positive outcomes. With appropriate support, children and young people demonstrate remarkable elasticity, adaptability, tenacity and reparative capacity in their development, and a natural ability to respond resourcefully to adverse challenges and changing circumstances and environments. Hence, children are naturally resilient (although this can be altered or hampered by neglect or abuse), and their resilience is closely and reciprocally tied with their development. Resilience can be observed in a person's ability to overcome exposure to environmental, developmental and other high risks, to persevere under pressure and adjust to trauma and negative events, in the context of high risk. It is important to note that resilience is defined based on an adaptive response to risk and harm and therefore, prospering in the absence of risk does not signify resilience, and resilience does not mean invulnerability to risk and negative outcomes.

Furthermore, although resilience is often misunderstood and is thought of as a static concept that is attributed to the individual as a trait or individual characteristic, this is inaccurate and represents a narrow vision of resilience. Instead, like risk, resilience is a variable and dynamic construct that is contextually shaped by the interplay between a number of psycho-socio-ecological factors and is the result of self within a network of relationships; that is, resilience includes environmental factors and the individual's network of relationships and resources, and is the response of a person-in-context (drawing on his/her resources, relationships, support networks and so on) that generates an exceptional performance in the face of significant adversity. Hence, by expanding and strengthening people's social and support networks and by increasing their resources, we can support and enable them to respond to adversity in more resilient ways.

Considering the constantly changing digital landscape and the unpredictable and evolving nature of digital risks, it is difficult to avoid online risks or to prepare a person for all possible online risks, and hence, it is especially important to harness the digital resilience of individuals. Digital resilience can reduce risk of harm and mitigate the impact of online risks, helping to enhance the person's coping strategies (enabling them to respond to risk of harm in a more resourceful manner).

Although at times it may be necessary to curtail young people's access to, or use of, digital and social media technologies, this should only be temporary and used as a solution of last resort rather than routine practice. The long-term digital exclusion of children can affect their ongoing and future learning, possibilities and life chances and outcomes. Practitioners should therefore ensure that adverse online experiences do not lead to the long-term digital exclusion of children, and that children are supported so they can recover from adverse experiences and are enabled to enhance their digital and social skills, reclaim their digital identity and presence, protect their digital rights and develop their digital citizenship.

Notwithstanding the significance of digital resilience, when thinking about or assessing individual vulnerabilities and resilience, practitioners should be mindful that this thinking does not lead to implicit or explicit victim blaming or recriminating the victim for their adverse experience; it is the perpetrator, and not the victim, who is responsible for the aggression, abuse or cyberbullying, and their effects and consequences.

Principle of relative and contextual online-offline equivalence

As noted in Chapter 2, there are important differences between online and offline environments and the implications of risks and behaviours in those contexts. Therefore, mindful of such differences, we suggest thinking about relative and contextual online-offline equivalence as a mindline for digital/online safeguarding. Therefore, taking into account the contextual differences of online and offline environments, from a safeguarding perspective, we suggest that interactions, attitudes and behaviours that are considered inappropriate, abusive or aggressive offline should be, *in a contextually relevant manner*, considered in the same way online, and by the same token, online interactions, attitudes and behaviours that are not considered inappropriate or abusive or aggressive offline should be, *in a contextually relevant manner*, considered in the same way online. We cannot overemphasise that such equivalence should be considered **in a contextually relevant manner**.

Defining online risks and the 10 C's risk typology

UK government guidance, *Child safety online: A practical guide for providers of social media and interactive services* (DCMS, 2016, Section 1.3), classifies online risk into three categories, namely, content risks, conduct risk and contact risk:

- **Content risk:** children receiving mass-distributed content. This may expose them to age-inappropriate material such as pornography, extreme violence, or content involving hate speech and radicalisation.
- **Conduct risk:** children participating in an interactive situation. This includes bullying, sexting, harassing, being aggressive or stalking; or promoting harmful behaviour such as self-harm, suicide, pro-anorexia, bulimia, illegal drug use or imitating dangerous behaviour. A child's own conduct online can also make them vulnerable – for example, by over-sharing their personal information or by harassing or bullying themselves.
- **Contact risk**: children being victims of interactive situations. This includes being bullied, harassed or stalked; meeting strangers; threats to privacy, identity and reputation (for example, through embarrassing photos shared without permission, a house location being identified, someone impersonating a user, users sharing information with strangers); and violence, threats and abuse directly aimed at individual users and/or groups of users.

Although helpful from service providers' perspective, this classification does not offer sufficient detail and a holistic view of online risks from a safeguarding perspective. Therefore, we propose a structured approach to online risks, protective factors, needs, rights and resilience that allows for further elaboration and detailing of online risks from a child-centric perspective. In specific, we suggest that practitioners can use the 10 C's risk and resilience typologies for thinking about and assessing risks, protective factors and resilience. The 10 C's risk and resilience typologies can also be used to assess the dimensions and implications of online identities, interactions, behaviours and posts. We should highlight that the 10 C's risk and resilience typologies is the fruit of a thematic analysis of the existing research and evidence, serious case reviews, case studies and consultations with children, people who access services and practitioners that explored and identified risks based on impact from a child-centred and person-centred perspective; that is, the risk impact is based on the child's/individual's identity, experience, communications, emotions and behaviour.

The 10 C's risk and resilience typologies are: confidentiality and personal disclosure risk; connection and social capital risk; context risk; content risk; contact risk (virtual and physical); conduct risk; consonance-dissonance and compatibility risk; consumption risk; commercial risk (risk of commercial exploitation and positive commercial potential); and composite and complex risks (see Figure 3.2). Each of these typologies offers the potential for positive development as well as negative outcomes. We should add that we have not numbered the 10 C's risk and resilience typologies as they can be used in any order, depending on the context and

Figure 3.2: The 10 C's risk and resilience typologies

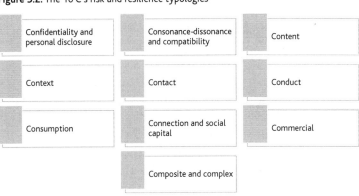

where the parent, practitioner or the child begins their reflection, conversation and/or risk analysis. Regardless of where one begins, 10 C's is an invitation to examine and reflect upon the child's identity, experience, communication, interactions, emotions, and behaviour, and to consider the different dimensions of risks and resilience based on their impact and from a child-centred or person-centred perspective.

Confidentiality and personal disclosure

This is the most common form of online risk (Staksrud and Livingstone, 2009) and refers to the risk of disclosing information that could compromise an individual's privacy or result in exposure to unwelcome, inappropriate, sexual, aggressive or harmful solicitation, contact or content, or amplify or facilitate other online risks. This includes information that may threaten one's privacy, identity or reputation, for example, sharing embarrassing/ inappropriate photos online, impersonating another person or identity theft, sharing one's password, phone number or home address, or sharing personal or private information with strangers. When using online media, it is important to decide the extent to which one wishes to share personal information and various activities and experiences online; this has important implications for safeguarding both practitioners and children and young people.

Connection and social capital

This refers to risk associated with relational aspects and the social capital dimensions of one's online identity. This encompasses the size (for example, the number of connections in one's social network, such as online friends or followers), quality (the quality of the young person's relationships and social network) and strength (the strength of bonds and relationships and whether the person can draw support from a given relationship or social network) of the person's social network, including their social capital. In practice, this requires an analysis and understanding of the person's relational identity and social capital including online and offline relationships with significant others, family, friends and peers, support networks, social networks and others, as well as the type, quality, accessibility, availability and reliability of support and resources that the person can receive from such relationships and social networks. Practitioners should also consider that although a large online social network may represent greater social capital it also entails a higher risk of exposure to age-inappropriate material, cyber-abuse, cyber-aggression and inappropriate solicitation or contact by perpetrators online.

Context

This refers to media-specific risks, those generated by the specific medium's environment and ecology. McLuhan's (1964) 'the medium is the message' highlights the importance of context and how the medium embeds itself in the message that it conveys, creating a symbolic relationship by which the medium influences the meaning and significance of the message and how it is perceived/understood. Indeed, different digital and social media platforms and apps create their own environment and ecology or system of interactions, language, meaning, etiquette (expected behaviours), ethics and associated risks. A visual examination of Facebook, Twitter, Instagram, Snapchat and YouTube will quickly reveal the significant differences between these SNSs. Each of these SNSs privileges a different type of communication, message and behaviour and has a different impact. (In Chapter 4 we offer a structured and systematic approach to analysis of the context and medium of online/video games.)

The following eight risk sub-categories generate and define the systemic risk ecology (Megele and Buzzi, 2018b) associated with a given medium, SNS, website, software application (app), or game; although practitioners are not expected to analyse these detailed risk sub-categories for defining context risks, the risk typologies below provide practitioners with a better informed and more critical and systemic appreciation of context risks:

- *Design risks* arise from the design of the software application or SNS – for example, Facebook, Instagram or Snapchat's design encourages different types of communication and risk taking.
- *Implementation risks* arise from the implementation and functionalities of the software application or SNS.

- *Configuration risks* are associated with the way a user configures the software application or SNS including privacy settings. Some software applications or SNSs do not offer adequate and appropriate configuration options; for example, there are significant differences between privacy options and settings in Facebook and Twitter and these have important implications for the users' activities, behaviours and postings.
- *Content risks* are associated with the type of information and content available or shared through that software application, SNS or medium. risk refers to the content that is privileged by and dominant on a given SNS. Content risk is covered more extensively below as part of the 10 C's risk and resilience typologies.
- *Structure risks* refer to the way the medium and data/information are structured. Structure can affect the meaning and significance of data/information (Huston and Wright, 1994); the same content presented in different structures can generate a different impact, meanings and response/reactions. Therefore, structure can have independent effects on the user. Indeed, interfaces for apps, SNSs, games, and so on are carefully designed and structured to achieve specific effects and objectives – think about the structure differences between Facebook, Twitter, Instagram, YouTube and Snapchat, and how that affects their impact and risk ecology. For example, the context risk associated with Snapchat Streaks can easily lead to problematic, excessive and obsessive use of Snapchat. Gamification is an important feature of many apps and many of the structural characteristics that influence gambling behaviour (for example, gambling frequency and expenditure) can be extended to gaming behaviour (Leino et al, 2015).
- *Mechanism risks* refer to the way the user interacts with the medium/app/SNS/game, ranging from the mouse, keyboard and touch screen to the joystick, virtual reality headset or other. The interface mechanism can have physical and psychological consequences for the user.
- *Narrative and culture risks* refer to the narrative and culture surrounding a given medium, software application, SNS or game; this includes the narrative used by the young person to describe the medium, app, SNS or game. Such narratives and culture condition the online behaviour and interactions

of digital identities within a given online space/environment (for example, a given SNS, game or app), and influence users' behaviours and identity; hence, they have an impact on conduct and consonance-dissonance and compatibility risks. They also moderate how online activity may impact offline behaviour. A visually induced response is a reaction to a given perceptual stimuli, while a thematically induced response is a reaction to the meaning of an event or stimuli (Laney et al, 2003). This distinction is important when examining content and context risks. These shape the user's interpretation and perception of their online identity and experience as well as their emotional response to that experience, and influence the psychological and behavioural impact and enactment of online identities, behaviours, attitudes and experiences offline; that is, narrative and culture around an online indentity, behaviour or experience can facilitate or hamper the extent to which a user may or may not enact that behaviour or experience offline (for example, postgame benevolence or violence as a result of an in-game experience). Identification with an online identity/persona increases self-activation and increases the chances of enacting that identity/persona in other contexts; this moderates the effect of the online experience on offline behaviour and may lead to conduct risk and consonance-dissonance and compatibility risk.

- *Knowledge gap* represents the risk of not knowing enough about the software application or SNS and the way it uses or misuses its user data and posts. This can result in sharing or misuse of information with unexpected consequences or without the user's informed consent.

Content

This is the risk of exposure to harmful, age-inappropriate or developmentally inappropriate online content, either intentionally or unintentionally. Examples include risk of children's exposure to online pornography and sexually explicit images; images of violence, trauma or terror; extremist material or content; other material or content that advocates and promotes harmful or antisocial behaviour (for example, Pro-Ana and Pro-Mia websites or websites promoting suicide), and others.

Contact

This is the risk of coming into contact with a threat, a perpetrator or source of harm/threat. These may range from online or offline bullying ('fairly commonplace') to sexual harassment or the risk of 'meeting online contacts ("strangers") offline' (Staksrud and Livingstone, 2009, p 6). To enable better and targeted safeguarding, we have divided contact risks into virtual/online and physical/offline. Indeed, virtual/online and physical/offline risks have different implications and entail different risks in safeguarding and require different targeted approaches.

Virtual/online contact risk refers to the risk of online contact between the perpetrator(s) and the young person. This includes experience of, or exposure to, virtual/online abuse or exposure to experience of abuse online, and includes all forms of inappropriate online behaviour and online aggression or abuse based on the principle of online-offline equivalence, as stated earlier in this chapter. Virtual/online contact risks encompass all online contact including friending and liking, re-posting or re-tweeting, communicating or interacting through text (for example, SMS, tweets, blog comments, etc), voice (for example, phone call, Skype call), image (for example, sending or receiving a photo), or video (for example, video calls or sending or receiving a video), or any other form of communicating or exchanging material or information or any other artefact online. Virtual/online contact risk also includes the risk of online abuse including cyberbullying, online sexual abuse (for example, exchanging indecent images or videos, masturbating or performing other sexual acts either via recording or in real time, such as in a video chat) or online physical abuse (for example, virtual beating or torturing, recording or displaying physical abuse online, self-inflicted physical or emotional harm via recording or in real time), or any other form of online abuse, aggression or trauma. The changes in digital and social media technologies may change the nature, content, behaviours, activities or risks associated with virtual contact.

Physical/offline contact risk refers to the risk of a physical/offline first-person encounter between the perpetrator or source of harm and young person. This includes exposure to aggression or abuse (experiencing bullying, harassment, stalking and physical or sexual abuse), or physical/offline first-person exposure to others' experience of abuse (witnessing bullying or sexual abuse), or meeting strangers who could present as a source of harm, etc.

Conduct

This is when the young person becomes an actor and perpetrator of inappropriate behaviour, harm, aggression or abuse, and engages in inappropriate, harmful, unlawful or abusive behaviour online or offline. This includes serving as a bait to recruit or entrap others for abuse – perpetrating abuse such as targeting, abusing or exploiting other children and young people – or any other inappropriate, abusive or exploitative activity.

Consonance-dissonance and compatibility

This refers to the degree of consonance or dissonance and the compatibility between the person's online and offline identities and behaviour. This raises a number of questions including authenticity. Identity development and social relationships are the central focus of young people's development, especially during adolescence, and cyberspace offers unlimited opportunities for exploring and experimenting with relationships and identities. Therefore, young people's online identities may represent their preferred-self-narrative or may be aimed at projecting and showcasing their strengths and positive qualities or compensating for what they perceive as lacking in their offline experience (for example, achievements, belongingness, validation, self-acceptance). This selective tailoring of identity provides an augmented yet limited perspective of reality (Griffiths, 2000), and is the essence of enframing (Megele, 2014b) aimed at enhancing one's social acceptance and social capital, and making thems feel good about themselves. This discrepancy between online and offline identities offers a developmental and potential space for growth (Megele, 2015; Megele and Buzzi, 2018d, 2018e). If the two identities are in consonance and compatible or complementary in some ways, the individual may gradually internalise their preferred identity and its qualities and this may lead to their growth and development (such qualities and growth may be positive or negative). However, strong dissonance and irreconcilable differences and incompatibility between the two identities may represent the person's internal conflict and anxiety and may lead to dissociation (Suler, 2004) or excessive and compulsive online engagement and activity (Billieux et al, 2015).

Exploring such discrepancies with young people can offer a valuable insight into their lives and thinking. Therefore, given the significant implications of young people's online identity for their relational identity and psychosocial and developmental growth and wellbeing, practitioners should establish a dialogue with young people to discuss and explore their identity narratives and behaviour (both online and offline). Understanding young people's online identity and behaviour offers a window into their desires, priorities and challenges, and helps practitioners develop stronger bonds with them while enhancing practitioners' understanding of the young person's experiences, identity narratives, values, mindset, social networks, behaviours and safeguarding opportunities and challenges from the young person's perspective. Such an understanding is important for the holistic and effective safeguarding of children and young people.

Consumption

This is the young person's behavioural pattern and the way they consume their time, and includes the risk of excessive, inappropriate or problematic internet use, as defined later in Chapter 5 of this book, including excessive or inappropriate use of the digital and social media technologies in a way that adversely affects one or more domains of their life, growth and development or wellbeing. These could range from excessive online/video game play affecting the young person's sleeping patterns or academic performance to compulsive gambling and other excessive online behaviour.

Commercial risk and commercial exploitation

This includes the risk of commercial exploitation as well as commercial child sexual exploitation. This also includes the positive commercial potential (including professional value) associated with online/digital identities and posts or artefacts. Although children and young people can generate such commercial or professional potential (for example, YouTube channels, blogs or websites by children offering products, services, advice or support to other children), given the primary objectives of this book and the focus in most safeguarding interventions, in this book we will mainly use the term 'commercial exploitation risk' including 'commercial sexual exploitation risk'. Although safeguarding interventions are usually focused on mitigating these risks rather than developing children's commercial potential, practitioners should not underestimate the importance of positive social media engagement; the case of Bethany Mota (NBC News, 28 April 2015) demonstrates the power of such engagement and its commercial potential. We draw on the definition of 'commercial sexual exploitation of children' by the Stockholm Declaration and Agenda for Action (1996) to define commercial exploitation of children as comprising all kinds of abuse that 'involve remuneration in cash or kind to the child or a third person or persons'. A key element in commercial exploitation is that the child is treated as an object or 'as a commercial object' while in case of commercial sexual exploitation the child is treated as a commercial and sexual object. Such exploitation 'constitutes a form of coercion and violence against the child and amounts to forced labour and a contemporary form of slavery' (Stockholm Declaration Agenda for Action, 1996, p 1). Therefore, commercial exploitation risk refers to the risk of a child being exploited in any way including as a sexual object for generating any sort of return, reward, remuneration or commercial benefit. Commercial and sexual exploitation of children is a huge challenge and we will explore this topic later in this book when we discuss grooming and child sexual abuse (see Chapter 6).

Composite and complex

This refers to the additional and cumulative risks that may arise from the combination and interaction between the above risks, including their outcomes and ramifications. This risk results from the interaction between the other risks but is distinct from them. Composite complex risk is in line with the systemic view of risk, and acknowledges that risk exists within complex psycho-socio-ecological systems, and that composite risks are more than the sum of their parts.

For each of the above dimensions and risk typologies, practitioners should also assess children and young people's awareness of that risk typology based on their own experience. An understanding of such risks and appropriate behaviour in response to them is an important protective factor that enhances children's resilience and is part of a good digital citizenship education. Therefore, assessments should include the above risk typologies as well as children's understanding of and responses to such risks as well as children's digital literacy and digital citizenship knowledge.

Depending on the legal context, the above risk typologies may or may not correspond to specific criminal or legal offences. However, from a safeguarding perspective, they offer a holistic and systematic understanding and structured approach to assessment and evaluation of online risks and their integration into a holistic safeguarding approach. The 10 C's risk and resilience typologies also offer a structured approach to evaluating online identities, profiles, posts and behaviours and their consequences and effects. Therefore, they can also be used in teaching and learning about risks and challenges and opportunities associated with digital and social media technologies. For example, the 10 C's model can be used by parents, teachers, lecturers, nurses, the police and other professionals for assessing the risks of a given online identity, profile, behaviour or posting for a young person or an adult. Furthermore, the 10 C's risk and resilience typologies can be used for teaching or in discussion with children and young people or adults to examine their current digital and social media presence, or to create a new social media account or online profile for them. Table 3.1 offers some helpful points and mindlines for creating an online presence/profile or digital identity.

Situating and assessing risks and protective factors

Human experience is situated in the sense that it finds meaning and significance within a given context and set of circumstances, and by the same token, risks and protective factors are not the product of individual behaviour in a vacuum. Indeed, risks and protective factors are situated and emerge as the result of complex interactions between individual and context and a set of relations and contingent and contextual factors/variables that shape the

Table 3.1: Using the 10 C's typology for creating an online identity

Risk typologies		Individual	Family	Friends and peers	Organisational	Community	Societal and social media
1	Confidentiality and self-disclosure						
2	Connection and social capital						
3	Content						
4	Context						
5	Contact (virtual/ online)						
	Contact (physical/ offline)						
6	Conduct						
7	Consonance-dissonance and compatibility						
8	Consumption						
9	Commercial exploitation						
10	Composite and complex						

relational layers of human experience. Therefore, a holistic view and assessment of children's lives and experiences should include an environmental, contextual and situated understanding of the child that spans from individual-self and child-in-family to child-in-community (including online and offline communities) and child-in-society (including SNS) contexts. Referring to assessment triangle, Jack and Gill (2003) argue that this represents 'the missing side of the triangle.' Hence, in analysing and synthesising risks and protective factors we draw on Bronfenbrenner's (1977, 1979) ecological theory to offer a holistic and contextual model for presentation and assessment of risks (RoH and PF), needs, rights and resilience, and their impact. In other words, the results of the 10 C's analysis should be transposed/mapped onto, and considered in the context of, the psycho-socio-ecological model (see Figure 3.3) to provide a meaningful and contextually relevant view of the experiences of the child or the young person as a person-in-context and considering the various factors/systems that affect their experiences at each level. These include the individual level, family level, friends and peers level, organisational level (for example, the school for children or workplace for adults), community level, societal and social media level. In Figure 3.3 we have presented digital and social media technologies cutting across each of the various levels of psycho-socio-ecological model to emphasise the impact and embedded nature of technology in human experience. This is made to emphasise that although social media operates at the social and society level it also permeates, shapes and is an integral part of the identities, relationships, activities and the context of

Figure 3.3: Psycho-socio-ecological model including digital and social media technologies

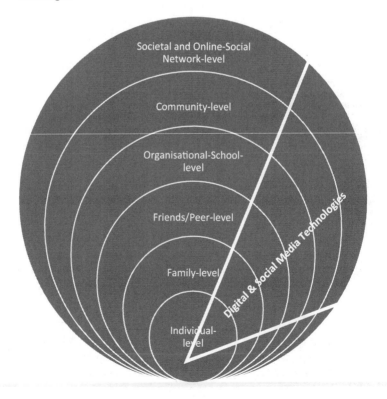

each of these levels from the child's self and identity to the larger society. This is particularly important, especially when we consider the networked and liminal nature of children's lives and human experience. Figure 3.3 presents the various levels at which risks, protective factors, needs, rights and resilience and their outcomes may be situated and operate.

The risks and resilience identified under the 10 C's typologies should be consdered and transposed onto the psycho-socio-ecological model to generate a holistic and contextual (person-centred and person-in-context) representation of risks and resilience. This can be done either diagrammatically or in table format. Chapters 4 to 10 include examples of the application of the 10 C's psycho-socio-ecological model and the diagrammatic presentation of some of the relevant risks, relative to the topic in each chapter, transposed onto the psycho-socio-ecological model. These are for representation purposes only, and should be expanded to include other risks, vulnerabilities, protective factors and resilience. For ease of use in everyday practice, practitioners can use the assessment summary table (see Table 3.2) as a starting point to produce a situated and contextual view of risks, protective factors, needs, rights and resilience in a table format.

Table 3.2: The 10 C's psycho-socio-ecological assessment table

Consonance-dissonance and compatibility risk
What is the purpose of creating this new identity or online/digital presence?
How does the person want to present themselves online? What will this new identity look like?
Is this identity in consonance or dissonance with the person's self/self-narrative? Are they compatible?
How will this affect the person's overall online presence?
How will this affect the person's self-narrative, identity, personality and overall sense of self?
Context risk
Which online SNS, medium or platform should I use?
What is the medium's risk ecology?
What is the medium's prevalent content, etiquette and ethics? What are the associated risks?

What are the potential positive outcomes associated with this medium? What is their likelihood?
What are the possible negative outcomes associated this medium? What is their probability?
How can the person leverage the potential for positive outcomes associated with this medium?
How can the person mitigate the risks of negative outcomes associated with this medium?

Confidentiality and personal disclosure risk

Is there a need to disclose personal information? What are the confidentiality risks?
What type of personal information will the person need to or want to disclose? What are the risks?
What are the risks of the person's personal or confidential information being breached?
What are the risks of the person's personal or confidential information being misused?
How can the person optimise confidentiality and personal disclosure risks?

Consumption risk

How much time will the person dedicate to this specific digital identity and online presence?
What will be the usage pattern? How frequently will the person uses this digital identity?
What are the risks associated with the amount of time and extent and pattern of use?
Does the amount of time and pattern of use enable the person to meet their objectives?
How can the person maximise the positive consumption potential and mitigate negative potential?

Content risk

What content is the person seeking? What would they like to be exposed to?
What is the prevalent content that I will be exposed to?
What are the risks of being exposed to inappropriate, harmful or illegal content?
How can the person mitigate the risk of exposure to such content? How can they optimise content risk?
How can the person enhance their resilience and improve their response to content risk?

Connection and social capital risk
Who and what sort of accounts will I connect with?
How does this digital identity influence the person's social network and relationships?
How does this digital identity influence the person's social capital?
What is the positive relational and social capital potential associated with this identity?
What are the negative relational and social capital risks associated with this identity?
How can the person mitigate risks of negative outcomes and leverage potential positive outcomes?
Contact risk
What are the contact risks?
What is the positive potential associated with contact risks? How can they be maximised?
What is the negative potential associated with contact risks? How can they be mitigated?
Are there any risks of physical contact for a child or vulnerable individual? How can this risk be mitigated?
Commercial risks
What is the positive commercial potential?
Is there any risk of commercial exploitation? How can this be avoided and stopped?
Is there any risk of commercial sexual exploitation? How can this be avoided and stopped?
Composite and complex risks
What are the composite and complex risks for positive or negative outcomes?
How can the positive potential associated with composite and complex risks be maximised?
How can the risks of negative composite and complex outcomes be mitigated?

Table 3.2 offers a two-dimensional view of risks (risk of harm, protective factors and resiliencies) and can include needs and rights. However, risks are not equivalent in their impact, intensity and duration/perseverance. The cumulative effect of harm or protection in time (probability, duration and frequency of occurrence) and intensity of impact represent the strength of a risk. Therefore, it is important to add the strength of risks as a third dimension to the above tabular representation of risks (third dimension of Table 3.2)

and resilience. This can be represented using the ROAG traffic light colour coding system to highlight the strength and impact of each of the above risks and resilience based on their outcome and strength into one of the five categories: knockout, high, medium, low strength, and virtually no risk. Knockout risks lead to significant and life-changing negative outcomes (for example, death, or loss of body parts, etc) while the high, medium and low strength risks should be defined based on professional, organisational or statutory guidance; for example, in the UK these could correspond to the various tiers of intervention, namely: child protection, child in need, and early help respectively; this ensures that definition and classification of risk is relevant to the specific practitioner and their professional and organisational context. Furthermore, this approach facilitates visual identification and prioritisation of risks based on their outcomes and strength. Finally, from a safeguarding perspective, it is important that practitioners consider the likelihood of occurrence and duration, intensity/severity and strength of risk of harm vis-à-vis the presence, intensity/quality and strength of protective factors.

A safeguarding framework

The 10 C's psycho-socio-ecological model offers a systematic approach to assessment of online risks, and should be considered in conjunction with the assessment triangle for a holistic approach to the safeguarding of children and young people. In other words, given the importance of digital citizenship and the online and digital dimension of children and young people's lives, identities and experiences, digital citizenship and the 10 C's risk and resilience typologies can be thought of as the fourth dimension of the assessment triangle (see Figure 3.4). Each of the 10 C's risk typologies represent potential for growth and development as well as risks of negative outcomes; therefore, they can be used to analyse online identities as well as online risks of positive and negative outcomes.

The risk and resilience typologies and dimensions and their evolution and ramifications over time should be considered within the context of children and young people's holistic (both online/digital and offline) development and achievement of appropriate developmental milestones and markers (these should include the achievement of digital milestones and markers in the context of digital citizenship and digital identity and growth). These dimensions are an integral part of children's liminal (both online and offline) lives and digital citizenship, and are essential to ensuring their healthy and holistic development and enhancing their current and future opportunities, potential and life chances and outcomes in an increasingly digital world.

Figure 3.4: The 10 C's risk typologies as the fourth dimension of assessments

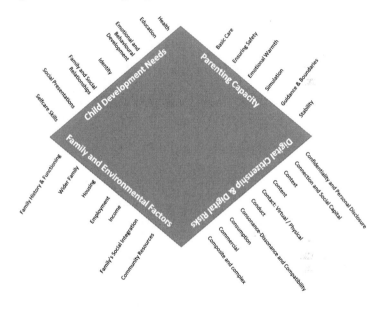

Different risk typologies require different interventions and safeguarding solutions and approaches. Hence, as suggested by the definition of 'safeguarding' in this chapter (see pp 51–2), to safeguard children and young people online requires a holistic view of risks, needs, rights, protective factors and resilience combined with targeted interventions that either recalibrate the relationship between risks and outcomes to tip the balance in favour of protection, and hence move away from risk of harm towards protection, or make sure that there is a sufficient combination of protective factors and resilience in place to minimise the impact of harm and ensure effective prevention, mitigation, coping and support that can produce a resilient response to risks and their outcomes.

Drawing on routine activity theory (Cohen and Felson, 1979), there are three key elements that must converge for risk of harm to lead to harm (that is, for harm or abuse to occur), namely, proximity or access to, or contact with, a motivated perpetrator or source of harm, individual vulnerabilities in interaction with environmental factors, and inadequate protection, guardianship or supervision (see Figure 3.5).

Figure 3.5: Triangle of harm

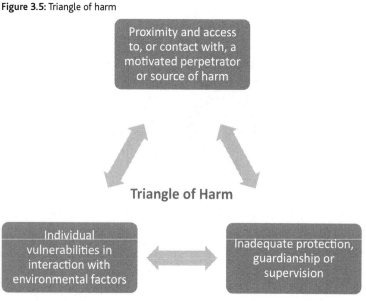

Hence, in most safeguarding cases , after detailing and analysing the relevant risks and resilience and their components, after detailing and analysing the relevant risks and resilience and their components, practitioners can use the triangle of harm and target their interventions in order to prevent the occurrence of harm by preventing the convergence of its three required key elements. For example, perhaps practitioners can ensure that the child or young person does not come in proximity of a motivated perpetrator or source of harm; this approach has been an important driver of policy and legislation in relation to online safeguarding in the UK

(Leaton Gray and Phippen, 2017). However, although such an approach may be possible and at times sufficient in closed systems and closed group settings, on the internet and the open web, this is much more difficult to achieve. Alternatively, practitioners may aim to ensure that the young person does not interact with harmful elements in their environment; however, this requires education and raising children and young people's awareness and understanding. Other approaches to safeguarding could involve enhancing the young person's resilience and mitigating their vulnerabilities to make them a less suitable target for perpetrators (remaining mindful that resilience does not mean invulnerability to harm), or ensuring that the child or the young person receives adequate and appropriate parental supervision and support, or a combination of these approaches. Interventions that can prevent the merging of these three key factors will help mitigate the occurrence of the risk factor concerned and its effect (Cohen and Felson, 1979).

To enable parents to better guide and support their children, it is important that parenting classes include digital literacy and digital citizenship, and that parents' digital literacy and knowledge and skills in relation to digital citizenship are considered and assessed as an integral part of parental capacity. Furthermore, practitioners should have clear guidance and training about e-professionalism or digital professionalism and digital/online safeguarding and should ensure that assessments and safeguarding are comprehensive and holistic and include both online and offline safeguarding.

Digital access, digital opportunities and engagement, digital risks and resilience, digital knowledge and skill (see Figure 1.2) and digital citizenship are the new sources of inequality in society leading to greater inequity and affecting children and their potential opportunities and development. Therefore, it is essential that assessments include careful consideration of the child or young person's digital access, digital opportunities and engagement, knowledge of digital risks, digital resilience, digital identity and digital citizenship as an integral part of their holistic safeguarding. Questions around private and public, audience, privacy, confidentiality, self-disclosure, digital permanence, deleting information, digital footprint and others can be conversation starters in practice, to assess and enhance children's digital access, digital resilience, digital literacy, digital identity and digital citizenship.

Thinking about the digital dimensions of identity and experience in to the context of digital citizenship and in relation to the assessment diamond/square (the integration of the assessment triangle and digital citizenship with the 10 C's risk and resilience typologies; see Figure 3.4), the 10 C's psycho-socio-ecological model invites us to consider the whole child and to think of children not as online or offline but as both (liminal), and this is encapsulated in the concept of 'cyborg childhood' and the pyramid of cyborg childhood (see Figure 3.6). This offers a holistic vision of children's identity, development and lived experience, and the 10 C's psycho-socio-ecological model provides a practical approach to think about the whole child and operationalises (that is, enables practitioners to apply) holistic child development and safeguarding in practice. The pyramid of cyborg childhood emphasises the need to think about the digital and liminal dimensions of each of the elements in the assessment triangle and the 10 C's risk and resilience typologies within the context of the psycho-socio-ecological model and the individual's digital citizenship. For example, when thinking about parental capacity, this model/approach invites practitioners to consider whether parents have the digital parenting capacity and are

Figure 3.6: Cyborg childhood pyramid

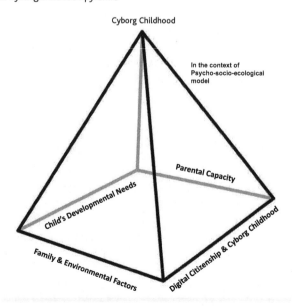

able and sufficiently engaged with and in their children's experiences in order to adequately protect and support them, both online and offline, and how they can be enabled to do so. Therefore, whereas the 10 C's psycho-socio-ecological model offers the dimensions of risk and resilience from a holistic child-centred perspective, the pyramid of cyborg childhood emphasises the digital and liminal dimension of each of the elements from the assessment triangle and the 10 C's risk and resilience typologies, in the contxt of the 10 C's psycho-socio-ecological model.

This conceptualisation is in line with both the systemic view and the psychosocial and relationship-based view of child development and protection; indeed, it bridges the gap between the psychosocial and relationship-based thinking and practice vis-à-vis systemic thinking and practice. We use the 10 C's psycho-socio-ecological model throughout this book to examine case examples and to analyse and assess online risks and protective factors; this model offers an integrated and integrative and holistic approach to assessment and safeguarding children and young people (see Figure 3.4). We have developed this concept for services' and from service providers' perspective elsewhere (see Megele and Buzzi, 2018e).

Given the widespread use of digital and social media technologies and their implications for children and young people's growth and development and their future possibilities and opportunities, it is urgent and crucially important that practitioners receive appropriate training, guidance and support, and are enabled to provide comprehensive assessment and safeguarding for children and young people. The 10 C's psycho-socio-ecological model offers such a framework for a systematic and analytic approach to holistic and evidence-informed assessment and safeguarding of children and young people. Therefore, in the remainder of this book we use the 10 C's psycho-socio-ecological model to examine and offer a critical and evidence-informed analysis of some of the challenging and frequently encountered digital/online safeguarding risks in practice.

4

Play and online/video games

Children discover the world and develop their sense of self through play and therefore, online games/video games can play a significant role in their development. However, there has been continuing debate and much concern about the world of online games and children's exposure to screen media (screen time), especially regarding video games with violent content and their effect on children and young people. While there has been extensive research in this area, some of the current arguments resemble moral panic. Indeed, concern for children's exposure to media with violent content is not a new phenomenon – for example, Bugs Bunny cartoons were contested as containing too much violence, and comic books labelled as corrupting young people and causing crime. Although Looney Tunes cartoons may have been 'more brutal than you remember' (Slate, 2014), and notwithstanding some level of moral panic, parents and professionals face the challenging task of safeguarding and supporting children in this dynamic and evolving landscape to ensure their healthy development.

The use of video games has consistently and significantly increased over time, and today they are a pervasive form of entertainment used by most children and young people (Pew Research Center, 2015), with continued debate about the negative effect of the games children play. A recent study found that four in ten adults believe that violence in video games leads to violent behaviour – 32 per cent play video games themselves, and 26 per cent self-identified as gamers (Pew Research Center, 2015). While a large body of research has found significant short- and long-term effects associated with video games, including a relationship between violent video games and post-game violence (Anderson et al, 2012), there are other studies that challenge these findings.

Given the large number of children and young people who play video games and the amount of time they spend playing them (Pew Research Center, 2015), it is important that practitioners have a critical and constructive approach and evidence-based understanding of the effects of online/video games and their associated risks and significance for children and their development. Therefore, in this chapter we offer an evidence-informed and systematic approach to examining the effects of online/video games. We begin with a brief description of gamification followed by a brief review of some theoretical explanations for the effects of online/ video games. We then use the 10 C's psycho-socio-ecological model and draw on existing research to provide a systematic framework for understanding the effect of online/video games. We conclude with a brief example of dark play and some practice reflections.

As video games can be played either online or offline, the social dimension of our analysis applies to video games that are played online and in a social mode.

Gamification

The main goal of games is reward or enjoyment. But, their impact on motivation and their widespread applicability has given them additional functions and applications in different areas of everyday life, ranging from training and education, to healthcare, and from social work and human sciences to engineering, politics, governance and management. These applications are known as 'serious games' and fall under the umbrella of 'gamification', Similar to serious games, gamification is the application of game elements for purposes other than sole entertainment.

Gamification and serious games are related in that both aim to leverage aspects of games to achieve something beyond playfulness. Indeed, they offer a fun way to solve real-world problems. Gamification has become a large industry and is widely used in everyday life and is embedded in most products and services ranging from earning loyalty points from supermarkets or airlines, to reward points on credit cards, to badges for doing sport activities, to raffles and prizes, and other forms of reward or discount. Indeed, most consumer transactions involve some sort of gamification.

Gamification goes beyond consumer products and is also used in education (from social work and human sciences to MBA studies and research degrees), behavioural change (for example, healthcare or Google PowerMeter that promotes energy saving), workforce development (for example, team building and professional development) or 'checking in' to mobile phone apps such as FourSquare and others. In general, gamification harnesses the motivational power of games in order to promote participation, persistence, performance and achievement. This is achieved by creatively crafting the reward, content, context, structure and mechanisms of the games to maximise enjoyment, flow, motivation and drive toward achieving the game's objectives. For example, cognitive behavioural game design is a new framework that combines social cognitive theory and theory of multiple intelligences as well as game design elements into a unified model that guides and helps designers create games for learning and behavioural change.

There is an ongoing debate about the impact of gamification, and that focusing on extrinsic motivation may have a negative effect on free choice and intrinsic motivation (Bielik, 2012). Others argue, however, that the negative effects are due to poor design rather than gamification (Bielik, 2012). The effects of the games' mainly extrinsic motivation mechanisms on intrinsic motivation are not clear and require further longitudinal research. Gamification is also combined with other techniques (for example, augmented reality) and SNSs and online/video games (see the example of Snapstreak in Chapter 1).

A brief theoretical framework

Several theoretical frameworks have been used to explain and understand the positive and negative effects of online/video games. One such theoretical platform is the General Aggression Model (GAM) (Anderson and Bushman, 2002), which has been widely used by many researchers to study media violence and its effects. The GAM draws on Bandura's (1973, 1983) social learning theory, and considers individual as well as personality and biological factors to explain the short- and long-term effects and processes that contribute to aggressive behaviour and personality. The GAM suggests that media violence (for example, violent video games) influences the person's internal state (for example, affective, cognitive and arousal states) and hence increases the short-term likelihood of aggression. GAM has been the dominant theoretical explanation used in research for aggression and violence, suggesting that violent games support the arousal and development of cognitive 'scripts' relating to aggression. However, although some have linked in-game violence to post-game aggression (Anderson and Murphy, 2003), others argue against such a link (Ferguson et al, 2008), while others highlight the need for further research in this area (Sherry, 2007). Nonetheless, meta-analyses by Anderson (2004) and Anderson and Bushman (2001) found a small but significant correlation between in-game and post-game aggression, serving as further empirical evidence for social learning theory.

In contrast to social learning theory, the catharsis hypothesis offers an alternative approach to examining the effect of violent video games. The catharsis hypothesis asserts that aggression may be provoked externally, but is fundamentally a biological drive that has been shaped by evolutionary adaptation and requires release (Lorenz, 1963). Humans may displace aggression in various ways and may express aggression in socially more acceptable ways (for example, by engaging in an aggressive sport rather than harming other people) (Megele, 2015). However, the catharsis hypothesis has also been challenged by several authors. For example, Sherry (2007) found that the intensity of effects decreased with longer video game exposure. This does not fully reject or support the catharsis hypothesis hence, Sherry suggests that it merits further investigation.

A qualitative study of young boys found that participants reported feeling calmer, less aggressive and less angry after playing video games (Olson et al, 2008); it seems that playing video games had a similar effect as using a punch bag or going for a run when feeling irritated or angry. Leisure activities can reduce stress and therefore, instead of catharsis hypothesis, it is possible that video games are used as a leisure activity and coping strategy for players to manage stress (Ryan et al, 2006).

Mood management theory offers an alternative perspective, and suggests that players select media that suits their prevailing mood and mitigates depressive feelings (Zillman, 1988). Hence, media that most effectively distracts players from negative emotions is the more likely choice. For example, young people experiencing a depressed mood may select games with violent content for the excitement and arousal offered by the game and, at times, this may improve the player's mood (Olson et al, 2008). We can conclude that people experiencing depressed mood or emotional difficulties may use media to make sense of their emotions (Nabi et al, 2006). Hence, when children play violent games, practitioners can use this as an opportunity to explore children's emotions, frustrations, sense of power and control vis-à-vis lack of power or control (many children derive a sense of control from playing video games), self-expression and voice, etc. It is important to appreciate how playing video games may meet these or other needs (for example, belonging and social validation) for children. For example, the achievement of tangible objectives within the game can be validating, and the social context of the game can amplify these effects. Therefore, it is essential that practitioners are able to assess and evaluate the effects and multidimensional impact of games within the specific circumstances of the child.

10 C's risk and resilience typologies and online/video games

Let us use the 10 C's psycho-socio-ecological model to analyse the risks and opportunities associated with online/video games.

Consumption risk (time spent and pattern of playing video games)

The amount of time spent playing video games influences the young person and can potentially lead to specific outcomes regardless of the content of the games. Although some of the effects of video games are not directly linked to the length of play time, increased video game play can have its own negative effects. While we discuss the challenge of excessive gaming and 'internet addiction' later, in Chapter 5, at this point, we should highlight that although the amount of time spent playing games or surfing the internet is an important factor in what is suggested as 'internet addiction', it is not a sufficient cause for 'addiction' (Gentile, 2009). Increased video game play offers increased exposure to the effects associated with the game, and therefore one would expect that it can reinforce the effects and outcomes associated with the other dimensions of video game play (for example, content, context, structure and the mechanics of the game). However, the overall effect of the game is a composite and complex risk that may have a different impact from the single components of the 10 C's psycho-socio-ecological model, as described later in this chapter.

Research suggests that time spent by children and young people playing video games can be linked to lower academic performance (Sharif and Sargent, 2006), while violent games are linked to violent behaviour but not school performance (Gentile et al, 2004). This is especially evident when the young person is engaged in excessive video game play, leaving little time for reading, learning and other activities. Although the consequences of the choice and trade-off between video game play versus academic learning is supported by research, it doesn't reflect the motivation behind the young person's choice. In other words, video game play can be a contributing factor to a young person's academic performance without being the primary cause. For example, young people who face difficulties and under-perform academically may spend more time playing video games and may derive a sense of validation from mastery of the game that compensates for their difficulty in academic performance and mastery. Therefore, although an excessive amount of time spent playing video games can have negative consequences, it is important to explore other meanings and possible factors, and to consider this information in the context of, and in relation to, the other dimensions of the 10 C's psycho-socio-ecological model. Furthermore, this suggests caution in generalising the effects of online/video games, and invites practitioners to keep an open mind and dialogue and to explore the effects and significance of the game for children with children.

Increased time spent playing video games may also result in other risks. For example, most video games are mainly sedentary, and therefore, increasing online/video game play time may mean decreasing time for physical activities, possibly leading to childhood obesity. However, practitioners could adopt a strength- and resilience-based approach and introduce the young person to movement-based games including Nintendo®'s Wii (for example, Wii tennis), Xerbike, LaserSquash, ApartGame, DanceDance Revolution, or perhaps Pokémon, to encourage movement and physical activity.

When evaluating the consumption risk for a game, patterns of consumption (for example, frequency/repetition and consistency) are as important as the total amount of playing time. A study of video game players spending an equal amount of time playing violent video games found that those who divided their video game play into regular and frequent intervals were more likely to react in an aggressive manner than those who played for longer hours but with less frequency (Gentile and Gentile, 2008). This highlights the importance of considering the consumption risk associated with children and young people's patterns of game play. We further explore the importance of time and patterns of consumption in Chapter 5.

Content risk (content of the game)

As described in Chapter 3, content risk is one of the most common and significant risks online. In the context of gaming, we consider content to refer to the script or themes of the game. Research demonstrates that game content leads to content-specific learning. For example, educational games have been used in schools and at home to support pupils and to facilitate learning various topics and school subjects (Corbett et al, 2001). Several studies demonstrate that playing violent video games can have causal as well as correlational effects. Indeed, some studies have shown that violent video games increase the likelihood of violent behaviour, while prosocial games increase the likelihood of helping behaviour. By the same token, many educational games can teach children and young people specific skills including reading and mathematics. Meta-analysis of various studies suggests that although the effectiveness of different games may vary, in general, educational games are very useful at teaching their content.

Examining 136 published and unpublished studies and research papers from both Eastern and Western cultures and involving more than 130,000 participants, Anderson and colleagues (2010) offer a meta-analysis of the effects of violent video games and their relationship to post-game aggression, and suggest that playing violent video games increases the likelihood of physiological arousal, aggressive thoughts, aggressive affect, physical aggression, desensitisation and low empathy and reduced probability of prosocial behaviour; these results were consistent across gender, culture and experimental design.

Context risk (context of the game)

The combination of the game scripts, themes, rules, goals and systemic risk ecology of the game define and create its context (see Chapter 3), and can influence the players differently. For example, most online games allow players to choose whether they wish to play against the computer or against other online players, and this has an impact on the contact risk and the connection and social capital risk. Many games also allow players to play either in single player mode (one player against all other players) or in team mode where the player pursues the same goals in a team together with other online players; this changes the context risk and has an impact on the way the players see themselves in the game, therefore affecting the consonance-dissonance and compatibility risk. These choices can influence the effects of the game. For example, the single player mode has no cooperative/collaborative feature and may therefore result in a more self-centred/individualistic focus compared to the team player mode that may promote other-awareness and perspective taking, although in both cases, the player may be exposed to the 'same amount' of violence.

The mechanics of the game influence both the context and content risks associated with the game. Practice can improve the player's skills in using the game's control device and may improve the player's physical skills such as gross motor skills (for example, using a Wii remote) or fine motor skills (for example, using one's thumb to control a joystick) or balancing skills (for example, using a Wii balance board); these can be used for non-game applications such as physical therapy.

Research shows that players produce a mental model of in-game elements that is enhanced with experience as they incorporate new learning, information and insights into this mental model (Graham et al, 2006). Indeed, 10- to 11-year-old children playing video games show 'expert' behaviour including self-monitoring abilities, pattern recognition, discipline in decision-making, qualitative thinking and superior memory (VanDeventer, 2002). This ability for self-monitoring and coordination of movement can be used in other circumstances including advanced modern surgery. Evidence (Rosser et al, 2007) shows that doctors performing laparoscopic surgery who had experience of playing video games for at least 3 hours a week were 27 per cent faster and made 37 per cent less errors on an advanced surgical skills course; indeed, video game experience proved to be a better predictor of surgical skill than prior laparoscopic surgical experience or the number of years that the person was in practice.

Context risk and character narratives in the game influence every aspect of the game including attitude formation, attribution of causality and players' perception and interpretation of the character's actions, and this mediates the effect of the game on players' post-game behaviour (Schwarz, 2007; Smith and Semin, 2007).

Connection and social capital risk (social context of the game)

Massively multiplayer online role-playing games (MMORPGs) include virtual reality and role-playing through online characters and involve large number of players (this can be thousands of players) – completing many of the game goals requires multiple players. Indeed, social games create their own social experience and context that provides the game context. Either formally or informally, groups and subgroups and cliques form within such games, generating a connection and social capital risk as well as contact risk; such groups are referred to as 'clans' or 'guilds' and are supported by the social features of the game. Social features refer to social context and the socialising aspects of video games, and include various game-related aspects and functionalities such as how players communicate with each other online and offline; features that allow the formation and maintenance of a community of players including rules of competition and cooperation (Megele and Buzzi, 2018e); support groups/networks that can help players learn about the game, and so on. Such a social dimension and support network allows experienced players to share their knowledge with others and to receive social recognition rewards, therefore influencing the players' sense of belonging, social capital and contact risks. These functionalities provide the social context for the game content and the shared challenge and online/telepresence inherent in playing MMORPGs. Such social structures and interactions combined with the cognitive and affective involvement associated with MMORPGs have an important impact for social identity, and serve as the social glue that binds online gaming communities around the game – online gaming communities are an important part of the game's appeal.

Adler (1992 [1931]) suggests that the fundamental motivation of humans is the need to belong, while Dreikurs and Soltz (1992 [1964]) explain that the desire to belong is inherent in children because they are social beings (see also Megele and Buzzi, 2018c). The social features and context of games such as MMORPGs offer mechanisms, groups, social tools and characteristics that can satisfy players' social and belonging needs (Cole and Griffiths, 2007). Indeed, the majority of players are part of a guild and play the game cooperatively for the possibility of sharing the winnings from the game – for example, about two thirds (66 per cent) of all players and 90 per cent of advanced players of World of Warcraft belong to a guild. Although few guild members may know each other personally, they are expected to adhere to group norms; failure to adhere to group norms and to meet one's obligation may have consequences ranging from loss of respect and social capital to expulsion from the group. For example, guild members may be asked to meet at specific times to play the game simultaneously and to continue playing until an in-game event (such as a 'raid') is complete. The game's social dimension and its systems of reward and punishment have implications for players' identities and the way they perceive themselves (consonance-dissonance and compatibility risk), and offer important added incentives for playing the game (consumption risk). However, these features may also result in inflexible commitments that may influence other dimensions of the young person's life (for example, sleep, studies, offline activities, face-to-face engagement with friends and peers).

Consonance-dissonance and compatibility risk

As mentioned above, the context, social dimension and script of the game influence the way players relate to and perceive their 'online identity/self', and this depends on the way the player interprets a given situation or behaviour. Therefore, attributing causal links to events may prove problematic; instead, in exploring the consonance-dissonance and compatibility risk of online/video games, practitioners should consider the meaning of children's behaviour and its significance for them. For example, children who perform poorly academically but who are successful in playing video games may find a sense of mastery and social validation, positive protective factors that may seem unachievable to them at school. Understanding the meaning of the game or behaviour for children, and how children see themselves online, enables practitioners to find more constructive approaches to safeguarding children while supporting them to maintain what is meaningful to them about a given experience.

Providing players with background information about the characters in the game provides a narrative context for the game and serves to immerse the player in its context. This also influences the players' interpretation of their in-game behaviour and their identification with the in-game character as well as their level of arousal and response to the game content and its effect on post-game behaviour (Fischer et al, 2010).

Personalising avatars and in-game characters increases identification with the character, although avatars need not be personalised to affect players and post-game behaviour. Yoon and Vargas (2014) found that regardless of the level of identification with their avatar, players who played heroic avatars were more likely to engage in prosocial behaviour than those playing an anti-heroic or neutral avatar. Furthermore, playing heroic avatars reduced hostile perception bias (the tendency to perceive neutral faces as hostile) and increased prosocial behaviour after the game (Happ et al, 2013). This demonstrates the importance of narrative context and how such narratives influence, moderate and alter the interpretation and effects of the game on players.

Composite and complex risks

Although each risk variable/dimension of the game can produce independent effects, they are also interlinked and have a cumulative effect on the experience of play and generate composite and complex risks; such combinations can even change the experience of the game. For example, in massively multiplayer online games (MMOGs) (for example, World of Warcraft), players who play in a team/group (guild) together with other players can access game content that is not available to individual players; this is an example of context influencing the content of the play and generating composite and complex risks. Furthermore, the social dimension to the game encourages collaboration and team working and increases connection and social capital as well as contact risks. For example, MMOGs can generate more complex effects as the social dimension of the game can influence and modify the game context and the meaning and significance of a given behaviour. For example, collective violence by guild members or being supported by guild members to use violence to achieve specific goals within the game may create a sense of acceptability of violence and therefore enhance the negative effects of in-game violence. However, the use of violence for prosocial purposes (for example, to save another team member) may be interpreted as heroic, and may therefore mitigate the effect of violence and encourage prosocial thoughts and behaviour. Hence, the contextual meaning of a behaviour is moderated and modified by its social context and the player's perception and motivations. This highlights the importance of avoiding generalisations and exploring such contextual meanings with children and young people.

Confidentiality and personal disclosure risk

Creating or selecting a game avatar/online persona and the social dimension of online/video games poses obvious confidentiality and personal disclosure risks. Try listing the confidentiality risks associated with an online/video game you know. Can the game itself or playing with others generate further confidentiality risks?

Contact risk

The context, connection and social capital dimensions of games pose virtual and physical contact risks. Indeed, many online/video games encourage such connections and contact by rewarding players who have many connections to virtually visit many of their connections. Such games often give the players the option of adding randomly assigned 'game friends', who can also be visited virtually. Since players can only visit each other every so often (for example, once a day), having many 'friends' (connections) offers the advantage of more visits and more rewards. These mechanisms help sustain and strengthen the online community around the game, however, they also pose contact risks for children and young people.

Conduct risk

The effects of the in-game experience on post-game behaviour is an example of the conduct risk associated with games.

Commercial exploitation risk

The convergence between online/video games and online gambling presents commercial exploitation risks for children. We explore this risk when we consider online gambling in the next chapter.

The preceding analysis of 10 C's risk typologies should be juxtaposed and mapped onto the psycho-socio-ecological model to provide a situated and holistic view of the risks and opportunities associated with online/video games (see Figure 4.1).

Figure 4.1: Play and online/video games: mapping risks, protective factors and resilience using the 10 C's psycho-socio-ecological model

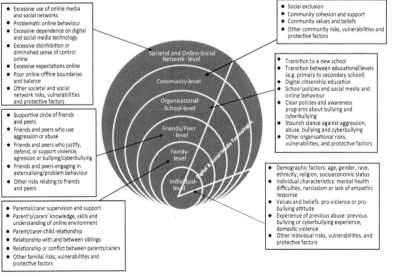

- Excessive use of online media and social networks
- Problematic online behaviour
- Excessive dependence on digital and social media technology
- Excessive disinhibition or diminished sense of control online
- Excessive expectations online
- Poor online-offline boundaries and balance
- Other societal and social network risks, vulnerabilities and protective factors

- Supportive circle of friends and peers
- Friends and peers who use aggression or abuse
- Friends and peers who justify, defend, or support violence, aggression or bullying/cyberbullying
- Friends and peers engaging in externalising/problem behaviour
- Other risks relating to friends and peers

- Parental/carer supervision and support
- Parent's/carers' knowledge, skills and understanding of online environment
- Parent/carer-child relationship
- Relationship with and between siblings
- Relationship or conflict between parents/carers
- Other familial risks, vulnerabilities and protective factors

Societal and Online Social Network - level
Community-level
Organisational-School-level
Friends/Peer -level
Family-level
Individual-level

- Social exclusion
- Community cohesion and support
- Community values and beliefs
- Other community risks, vulnerabilities and protective factors

- Transition to a new school
- Transition between educational levels (e.g. primary to secondary school)
- Digital citizenship education
- School policies and social media and online behaviour
- Clear policies and awareness programs about bullying and cyberbullying
- Staunch stance against aggression, abuse, bullying and cyberbullying
- Other organisational risks, vulnerabilities, and protective factors

- Demographic factors: age, gender, race, ethnicity, religion, socioeconomic status
- Individual characteristics: mental health difficulties, narcissism or lack of empathic response
- Values and beliefs: pro-violence or pro-bullying attitude
- Experience of previous abuse: previous bullying or cyberbullying experience, domestic violence
- Other individual risks, vulnerabilities, and protective factors

For larger version please see p 255

Dark play

In spite of its many positive potentials, digital and social media technologies and SNSs are fluid spaces that are also used for aggression, abuse and transgressive games and experimentation such as cyberbullying, online grooming and 'dark play'. The following case example offers a glimpse into dark play, and an example of when the children and their families' rights and boundaries are violated.

#BabyRP

Games such as #BabyRP are examples of the boundary transgressions and challenging problems that can occur online. #BabyRP is a game in which photos of babies are harvested/copied from other people's accounts (usually Instagram or Facebook) and re-posted under a different account with a new name and imaginary storyline, including virtual adoption, inviting others to role-play being daddy, mummy or the child.

Clearly, this can be quite distressing for parents who are oblivious to the fact that the photo of their child is being used in that manner, and usually find out only too late. However, players argue that they get the pictures from Instagram accounts that are public, and the fact that the accounts are public means that the pictures are public too, and so they are allowed to use them.

Players offer a variety of motivations for engaging in #BabyRP, ranging from wanting to be someone else who is loved, to missing being a child, to just having a good time. Most of the players seem to be young people role-playing as parents, but it is not difficult to find sexualised versions of #BabyRP.

Some possible good practice mindlines for parents and practitioners to avoid/prevent being victimised by #BabyRP include:

- being mindful and thinking about what one is posting and who it is shared with (content and conduct risks)
- keeping an account private and not accepting friends or followers one doesn't know (confidentiality, connection and contact risks)

- watermarking all images/photos, especially if they are being shared more widely (context risk)
- ensuring that location tagging is turned off (confidentiality and context risks).

Conclusion

Although social media and online/video games are in constant evolution, it is important that practitioners have an informed perspective and critical approach to examining and understanding the implications of online/video games for children and young people. To this end, in this chapter we have drawn on dominant theories and research to offer a structured, critical and evidence-informed approach for practitioners to think about and assess the positive and negative effects of online/video games and their implications for children and young people from a safeguarding perspective. This also enables practitioners to have an open and informed conversation with young people about online/video games.

Additional mindlines and reflections

The following additional mindlines and reflections may be helpful in practice.

- Children explore and learn about their world through the medium of play and are often excited about the games they play. Therefore, speaking about online/video games can help establish an open dialogue with children to explore their thoughts, emotions, experiences, preferences and priorities, as well as any challenges and strengths.
- Practitioners should carefully consider the social and narrative dimensions of online/video games and their impact and meaning for children. These are a source of social validation or challenge and risk for children, and are often much more significant and important than the actual content, structure or mechanisms of

the game. These aspects can be a source of both resilience and risk.

- It is essential to understand the effect of online/video games and its associated behaviours from children's perspective, and to consider their meaning and significance for children. This will enable practitioners to adopt alternative and constructive rather than restrictive approaches to protection, and to safeguard children in ways that the children can relate to and understand. In practice, this is a strength- and resilience-based approach that builds on positives, strengthens protective factors and enhances children's resilience to counter possible risks of negative outcomes. When necessary, using this approach practitioners can try to redirect the children's curiosity, passion and energy to other games and new forms of play to avoid specific risks that raise important concerns. In some cases, some form or level of restriction may become inevitable and indeed necessary; however, as a general rule, restrictive approaches should be used as a last resort rather than routine practice.

- Although we cannot assume that there is a stronger link between in-game and post-game violence in interactive games than other media, games encourage their players to engage with their in-game identity (for example, an avatar, character or entity that represents the player within the game); this generates content, context and consonance-dissonance and compatibility risks. Therefore, when considering the effects of the game and its content on children (effects on cognitions and behaviours), practitioners should go beyond what children do through their in-game identities/characters and consider the narrative and motivation of the children and the context for their actions and behaviour. It is the children's contextual meaning and interpretation of their in-game action that alters and mediates its positive or negative effects.

- Practitioners should distinguish between the goals of the game and the motivation of the in-game character played by the child vis-à-vis the child's motivation for playing the game. Although all three influence children's responses to the game and its effects, they are not the same, and each can produce an independent effect on children (Ryan et al, 2006).

Online games are praised by their proponents for their benefits and vilified by their critics for their negative effects, and interestingly, both parties are correct about online/video games having both positive and negative effects. The problem is when the complex and nuanced relationship between in-game features and post-game behaviour is extended in a simplistic and deterministic manner as blanket statements about online games and their effects. Considering the importance of empowerment and individual agency and adopting the 10 C's psycho-socio-ecological model for assessing the different risks and dimensions of online/video games allows us to move away from the simplistic dichotomy of good and bad and toward a more nuanced and multidimensional understanding of online/video games and their effects. This understanding encourages practitioners to avoid restrictive approaches that limit children's potential growth and digital citizenship, and instead enables them to adopt an evidence-informed strength- and resilience-based approach to supporting and safeguarding children and young people.

5

'Internet addiction': problematic and excessive internet use and online gambling

'Internet addiction': history and background

It was the work of Kimberley Young that drew the attention of researchers to investigate 'internet addiction'. Her first paper (Young, 1996) on internet addiction was a case study of a 43-year-old woman whose husband was seemingly addicted to AOL chatrooms, spending 40 to 60 hours online at a time. It should be noted that at that time internet connections were dial-up connections (computers were connected through the landline phone line), with an estimated hourly cost of about US$2.95 per hour. This created a financial burden for the family and eventually led to divorce as the husband met other women in these online chatrooms.

Replicating and adjusting the criteria for gambling in the *Diagnostic and Statistical Manual of Mental Disorders* (4th edn) (DSM-IV) (APA, 2000), Young (1998) proposed a set of criteria for diagnosing what she called 'internet addiction' (IA). She selected eight of the ten gambling criteria from DSM-IV that she thought also applied to internet use as the criteria for identifying IA, namely, preoccupation with the internet, a need for an increasing amount of time spent online to achieve the same amount of satisfaction, repeated efforts to curtail internet use, irritability, depression or mood lability when internet use is limited, staying online longer than anticipated, putting a job or relationship in jeopardy to use the internet, lying to others about how much time is spent online, and using the internet as a means of regulating mood. She argued that exhibiting five out of these eight criteria should be diagnosed as IA and the individual considered internet-dependent. Young admitted that her data collection strategy based on voluntary online or telephone surveys was somewhat biased, and that most people formed an 'addiction' to specific applications, services or networks on the internet rather than the internet itself. Nonetheless, her results highlighted several differences between 'addicted' and 'non-addicted' groups in her study, with implications for psychological and occupational wellbeing.

In parallel to Young's work, in Europe, research into IA began with the publication of Griffiths' (1995) paper on 'Technological addictions' that prompted further investigation into IA (Griffiths, 1996a, 1998) as well as specific online 'addictions' such as internet gambling 'addiction' (Griffiths, 1996b). This was followed by others studying prevalence, correlates and development, and validation of psychometric measures and instruments for IA. For example, Beard and Wolf (2001) suggested a modification of Young's (1998) criteria, stating that her first five criteria did not necessarily detect IA, and that at least one more from the remaining three criteria would have to be met in order to clearly confirm and define IA.

The American Psychiatric Association (APA) included 'internet gaming disorder' in DSM-5 as a 'condition for further study' (APA, 2013), which means that 'internet addiction', or more specifically, what DSM-5 calls 'internet gaming disorder', is currently not considered a 'disorder' in psychiatric terms, and requires further research and evidence, after which the APA will decide whether or not to make this an official 'disorder'. It should be noted that internet-based gambling is included in DSM-5 under 'gambling disorder', and is therefore not part of the new 'internet gaming disorder'.

The DSM-5 criteria for 'gambling disorder' are listed below. If an individual:

- gambles with an increasing amount of money in order to achieve desired excitement
- becomes irritable or restless when attempting to interrupt, reduce or stop gambling
- has made repeated unsuccessful attempts to control or reduce or stop gambling
- is often preoccupied with gambling (reliving past gambling experiences, planning for the next time gambling, thinking of ways to get money to gamble)
- often gambles when feeling distressed (for example, experiencing helplessness, guilt, anxiety, low mood)

- after losing money, often returns to win back the money/get even ('chasing' losses)
- lies to hide the extent of their involvement in gambling
- has jeopardised or lost a significant relationship, job, educational or career opportunity because of gambling
- relies on others to provide money to relieve desperate financial situations caused by gambling

and meets four or more of these criteria within 12 months, and their gambling behaviour is consistent and not sporadic, from a psychiatric perspective they are diagnosed with gambling addiction. The intensity of 'addiction' is rated based on the number of criteria met, that is, four to five criteria met = mild, six to seven criteria met = medium, eight to nine criteria met = severe.

The DSM-5 defines 'internet gaming disorder' as 'repetitive use of internet-based games, often with other players, that leads to significant issues with functioning', and suggests that for a positive diagnosis the individual must exhibit five or more of the following criteria over 12 months:

- preoccupation or obsession with internet games
- withdrawal symptoms when not playing internet games
- a build-up of tolerance – more time needs to be spent playing the games
- the person has tried to stop or curb playing internet games, but has failed to do so
- the person has had a loss of interest in other life activities, such as hobbies
- the person has had continued overuse of internet games even with the knowledge of how much they have an impact on their life
- the person lied to others about his or her internet game usage
- the person uses internet games to relieve anxiety or guilt – it's a way to escape
- the person has lost or put at risk an opportunity or relationship because of internet games.

The first inpatient facility for 'internet addiction' was opened in 2006 in Beijing, China (Jiang, 2009), and the first US national study of problematic internet use showed that one in eight Americans met at least one criteria for problematic internet use (Aboujaoude et al, 2006).

This is a brief history and current view from a psychiatric perspective. From a safeguarding perspective, although the evidence from psychology and psychiatry can help inform practice, practitioners should avoid medicalising the problem, and instead adopt an evidence-informed humanistic and person-centred approach to practice. Therefore, in this chapter we examine the challenges of excessive and problematic use of online media followed by a discussion of gaming and gambling and their implications for safeguarding from a psychosocial and evidence-informed perspective.

Changing and challenging context and concept

The advent of Web 2.0 and social technologies and social networking sites (SNS), such as Facebook in 2004 and Twitter in 2006, combined with 24-hour connectivity and developments in mobile technologies, have weaved the use of social media into the fabric of people's experience. Indeed, social technologies permeate and influence every phase and aspect of everyday life from home to work, from education to entertainment, and from shopping to personal and healthcare, and so on. The increasing convergence of technology, media, content, contact and devices are worlds apart from the dial-up internet access described in Young's (1996) initial case study, and pose new questions and challenges with regards to any possible definition of 'internet addiction'. Therefore, while recognising the challenges of excessive or problematic use of online media, it is important to note that any such indications should be considered as a question of the quality of the individual's engagement within the context of the 10 C's psycho-socio-ecological model rather than the sheer amount of time they are connected to the internet. Indeed, practitioners should exercise caution not to pathologise or stigmatise individual passion and preference or difference in behaviour as an 'illness' or pathology.

Furthermore, the notion of IA is unhelpful and confusing as it seems to suggest that somehow the individual is 'addicted' to the internet, while in practice individuals do not access the internet for sake of access to the internet itself; instead, they use the internet as a medium to access specific SNSs, apps, games, websites, etc, each of which represent a different consumption risk and can therefore be considered as a different behavioural 'addiction' (for example, online gambling; see Griffiths, 1996b). Young (1999) tried to address this problem by distinguishing several types of IA, such as 'cybersexual addition' (excessive and obsessive use of online pornography or obsessive engagement in cybersex often accompanied by the use of adult chatrooms); 'cyber-relationship addiction' (obsessive engagement in online relationships often at the expense of face-to-face relationships); 'net compulsion' (this includes a range of behavioural patterns such as obsessive online gambling, compulsive engagement in online social networks or online communities, obsessive online shopping, online stock trading, etc); 'information overload' (obsessive search and surfing of online databases and online information; Young suggests that those affected spend an increasing amount of time searching and organising data to the extent that this forms an obsessive compulsive tendency); and 'computer addiction' (obsessive use of technology, computers and other devices, including obsessive computer game playing in a work setting). The APA's (2013) adoption of the term 'internet gaming disorder' instead of 'internet addiction' is an implicit recognition that, from APA's perspective, this phenomenon is about specific behavioural patterns ('addictions') rather than 'addiction' to the internet itself.

'Internet addiction': some safeguarding considerations and mindlines

There is currently no general consensus regarding the conceptualisation and diagnosis of internet-related 'addictions' or difficulties (King et al, 2013). Hence, from a safeguarding perspective it is important to distinguish the specific pattern of excessive and problematic internet use based on a spectrum of related but independent patterns of behaviour. Therefore we can summarise the debate around IA as follows:

- The APA only included 'internet gaming addiction' in Section 3 of DSM-5 as an emerging phenomenon requiring further research and evidence (APA, 2013). Therefore, as of this writing, there is no official evidence-based 'diagnostic' consensus about IA.

- Research suggests that children and young people who use online media 'obsessively' may also experience other challenges such as bipolar experiences, social anxiety and difficulties with mood management (Shapira et al, 2000). Furthermore, Anderson (2001) argues that a large number of people using online media excessively may also meet or have met the criteria for substance abuse 'disorder' from a psychiatric perspective. This is consistent with patterns of behaviour noted in individuals with behavioural addictions such as online gambling, and suggests that those who experience addiction or certain excessive or 'obsessive' behaviours also have a higher likelihood of overusing online and social media technologies (Pratarelli and Browne, 2002).

- Given the vast use and applications of social media and their deep embedding in every aspect of everyday life and experience, it is important to avoid dichotomous thinking and blanket statements that confound human passion and individual preferences for self-expression with obsession and to pathologise common behaviours.

- Play is a complex medium that offers a host of opportunities for learning, self-expression and growth, and cyberspace offers infinite opportunities for play. Indeed, the virtually unlimited possibilities and continuous flow of online experiences are a natural magnet for children's curiosity and desire for learning and discovery, and an important part of their identity, new digital knowledge and skills, and digital citizenship. Therefore, early online engagement by children and young people should be considered and understood within the context of their curiosity and digital citizenship and development.

- Cultural differences play a significant role in defining and conceptualising childhood and its significance within different societies. Therefore, practitioners in different countries or cultural contexts should think about the meaning of childhood within the young person's culture and social setting, and act in ways that safeguard children and young people's universal rights in a culturally sensitive manner, enabling young people to strike and maintain a balance between different emotional, cognitive, functional, developmental, social and cultural domains in their lives.

- From a practice and safeguarding perspective and drawing on existing evidence, we can define problematic and excessive use of the internet and online digital and social media technologies as any pattern of use that results in disruption, neglect, underperformance, underachievement or underdevelopment in one or more dimensions and domains of people's lives and development (that is, a balance between emotional, cognitive, functional, developmental, social and cultural domains). Hence, if the young person is engaged and performing well in different life domains, then chances are that their online digital and social media engagements are not excessive or obsessive.

- Furthermore, it is important to understand the reasons and motivations why a young person may use a given SNS, software application (app), online service or community in an excessive or obsessive manner and have an evidence-informed understanding of its implications, correlated risks of positive and negative outcomes, protective factors and resilience.

- Practitioners can use the 10 C's psycho-socio-ecological model for holistic assessments as well as a structured and critical approach to examine online identities/profiles, behaviours, interactions and posts, and to identify the online risks of positive and negative outcomes, needs, rights, protective factors and resilience. For example, a high level of consonance-dissonance and compatibility risk may suggest excessive or inappropriate online activity.

- Online media can be quite self-absorbing and can influence the young person's needs and development in other domains of life. Therefore, practitioners can use the 10 C's psycho-socio-ecological model in conjunction with the assessment triangle to gain a holistic view of the child (see Chapter 3, Figure 3.4). Practitioners should consider children and young people's daily routines, and assess how their use of online media is having an impact on their needs and development. This includes the young person's eating and sleeping patterns, academic performance, engaging offline with family, friends and peers, etc, and how these aspects may be affected by online activity.

- For example, research indicates that adolescents need more than nine hours of sleep a night (Carskadon, 1999). Mobile phones and other digital devices can influence the young person's sleeping hours and its quality, and studies indicate that lack of sleep can lead to a host of physical, mental and emotional difficulties, from poorer memory to difficulty with attention and impulse control and information processing, substance misuse, anxiety, depression and suicidal ideation. Furthermore, chronic sleep problems can rewire the prefrontal cortex, and this can extend poor sleeping patterns into adulthood (Calamaro et al, 2009). Therefore, it is important that in conversation with young people, practitioners explore constructive approaches and a healthy balance between online and offline activities; this could include approaches to restoring boundaries and balancing online-offline engagement, as discussed later in this chapter.
- Davis's (2001) cognitive behavioural model suggests that psychological factors can generate vulnerabilities that can lead to cognitive distortions and dependence on online content. Therefore, practitioners can also use psychosocial and relationship-based approaches (Megele, 2015) such as cognitive restructuring, as described later in this chapter.
- Furthermore, young people's perception and cognitive schema of social media and online environments as friend' represents a cognitive bias and blind spot that can increase their vulnerability (Davis, 2001).

Young people may tailor their online identity differently from their offline/'in-person' identity, and this may represent their preferred-self-narrative or may be aimed at compensating for what they perceive as lacking in their offline experience. This discrepancy offers a potential space (Megele, 2015) for development, and raises potential consonance-dissonance and compatibility risks (see Chapter 3). This alters one's consciousness (Griffiths, 2000) and, for young people experiencing behavioural addition, can lead to dissociation (Suler, 2004) and inappropriate or excessive use of digital and social media (Billieux et al, 2015). Therefore, it is essential that solutions and safeguarding plans are co-produced between practitioners, the young person and their families and other professionals in a holistic and integrated, multiprofessional and interagency approach.

Online gambling

Technology has always played an important role in games, but over the past few decades we have seen an increasing overlap between games and gambling combined with new forms of gambling and their online spread (King et al, 2013). The widespread use of gamification enhances extrinsic motivation and reward-seeking behaviour, while the blurring of boundaries and increasing convergence between online/video games and gambling poses new and complex safeguarding challenges. The overlap between video games and gambling and between social games (for example, MMOGs) and social gambling increases the exposure of young people to, and the likelihood of their involvement in, gambling at a younger age (King et al, 2010). Therefore, in this section we briefly examine some of the effects of digital technologies on types, mechanisms and the spread of gambling, and their implications for safeguarding children and young people.

While governments usually regulate access to legalised gambling, digital technologies enable gambling operators to register websites in unregulated or poorly regulated jurisdictions, and offer gambling products across the globe to anyone, anywhere, anytime (Eadington, 2004). Furthermore, thinking of smart technologies, every digital device (from a mobile phone to digital pads, and from laptops to gaming devices such as PlayStation, Xbox, PSP and others) that can connect to the internet can serve as a potential digital gambling device and can also access SNSs. This brings 24-hour gambling, including social gambling, within easy reach of young people, and increases the risk of problem gambling.

The UK Gambling Commission's *Young people and gambling 2016* report (Ipsos MORI, 2016) indicates that 450,000 children (21 per cent of boys, 11 per cent of girls) are gambling in England and Wales every week, and around 9,000 of these are likely to be problem gamblers. The findings indicate that overall about 16 per cent of 11- to 15-year-olds gamble; this figure is higher than the number of 11- to 15-year-olds who had smoked (5 per cent) or drank alcohol (8 per cent) in the week preceding the survey, or who had taken drugs (6 per cent) in the month preceding the survey.

Problem gambling can be defined as behaviour that seems beyond the person's control and that disrupts or has a negative impact in various domains of the person's life including personal aspects, relationship with family and friends, financial and employment relations, and other functional, social, emotional, psychological or developmental domains. Problem gambling is often linked to a host of other difficulties including financial problems, crime, depression and suicide.

Online gambling: some safeguarding considerations, mindlines and practice reflections

Online gambling is pervasive and involves more complex considerations than offline gambling as a number of different factors can influence and compound its challenges. Therefore, below is a summary of some of these challenges that may affect children and young people.

To begin, it is important to note that given the increasing overlap between online/video games and gambling, many of the approaches to analysing online/video games, as described in Chapter 4, also apply to online gambling. Early introduction of young people to online gambling, and mobile phones or apps that provide easy 24-hour access to mobile gaming (mGaming) regardless of age and ability, can generate safeguarding concerns. Indeed, the Ipsos MORI (2016) survey shows that among the respondents who gambled, 73 per cent used apps and mobile phones to do so (up from 64 per cent the previous year). Online disinhibition and dissociative effects compound the problem as they increase individuals' impulsive tendencies and behaviours (Suler, 2004). Indeed, evidence suggests that a higher percentage of online gamblers meet the criteria for problem gambling than non-internet gamblers (Griffiths and Barnes, 2008); this is part of online gambling's context risk.

Digital and interactive televisions and television programme hashtags on social media allow consumers to engage and interact with broadcast programming using a variety of possibilities. This enables television programmes to obtain feedback and enhance participation through various media ranging from SMS (short messaging service) text to online social media posts or interacting with a programme's hashtag (for example, the hashtag #BBCQT for BBC's Question Time). This two-way communication offers a host of opportunities for engagement, including the possibility of purchasing merchandise from broadcasters, subscribing or purchasing access to programmes, voting on programmes, and entering competitions or gambling (for example, betting on games or races); this generates context, content, contact, conduct and composite and complex risks.

Simulated gambling refers to online interactive gambling that offers the same features and setting (context, content, structure, etc) as the actual game without requiring monetary investment. We refer to gambling that does not involve monetary investment as non-monetary gambling. There is little regulation for simulated gambling and non-monetary social gambling on social media sites; this represents composite and complex risks.

Traditional online/video games have a limited number of possible game outcomes, and so there is a clear connection between the player strategy and actions vis-à-vis the game outcomes; hence, practice and repeating the game can improve performance in the game. While gambling outcomes are randomised and uncertain, therefore, a player's actions and strategy can result in variable outcomes; hence, practice and repeated play do not necessarily improve performance (this represents context risk). However, the increasing overlap and similarities between video games, simulated gambling, non-monetary and monetary gambling may result in normalisation of gambling as 'just another game', with a possible implicit misconception about predictability or controllability of its outcome and that practice can improve performance – an obviously false assumption that can lead to financial losses and other risks and adverse outcomes (representing content, conduct and composite and complex risks).

Many online games on SNSs such as Facebook offer gambling-like features or wagering opportunities for virtual credit or points that can be paid for with money, and many online gambling sites and apps offer simulation and free-to-play games that are similar to online/video games. Winning and accumulation of virtual credit/money or points on SNSs may allow players to buy virtual goods or services, give virtual gifts or obtain added privileges (for example, extended play time or premium services); these can lead to higher status and may represent meaning and significance that go beyond their monetary value (Downs, 2008) (representing complex and composite risks). There are also numerous apps and sites that offer both monetary and non-monetary simulated gambling, and although online gambling may not necessarily lead to problem gambling, increased access to gambling increases the risk of problem gambling (Lund, 2008; Griffiths et al, 2009). Forrest et al (2009) found that non-monetary gambling was also correlated with problem gambling among young people. Even when games do not involve money (for example, playing poker for points on Facebook), they introduce young people to the idea and principles of gambling, and can have a normalising effect. Indeed, King et al (2014) ($n=1,287$, 12- to 17-year-olds) found that simulated games generate familiarity with gambling, and this can make young people more inclined to engage in gambling with monetary involvement. These represent content, conduct and complex and composite risks.

Smeaton and Griffiths (2004) examined 30 gambling websites in the UK, and found that more than half did not verify the age of the players, and 29 out of 30 did not have a self-limiting option, and 26 out of 30 did not have reference to gamblers help or consumer protection. Indeed, many websites use aggressive marketing strategies to continue to engage the players even if they are trying to quit or leave the site. Furthermore, Griffiths and Parke (2010) argue that many of the penny auctions that are not considered gambling actually represent a form of gambling with the obvious risk of losing money. These represent content, conduct and complex and composite risks.

Griffiths (2013, pp 84-5) highlights that although games like FarmVille are not considered gambling, like gambling, such games use operant conditioning (Skinner, 1953) and random reinforcement schedules as behavioural reinforcement techniques to keep players engaged for the maximum amount of time possible. Operant conditioning is a form of learning that assumes that the strength of a behaviour is modified by the behaviour's consequences (for example, reward or punishment), and that the behaviour is controlled by its antecedents (that is, discriminative stimuli) that then signal those consequences. For example, a child can learn to open a box to get the candy inside the box, or learn not to touch a hot stove to avoid burning. In this case the box and the stove are discriminative stimuli. However, when the stimuli signal significant reward or punishment, the associated response or behaviour can become reflective (for example, the dog in Skinner's test [1953] salivating at the sound of a bell). The use of random reinforcement schedules in the game results in unpredictability of rewards/winnings (Griffiths, 2013), and this generates constant excitement and expectation that the next round in the game may be the winning round; this encourages the player to play with the hope of just one more round. Hence, some gaming companies have been accused of using the mechanics and psychology of gambling to build and maintain their customer base (Griffiths, 2013). This may explain why players may find it hard to interrupt the game (for example, interrupting children and young people's play may lead to a tantrum or irritation) (Hiniker et al, 2016). Hence, choice of digital games that are engaging for a dual audience (parents and children) with built-in 'pauses' may allow for better balance and social and learning interactions (Hirsh-Pasek et al, 2015). For example, Bedtime Math offers a platform that encourages such dyadic activity in which parents and children read stories and answer maths questions together on a nightly basis, and research has demonstrated its benefits (for example, Berkowitz et al, 2015). Indeed, game design that taps into social interactivity for functionality holds great positive potential, although most games are still focused on individual players (Wartella, 2013). These factors generate context, conduct and composite and complex risks.

Parents, family and friends can play an important role in normalising and introducing young people to gambling. Parents who introduce children to gambling at an early age, or parents who are heavy gamblers, are a key social risk that increases the probability of problem gambling in the future (Ipsos MORI, 2016) (contact, conduct, and composite and complex risks).

Apart from parental influences on young people's access to and involvement in gambling, evidence suggests that online gambling offers new ways and greater potential for young people to explore and engage in gambling without parental supervision. In their study of parental influences on adolescents' commercial (monetary) and simulated (non-monetary) gambling and 'the association between parental influences and problem gambling', King and Delfabbro (2016; n=824) found that although gambling was usually facilitated by a parent, particularly for scratch cards and sport betting, simulated gambling and social gaming were reported as mostly unsupervised. More importantly 'Young people's perceptions of parents' measures to limit, restrict or oversee online and electronic activities were not significantly associated with youth simulated gambling. Their perceptions of parental influences were not significant predictors of problem gambling behaviours.' King and Delfabbro's (2016, p 424) study 'underscores the need to examine potential differences in how adolescents develop an understanding of different gambling activities without parental influences, and adds to the continuing debate on the necessity of regulation and other countermeasures to limit young people's access to simulated gambling activities.' This is a further reaffirmation that online gambling presents a complex and multidimensional problem and requires a more sophisticated and integrated policy and practice approach, presenting composite and complex risks.

Practitioners can draw on the combination of learning and ideas from Chapter 4 and this chapter to critically assess the risks associated with video games and gambling. It is important to note that the social dimension of video games and gambling add a performative dimension to individual behaviour and amplifies their associated risks (Megele, 2014b; Megele and Buzzi, 2018b, 2018e). Furthermore, the social dimension of games and gambling raises contact risks, and can augment the impact and significance of content, context, conduct and composite and complex risks.

Below are a few additional considerations and mindlines for practice reflection in relation to excessive or problematic internet use and online gambling from a safeguarding perspective.

Studies have shown that loneliness, anxiety, low mood and depression can increase the likelihood of excessive or problematic internet use. Therefore, it is important to think about the young person's emotional and mental state and psychological wellbeing in relation to their online activities and engagement. Hence, consideration of connection and social capital risk with measures that enhance the young person's social capital, such as healthy relationships and offline relationships, as well as consideration of composite and complex risks with measures that reduce the person's anxiety or low mood, can be helpful to mitigate excessive or problematic use of online media. Furthermore, young person's participation in an age-appropriate support group can be an effective complementary safeguarding strategy.

If the young person is of an age that they can keep a daily journal, it may be helpful for them to keep a journal to capture their emotional experiences online and offline. For example, when the young person feels an urge to go online, they can take note of the emotions they experience in that moment, or if they are online, they can note their experience and emotions afterwards. Such a journal will help document and explore the emotions and mental states experienced by young people when they feel the urge to 'go online', after they have been online and have 'just come offline'. Do they experience reduced anxiety, feel more upbeat, smarter or more confident online than offline? Do they feel irritated, anxious, depressed or isolated when they are not online? These are important cues that can help practitioners better understand and address the young person's needs and experiences.

The young person may need specialist support (for example, therapy or psychiatric support) in relation to their excessive or problematic use of online media or gambling. It may also be necessary to make a referral to a rehabilitation centre where trained professionals can support and guide the young person toward a healthier and more balanced lifestyle. Ensuring a strong team around the child that can meet their needs, mitigate their vulnerabilities and support their growth and development is essential for effective safeguarding.

Practitioners can use the 10 C's psycho-socio-ecological model in conjunction with the assessment triangle (see Figure 3.4) to gain a holistic view of the child (see Figure 5.1), and to ensure a holistic approach to assessments and safeguarding. Thinking about the situation from a psychosocial and relationship-based perspective, practitioners can also draw on various approaches (see Megele, 2015) including using cognitive behavioural approaches such as cognitive restructuring, behavioural exercises or exposure therapy techniques to influence the young person's thinking and to bring about positive change. Therefore, given its usefulness for a range of interventions, we briefly describe the use of cognitive restructuring as a tool to support practitioners' communication

Figure 5.1: 'Internet addiction': mapping risks, protective factors and resilience using the 10 C's psycho-socio-ecological model

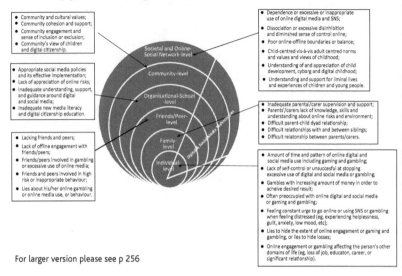

For larger version please see p 256

and intervention with young people. It is important to note that although this approach may be helpful in supporting young people, it doesn't substitute the need for counselling and specialist support, and depending on the level of risk involved, practitioners may need to engage a cognitive behavioural therapist.

Cognitive restructuring technique

Cognitive restructuring is a helpful approach for working with young people with excessive or problematic use of online media or those who experience a sad mood and unhappy feelings. It can also be used to manage stress as well as mental health challenges such as depression, anxiety, post-traumatic stress, relationship difficulties, social phobias, binge eating and other difficulties. This approach can be useful for practitioners and for young people, and can be applied in everyday situations, ranging from managing everyday stress or preparing for a stressful task to resolving family or interpersonal conflicts.

Technically this approach is meant to challenge and reframe what is referred to as cognitive distortions or 'automatic beliefs' that are usually the reason behind the problem. Although helpful, this approach doesn't address the unconscious or deep-rooted trauma or challenges faced by the individual. Cognitive restructuring is aimed at reframing unnecessary negative thinking or negative feelings that we all occasionally experience. By reflecting and reframing the situation, this technique helps the person approach the situation with a more positive mood and frame of mind. In effect, cognitive restructuring teaches the individual to notice their automatic thoughts and to examine them to see whether they are rational. This also makes the person aware of automatic triggers and enables them to engage in active and reflective thinking in order to disrupt the automatic thoughts and reactions. Below is a step-by-step approach to using cognitive restructuring in practice.

Step 1: Calm the young person: Upset, agitation or anger reduce our cognitive capacity and ability to reflect and explore our thoughts and feelings. So, if the young person is still upset, angry or stressed by the thoughts and feelings that you need to explore, they will find it difficult to reflect on them. Use a calming technique such as deep breathing, mindfulness or meditation techniques, or an activity that is calming or allows releasing stress (for example, play); the selection of calming technique should be developmentally appropriate and suit the specific context (for example, using drawing or toys to engage smaller children).

Step 2: Identify the antecedent event: Ask the young person to describe the situation that triggered their negative mood and note down the details. This should be done in an age-appropriate manner – for example, while young adults may be able to write down their experience in a more or less reflective manner, young children may not be able to write down the details of the situation. Therefore, for younger children you can use emoji-like expressions or a simple drawing with simple writing to highlight the key points that they describe.

Step 3: Analyse the person's mood and feelings: Ask the young person to describe in an age-appropriate manner the moods and feelings that they experienced during the situation. Here the focus should be on the young person's feelings (what they felt) and not their thoughts (what they thought) or behaviour (what they did) during the situation. An easy way to distinguish between moods and thoughts is to remember that we can usually describe a feeling or mood in one word, while thoughts are more complex and cannot be condensed in one word. For example, 'Mummy told me off in front of my friends' is a thought, while a relevant feeling or mood may be humiliation, anger, frustration, insecurity, rejection, etc.

Step 4: Identify automatic thoughts and beliefs: Ask the young person to describe the immediate reaction or 'automatic thought' when they felt the mood or feeling that they experienced. Examples of some 'automatic thoughts' relating to the preceding paragraph may be: 'Mummy doesn't like me.' 'Mummy hates me.' 'Mummy is rude.' 'Mummy is aggressive.' 'No one likes me.' 'I can't do anything right.' 'It is just like mummy.' 'I can never face my friends again.'

It is important to identify the young person's 'hot thoughts' – the thoughts that come almost instantaneously with a negative emotion; it is as if the thought is inseparable from the emotion experienced. For example: I hate you = anger; anger toward a person may be accompanied with the thought of really hating the person. 'I am a failure' or 'I always mess it up' = depression. 'God, is that a snake?' = fear. Although, seeing a snake can provoke significant fear, if the person is looking at a hose pipe and thinking it is a snake, that represents a cognitive distortion.

Step 5: Disputing automatic thoughts and identifying supportive and contradictory evidence: Divide a sheet of paper into two columns and write the heading 'Supportive evidence' in the first column and 'Contradictory evidence' in the second. Ask the young person to identify and describe evidence that effectively supports their automatic thoughts and list these in the first column. In the case of our earlier example, this could be 'After my friends left, mummy continued ignoring me and didn't answer me, even when I asked her something several times', or 'After my friends left, mummy continued mocking me.' The main focus in this step is to identify and note specific actions, events, comments or other indications that support the automatic thought that the young person experienced.

Ask the young person to think about and identify evidence that contradicts the automatic thought and note these down in the second column. In the case of our example, this could be

'Afterwards mummy said nice things about me to my friends.' 'Mummy often praises me.' 'Mummy was nice to me afterwards and gave me my favourite snack.'

Step 6: Identify and formulate alternative explanations and more balanced thoughts: Review and re-evaluate the supportive and contradictory evidence together with the young person, and ask them to formulate and describe a fair and more balanced thought about the situation. If the young person remains unsure about the situation, try further reflection and drill deeper into each step, and test each question in some other ways. In the case of our example, a balanced thought may be: 'I did something that was inappropriate which made mummy intervene. I have learned my lesson and mummy loves me and my friends respect me.' 'Mummy should have been gentler. But mummy loves me and my friends respect me.'

Step 7: Check the present mood: Take a moment with the young person to reflect and re-assess their present mood. Are they feeling better and have the preceding steps helped provide a better and more balanced view of the situation? Are there any further actions that you or the young person need to consider? Re-examining these questions can help assess the situation and decide on the next step and any additional actions that may be needed.

This approach is a central cognitive behavioural therapy (CBT) technique that can be used in a purposeful and solution-focused manner to help and support people who access services. In her book *Psychosocial and relationship-based practice*, Megele (2015) offers a range of holistic and evidence-informed approaches with detailed case studies that may be helpful for those interested in effective and evidence-based practice and interventions.

Restoring boundaries and balancing online–offline engagement

Parents and practitioners can adopt either active mediation (for example, explore and discuss the positive and negative aspects of various contents, contexts and behaviours) or restrictive mediation (for example, pose limitations for young people's use of the internet including hours, content, SNSs or websites) to safeguard young people. Active mediation and taking the time to explore the risks and consequences of online behaviour help inform parents and young people, and are greater protective factors than restrictive rule-setting that only limits young people's access and behaviours. Nonetheless, a balanced combination of active and restrictive parental mediation often offers the most effective approach and protective measure for young people. Below are some suggested approaches to restoring boundaries and balance between the online and offline engagement of young people (it is important to note that each item below requires discussion and agreement with the young people and their parents and carers):

Create screen-free zones in the home: Having areas of the home screen-free is important for maintaining a balance between online and offline activities. In discussion with the young people and their parents and carers, agree for specific areas of the home to remain screen-free, such as the kitchen or bedrooms, etc.

Agree screen-free time: As part of the daily routine, agree making devices such as TVs, phones, computers, games or other electronics off limits at specific times, for example, dinnertime and before bedtime. It may be necessary to establish more extended breaks from technology each day, especially for families with very young children.

Agree family time: This can offer opportunities for family bonding and providing a time and space when young people can discuss their experiences, emotions, daily activities or any other conversations. It may be necessary to support parents in achieving this goal, for example, you may have to participate in initial family time meetings to help establish a balance and support children and their significant others.

Device curfew: Each family is different, but considerations about where computers are located, access to mobile devices and levels of conversation between parents and children regarding their usage are important. Deciding when all devices are turned off or agreeing that phones and other digital devices will charge overnight in the parents/carers' bedroom can also be a way of limiting overnight access, ensuring children and families get undisturbed and uninterrupted sleep. Depending on the situation, for example, when there is excessive use of online media or problem gambling problems, curfews may need to be extended over longer periods.

Diversify children's media use and games: Completely blocking children and young people's media use should only be a last resort, and can be ineffective and may result in covert online access through friends' phones or other sources. An alternative is to redirect young people's interest and media use in ways that promote learning, interaction, connection and creativity. Diversifying media time can help mitigate the risk of excessive focus on one single activity; this reduces the impact of a single activity and helps avoid some of the negative consequences of excessive or obsessive attention and use. There are also many interactive educational media that use gamification. Introducing young people to such media in an age-appropriate manner can help redirect their attention to a more helpful and positive online engagement.

Co-view and co-play: Parents and carers should invest time for co-viewing shows (online or on TV) or co-playing games with children. Co-viewing and co-playing allow the support of young people and enhance child–parent relationships and bonding while ensuring that the programmes are age-appropriate. These also help parents better understand and support their children's experiences, thinking and challenges.

Lead by example: Establishing and following simple rules that create a better balance between online and offline engagements is important, and parents should lead by example. This includes not bringing phones to the table at meal times, not looking at the phone or texting while speaking with others and apologising if it is necessary or urgent to respond to a message or phone call.

Being a good digital citizenship: In collaboration with parents, support children and young people to be good digital citizens. This includes discussion of privacy and online challenges, and speaking with children about digital citizenship and its consequences, acknowledging and supporting their struggles and concerns while promoting and guiding their curiosity in a developmentally appropriate manner.

Separating the young person from the source of the problem: When there is risk of harm or abuse (for example, cyberbullying or other abuse), agree specific measures with children and young people and their parents and carers to separate and protect the young person from the source of harm/problem.

Conclusion

In conclusion, with 24-hour connectivity and when digital and social media technologies are an integral part of children and young people's experiences and identities, it is the quality and nature of engagement rather than its quantity that determine inappropriate use of digital media or the internet. However, any such assessment should be made with careful consideration of the 10 C's risk typologies and in the context of the lived experience of children and young people. Therefore, practitioners can use the 10 C's psycho-socio-ecological model for holistic safeguarding and to discuss, explore and recognise the types and patterns of the young person's behaviours and activities, and the motivations and gratifications that drive those behaviours and activities as well as their implications and associated risks. This information can then provide the basis for a more effective support and safeguarding plan that can mitigate risks including the young person's risky behaviour (for example, problem gambling, financial risk taking) and the drivers of those behaviours. Furthermore, it is important to accurately identify and mitigate the cognitive distortions that support problem gambling or other excessive, inappropriate or obsessive behaviours. As discussed in this chapter, where possible, practitioners can use cognitive restructuring techniques to contain young people's anxieties and cognitive distortions. However, each situation is unique and should be carefully and critically considered, and most cases may require interagency and multiprofessional working including the involvement of a cognitive behavioural therapist or other professional to support the young person and to address the identified risks and challenges.

6

Sexting

The *Oxford English Dictionary* added 'sexting' to its lexicon in 2010, defining it as 'the sending of sexually explicit photographs or messages via mobile phone'. However, given the increasing impact of social technologies and shifting boundaries, as discussed earlier in Chapter 2, today the concept of sexting extends far beyond SMS messages and the use of mobile phones, and includes a large number of different media and devices. Hence, Ringrose et al (2012, p 9) define sexting as 'sexually explicit content communicated via text messages, smartphones, or visual and Web 2.0 activities such as social networking sites'. To ensure compatibility with current and emerging technologies, we define sexting here as any sexually indicative artefact shared with or communicated to others, or any solicitation or encouragement for others to do so. In this definition, we have used the term 'sexually indicative' instead of 'sexually explicit' to better emphasise the semiotic and symbolic aspects of sexually toned sexting images. We must emphasise that taking, making, sharing and possessing indecent images and pseudo-photographs (images made by computer graphics or otherwise which appear to be or are similar to photographs) of people under 18 is illegal. To be clear, although 'indecent' is not defined in the UK legislation it includes penetrative and non-penetrative sexual activity; 'making' includes opening, accessing, downloading and storing online content; while 'sharing' includes texting, emailing, offering on a file-sharing platform, uploading to a site that other people have access to, displaying, and possessing with a view to distribute.

Sexting poses a range of problems and risks, and one of the most concerning aspects is the risk that shared images and sexts could be forwarded to an audience wider that the one originally intended by the producer of the sext. This can damage the person's image and lead to a host of problems including cyberbullying, sextortion (sexual extortion and exploitation) and pornography.

Although the exchange of self-produced sexually explicit images within the context of relationships or harassment cases is not a new phenomenon (Chalfen, 2009), digital and social media technologies have dramatically transformed its potential for replication and further distribution as well as its consequence for the person's image and identity. This significantly amplifies the risks of negative outcomes associated with sexting. Dissemination of sexting can be done on several levels, ranging from showing a sexually explicit image of a peer to one's friends to forwarding the sext message to others, to posting the sext content or image on blogs or SNSs or other websites. Indeed, some websites are dedicated to such transgressive and inappropriate posting of images, messages or screen shots of other people's images and messages of various nature.

Such actions could be motivated by a host of factors, such as demonstrating one's popularity, gaining peer approval, as a game and 'just for fun', expressing intimacy or one's sexuality or revenge porn for a relationship gone sour. However, regardless of motives, sexting can have significant and far-reaching consequences. Once an image or message is posted online, the dissemination and sharing potential of social media technologies poses significant challenges for possible remedial actions or safeguarding interventions – once an image or a message is transmitted or posted online, it becomes almost impossible to retrieve and fully delete, or to know how many people have seen, copied or redistributed it. This is a great challenge for safeguarding and managing the consequences of sexting.

Studies indicate (Dake et al, 2012; Rice et al, 2012) that sexting is correlated with a number of other risk-taking behaviours, such as:

- Young people who engaged in sexting had a greater likelihood of sexual activity and of having unprotected sex.
- Young people who engaged in sexting had an increased risk of becoming target of cyberbullying.
- Sexting has also been associated with the use of alcohol, marijuana and smoking cigarettes.

Furthermore, the EU Kids study (Livingstone et al, 2011) found a direct correlation between several risk factors, including exposure to sexual images online; having experienced hurtful behaviour online; seeing or receiving sexual messages; online contact with strangers; meeting an online contact offline for the first time; exposure to potentially harmful user-generated content online; experience of misuse of personal data/information; having acted in aggressive or hurtful ways towards others; sending or posting sexual messages; and any one or a combination of these factors. Research in the US involving 12- to 18-year-olds suggests that sexting may lead to sadness, hopelessness, suicide and suicide ideation. However, it is not clear as to whether sexting precedes and contributes to, or follows and is a consequence of, such risky behaviour, and so further research is needed in this area.

Notwithstanding the above, there are divergent interpretations of sexting. Some argue that sexting is a standalone safer sex alternative to sexual intercourse, while others suggest that it is a way of documenting one's sexuality. Therefore we can conceptualise sexting from a psycho-socio-ecological perspective as a by-product of technological convergence and a form of sexual expression that re-mediates and inscribes one's sexuality as a digital artefact and user-generated capital in the attentional economy of contemporary digital culture. This implies that sexting is a user-generated expression of one's sexuality aimed at attracting social recognition/attention and increasing an individual's social capital. In the remainder of this chapter, we use the 10 C's psycho-socio-ecological framework to unpack the relevant risks, protective factors and resilience associated with sexting.

Selfies: some mindlines

Most sexting images are 'selfies'. A selfie is an example of digital embodiment capturing and inscribing the physical (one's self and surrounding/environment) onto the digital and virtual realm. Selfies have a wide range of purposes and can be helpful in documenting, storifying or narrating one's experience, mood, physicality, presence, surrounding, relationships, and so on. A selfie is a powerful mode of self-expression with multiple layers of meaning and information. Some argue that selfies are a mode of sharing and that sharing is caring. Although that is true to some extent, when we overshare or share the wrong information or unintentionally share private information online, it can lead to tricky conversations and present unexpected risks and unintended consequences.

The following mindlines for sharing selfies may therefore be helpful in mitigating unwelcomed consequences or negative outcomes that may arise as a consequence of posting a selfie.

- *Sexually toned selfies:* as discussed in Chapters 1, 2 and 3, once you share a given image or information online, even through private channels, it can be shared and distributed beyond the original audience or used/misused in ways that were not originally intended with unexpected consequences. Therefore, as a general rule if you are not able to share the information openly with your friends and family, then don't share it in a selfie or private sext or on other social media private channels.
- *Turn off geo-location settings*: sharing geo-location may be helpful for using digital assistants such as Alexa, Cortana, Google Now or Google Maps; however, when geo-location is on, all your data is tagged with your location. That means your selfies too will have your location saved with the image, so as you share the image you are also sharing where you took that image. This data can be misused in several ways: for example, sexual offenders can use such information to learn about the places a child visits, or burglars can use the information to know when you are away on holiday. So make sure you turn off geo-location before taking a selfie.
- *Be mindful of the information you share in a selfie*: a selfie can reveal much more information than your location. For example, a logo or other signs can reveal the place of your work, or an emblem on a child's school uniform may identify the child's school; buildings and landmarks may still identify your location; selfies may tag not only your location but personal attributes such as age and gender. Hence, it is important to be mindful of what you are sharing before doing so, especially if you are sharing it on 'My Story' on Snapchat, which means it is sent to everyone on your list.
- *There are no free apps*: The saying 'there is no free lunch' applies also to free apps. Free apps offer free use of their functionality in exchange for gathering your data and behaviour. They often collect detailed information about you, ranging from your name, your age, your location, personal contact details, content you share, your interests, your contacts, and so on, and build a

profile of you that is then used to sell advertising. Therefore, it is important to weight the benefits of the app against the data and privacy you are giving up.

• **Check privacy settings and be mindful of the 'social' in social media**: An important characteristic of social media is that all that is posted online is social and shared by default. Therefore, the onus is on the user posting the information to ensure that there are appropriate privacy settings in place and that the specific information being posted does not breach the privacy, confidentiality or contextual integrity of anyone associated with that posting.

Sexting: implications for practice and safeguarding

Although the exchange of sexually suggestive/explicit images is not a new phenomenon (Chalfen, 2009), digital and social media technologies have heightened the potential for their reproduction and dissemination. The adverse effects of sexting go beyond risk of exposure to inappropriate material, and can include significant, lasting and far-reaching implications, with multiple negative outcomes for its victims (Ringrose et al, 2012).

Given that most cases of adolescent sexting begin with one's peer group, the school plays an important role in prevention as well as intervention and support plans in response to sexting cases. In terms of prevention, schools should have clear anti-sexting policies and prevention strategies, and should inform and educate young people about the negative consequences of sexting. Given the importance of open discussion about sexting, and considering the complexities and sensitivities involved in sexting behaviour and its gendered dynamics and implications (Ringrose et al, 2012), it is also important that schools offer separate (same-sex/single-sex) classes when discussing sexting.

Furthermore, while the perpetrator will need re-education and rehabilitation in relation to sexting behaviour, it is important to engage the perpetrator to explore and understand its ramifications in terms of associated risks; this can help determine the spread of the problem (the extent of the dissemination of sexting messages), and may also reveal other victims who may need intervention and support. However, it is essential to avoid a 'blame the victim' attitude where the producer(s) of sexts (these are mostly girls) is/are blamed or shamed for the consequences of sexting. There are a number of video testimonials on YouTube in which victims of sexting speak about their ordeal and how they coped with it. Watching these testimonials together with the victim can serve as an ice-breaker and offer a point of departure for discussing the impact of sexting and the spread of messages (Ringrose et al, 2012; Lippman and Campbell, 2014).

Just as is the case with cyberbullying, it is important to note and to inform sexting victims that retaliation against the perpetrator is not an effective strategy, as this may intensify and aggravate the problem (Mason, 2008; Perren et al, 2012). Instead, practitioners should contact the perpetrator and his/her parents/carers and ensure that appropriate measures have been taken to address the perpetrator's behaviour and that support and rehabilitative measures have been put in place.

Many young people think that sexting is the norm among their peers (Lippman and Campbell, 2014), and therefore, it is essential to highlight to them that this is not the case, and that many of their peers do not engage in sexting (Ringrose et al, 2012). Practitioners should also consider that at times young people receive a sext message without having sought or solicited it, and may experience peer pressure to forward/disseminate the message.

Furthermore, we see a resurgence of patriarchal values and a division of gender roles in sexting behaviour. Therefore, practitioners should be aware of the gendered implications of sexting. Whereas young men may collect sext message or even post their own sexually explicit images as a sign of their popularity and masculinity, and this may often lead to their increased social capital and popularity among their peers, young women are usually the subject of sexting, and posting their sexually explicit images is generally viewed negatively by their peers, leading to their unpopularity with other young women.

Similar to bullying, peer group reactions have significant implications for sexting behaviour and its impact on young people, so educating young people to challenge and report peers who spread sexting messages can serve as an important protective factor. Young people should feel enabled and supported to express open disapproval of sexting messages, and to refuse to forward such messages. They should also feel empowered to report and seek help about such behaviour.

Social work and safeguarding practitioners working in children's services should have appropriate training and a clear strategy as well as specific and flexible guidelines and emergency plans for responding to sexting and other forms of negative 'online' or 'offline' behaviour. Practitioners should recognise the sensitivities, impact, implications and legal liabilities for those involved in sexting behaviour. Sexting victims may need counselling for coping with the situation, and practical support and advice from practitioners or other professionals with regards to an appropriate course of action and related risks and resilience, including confidentiality and personal disclosure risk and identity management. It is important to work sensitively, supportively and collaboratively with victims of sexting to gather relevant evidence and to stop and remediate the situation and its consequences.

Alice's story

Alice is a white middle-class girl in Year 8. She is doing well in school and achieves good grades. She lives with her parents and two younger siblings just outside London. Charlie attends the same school as Alice and is also in Year 8. Alice and Charlie have started to spend more time together and have been out a couple of times together. Charlie asks Alice if she will give him a blow job, but Alice says no – she hasn't done anything like that before, and doesn't feel comfortable with it. Charlie asks Alice every day for a month to give him a blow job, and after daily requests, including frequent WhatsApp messages, Alice 'caves' in and agrees. Charlie films Alice giving him a blow job and she asks him to delete it and he agrees but doesn't delete it, and instead sends it to a group of his friends who share the video, and before the end of the week the video is being circulated widely at school.

The girls in Alice's year group see the video and call her a 'dirty slag' and laugh at her each time she walks by. At first Alice's friend Lottie supports her, but as the name calling and teasing continues, she feels more and more uncomfortable, and stops sitting with Alice. Alice finds herself ostracised by her peers and ridiculed at school.

Ashamed, isolated and embarrassed, and feeling she has nowhere to turn to, Alice tries to take her own life. Alice is taken to A&E where her stomach is pumped and she is referred to a psychiatrist and mental health team who refer Alice to children's social care, and the police are called. Alice is interviewed by the police and social worker, and the police arrest Charlie.

Alice is scared that she's got Charlie into trouble and that he will only make things worse for her.

Reflection and analysis

We will leave the specific analysis of the above example for readers' reflection, and instead use the 10 C's psycho-socio-ecological framework, listing some of the relevant questions that practitioners may need to consider (this is meant to encourage reflection rather than being an exhaustive list).

Consumption risk:

- Are there any concerns with regards to excessive or problematic use of online media?
- Are there any concerns about the pattern of use and its associated risks?
- Do the victim/Alice or the perpetrator/Charlie need additional support or safeguarding measures in balancing their online–offline engagement/activities?
- Do significant others and the home environment adopt and maintain a healthy digital vs physical balance? (See Chapters 2 and 5.)

Confidentiality and personal disclosure risk:

- What information is available online about the victim/Alice? Is there any personal information about the victim/Alice online?
- How sensitive are the information and personal disclosures online?

- What is the impact and possible ramifications of this information (over time and in relation to other risks)?
- Can any information that poses confidentiality and personal disclosure risk be removed? What can be done to mitigate the risk of future negative outcomes associated with the information available online?
- Does the victim/Alice need a better understanding of confidentiality and personal disclosure risk?

Context risk:

- What was the context and purpose of sexting (for example, game, flirting or romantic gesture, intimate relationship, sexual attention seeking, bullying, intimidation or intent to harm, voyeurism, etc)?
- What is the medium/platform(s) used for sexting? What was the original platform (for example, SMS)? How was it breached and disseminated further (for example, distributed to a group via SMS or WhatsApp, or posted on a website or SNS)?
- What are the characteristics, risks and protective factors associated with these media/platform(s)?
- What is the victim's/Alice's background? Does the victim have a history of past abuse? Is the victim a child in need, looked after, etc? Do they experience any specific vulnerability (for example, learning difficulties or difficulties with body image, etc)? Any police or criminal justice background?
- What actions are needed to stop further dissemination/circulation of this content?
- What other remedial or preventive actions are required?

Consonance-dissonance and compatibility risk:

- What are the ages and developmental stages of the victim/Alice and perpetrator/Charlie?
- Was the victim/Alice influenced by the behaviour of an influential adult (that is, someone with easy access or in position of power relative to the victim)? What is the implication of this for safeguarding?

- What is the impact of sexting on the victim's/Alice's identity (online and offline), emotional wellbeing and mental health?
- What support and safeguarding measures are needed (for example, re-education, individual counselling, peer support, group therapy, etc)?

Connection and social capital risk:

- What is the spread of the problem? How widely have the messages/content been shared (for example, victim's peer group, school, community, SNS, wider public)?
- Who was the original addressee of the sext message? Who and how many people are involved in sexting now? How may these numbers change in the future?
- Are there any other victims?
- The victim's/Alice's school plays an important role and should therefore be involved in the process. However, is there any other school involved (for example, the perpetrator's school)? Was the sext message/content distributed in that school as well?
- What measures are needed to stop further spread/dissemination?
- What is the impact of the message on the victim's/Alice's relationships and social capital? How can this be remedied and restored?
- What are some helpful contacts and resources or organisations that can help and provide support for the victim/Alice?
- Is there a need for further awareness and training?

Content risk:

- What is/are the content of the sext message(s) that has/have been sent? What has been breached/disseminated and what may still be disseminated (for example, image, video, personal information such as home address, phone numbers, partial or fully nude pictures, image of sexual intercourse, screen shot of an image/post)?
- How can the content be removed, deleted or contained? (For example, in cases of indecent images of children, websites or SNSs can be contacted to remove the content.)
- What other safeguarding measures are required?

Contact risk:

Virtual:

- Is there ongoing online contact between the victim/Alice and the perpetrator/Charlie?
- What are the specific virtual contact risks? What is needed to mitigate virtual contact risks?
- What needs to be done to stop further spread/dissemination of messages/sexts?

Physical:

- Was there any physical contact?
- Are there any future physical contact risks?
- What measures are needed to support the victim/Alice?

Conduct risk:

- Adolescents experiment with their identity and sexuality, but how about younger people? Was the activity age-appropriate and developmentally appropriate, or is it out of norm or an extreme behaviour? Does it raise any concerns? What are its safeguarding implications?

Contact risk:

- Was this a one-off incident or was there repetition?
- Was there any revenge porn or revenge sexting by either party?
- Are there any other conduct concerns? These could include conduct such as being withdrawn or anxious, casual sexual relationships with different partners, simultaneous sexual activity with more than one partner, substance misuse, etc.
- Was the incident accidental, reckless or the result of not thinking about the ramifications of one's actions, or was it intentional or premeditated?
- Was the relationship reasonably equal and was sexting consensual? (Children younger than 13 cannot legally give consent to sexual activity.)

- Was there a power difference/imbalance? Power difference has many forms, for example, was an adult involved? Was there an age difference of more than three years?
- Was there sexual grooming? Was there a relationship of trust? (A legal definition is provided in Section 27 of the Sexual Offences Act 2003.)
- Was the victim/Alice threatened, coerced or bullied in any way?
- Was there criminal conduct?
- Is there a need for further awareness, re-education or rehabilitation of the offender(s)?

Commercial exploitation risk:

- Was there an element of bribery or numeration or other persuasions in any way, either in cash or otherwise (for example, alcohol, either physical or virtual gifts, ticket to an event, promise of a reward)?
- Was there any commercial exploitation risk?

Composite and complex risk:

- Does either the victim/Alice or the perpetrator/Charlie have a disability or experience mental health difficulties in any way?
- Are there any religious, cultural, ethnic, racial or other issues that may have an impact on the situation? Is this a hate crime?
- Are there any other associated risks or issues (for example, aggression or abuse, inappropriate use of media, cyberbullying, sextortion or cyber-extortion)?
- What are some of the complicating factors? Does timing make a difference? For example, if the incident is reported on Friday, is any action needed immediately to avoid escalation over the weekend?
- How has this experience influenced the victim's/Alice's family relationships and relationships with significant others? What can be done to enhance and restore these relationships?
- How has this experience influenced the different domains and other aspects of the victim's/Alice's life? (See the dimensions of risks and assessment in Chapter 3.)

- How do the combination of the above factors influence the victim/Alice? Do they give rise to new risks, and how can these be mitigated?
- Are there any other composite risks or protective factors?
- What safeguarding measures are required to address the composite and complex risks?
- How can the composite and complex protective factors and resilience be leveraged to support the victim's/Alice's healthy growth and development?

Mapping onto 10 C's psycho-socio-ecological model

The response to the above and its analysis should be transposed and considered in the context of the psycho-socio-ecological model in order to fully appreciate their effect and implications (see Figure 6.1). Therefore, in mapping the result of the above analysis onto the 10 C's psycho-socio-ecological model, practitioners should consider the following mindlines and practice points.

- In the UK, Section 67 of the Serious Crime Act 2015 makes it a criminal offence for an adult to send sexually explicit messages to a child under 16 years old.
- Although possession of sexually explicit images of children by adults or children is a criminal offence in the UK and the US, to avoid criminalising young people, the UK police and Crime Prosecution Service (CPS) has a clear policy not to pursue the prosecution of children and young people.
- As mentioned in Chapter 3, there are significant differences between children and adults' understanding and perception of risk, and for effective safeguarding it is important to understand children's experiences and perception of risks, protective factors and resilience.
- Sexting can be in many forms and can include different media, devices and content. Sexting often involves peer pressure and may include some level of coercion; when there is coercion it is tantamount to sexual bullying. Therefore, the exact dynamics and nature of sexting should be explored with those involved.
- Once engaged in sexting, the young person can be drawn into a complex and vicious cycle of solicitation, coercion and further

sexting. This can lead to sexual abuse and sextortion, where lack of compliance can result in public disclosure of personal and compromising images and information, while compliance will only escalate into increasing vulnerability and sexual abuse.

- The increasing sexualisation of childhood and young people's lives, and the demand for increasing attentional and user-generated capital in the attentional economy of the digital age, has resulted in a cultural transition to a much more sexually permissive society, normalising self-disclosure and sexual attention-seeking and experimentation (Megele and Buzzi, 2018d). This has significant implications for social norms, cultural values and the moral fabric of society, which, in turn, defines childhood, and shapes children and young people's lives, experiences and behaviours. In this sense, sexting is a techno-cultural by-product of the digital age permeating the lives of younger and younger children.

- Sexting is influenced by gendered dynamics of the peer group and popular culture norms in which boys brag about sharing their masculinity and their 'sexual conquests' while sexually active girls are labelled and denigrated. In this sense, collecting sexually explicit image of girls is the digital extension of the patriarchal notion of owning and dominating the female body. The consequences of sexting can be particularly severe for girls; if they don't engage in sexting, they are pressured by prodding such as 'grow up' and 'don't be a baby', but if they engage in sexting, they suffer reputational damage and are labelled 'sluts', 'slags' or lacking self-respect. Therefore, it is important that safeguarding and support provisions are gender-sensitive to ensure they meet everyone's needs.

- Although social workers cannot inspect children's phones, under certain circumstances, teachers in the UK can inspect and confiscate a student's mobile phone or digital device or delete images from the phone/digital device. However, it is important to note that such a search should be carried out only when there is serious risk of harm to the child, his/her peers or others. This power exceeds the stop and search powers granted to police in the UK and should be used with great care and only when absolutely warranted. Furthermore, in respect of children and young people's right to privacy and to minimise possible abuse of such powers, we suggest that a record of any such inspection, detailing the reason and outcome, should be kept in a school logbook and countersigned by the head teacher.

- As we have pointed out previously, it is important to note that, given the fluidity and ease of accessibility of digital and social media technologies, repressive and restrictive approaches to safeguarding can lead to false compliance and covert behaviour. It is only through appropriate education, open conversation and positive engagement and support that children and young people can be empowered and enabled to develop their own developmentally appropriate understanding and understandable code of ethics, appreciation and solution to safeguarding challenges, and resilient responses to possible risks of harm.

- The complex, varied and multidimensional nature of sexting and its ramifications underline the need for strong partnership multiprofessional and interagency working. Specifically, school plays a huge role in preventive and remedial action and education for young people. Therefore, close collaboration with the school is indispensable, as preventive and corrective safeguarding measures and to ensure continued support for the victim. School intervention is also important in mitigating and repairing reputational damage resulting from sexting. To ensure the relevance and effectiveness of any safeguarding plans, solutions or interventions it is important that they are developed in consultation and with the active participation and collaboration of children and young people, their families and all stakeholders.

- Although parents are generally concerned about sexting, many may struggle to stay up to date with technology and its applications and implications. Therefore, many parents may feel that they are not in a position to advise their children about healthy and appropriate use of digital and social media technologies. Hence, schools can offer specific workshops to acquaint parents with technology and to enhance their understanding of social media, digital boundaries and digital citizenship. In the current digital context and culture, such training should be considered an important and complementary part of parental capacity.

- Aside from the police's role in cases involving adults or criminal behaviour, informing and involving them even in non-criminal cases can be helpful. For example, at times a verbal and informal warning by a police officer can be helpful. It may also be helpful to ask a police officer to speak to the victim's class about sexting and its associated risks, emphasising that possession of sexually explicit images of young people by either adults or young people is a criminal offence.

- Furthermore, sexting may influence young people's mental health and psychological wellbeing. Therefore, practitioners should consider referring the victims for individual or group counselling or both, depending on the victim's circumstances and preferences.

- Notwithstanding the above, it is important to acknowledge and remember that, to an extent, sexting is the new expression of online/digital intimacy. Therefore, demonising acts of sexting or any messages with a slightly sexual tone, or misunderstanding young people's curiosity about their body and sexuality and their evolving relationships is a repression of their rights that weakens their self-esteem and spirit of discovery and hampers their healthy and holistic development.

- Given the significance of peer group and social identity for young people and their healthy development, and considering the reputational damage that may result from sexting, practitioners should ensure a robust and holistic (both online and offline) support and safeguarding plan that addresses risks and builds on young people's strengths and resilience. Furthermore, the dynamic nature of risks and their ramifications in time (see Chapter 3) require careful reflection and consideration, as sexting can lead to multiple and complex negative outcomes including reputational risks, sexual solicitation, involvement in online pornography, cyberbullying, sextortion (sexual extortion) and other cyber-abuse, low self-esteem, withdrawal, low mood, depression, self-harm and suicide.

- As mentioned in Chapter 2, technology magnifies power imbalance and amplifies vulnerabilities and, combined with the relative permanence of online postings and their potential for replication and dissemination, exacerbates the consequences of sexting and its ramifications.

Figure 6.1: Sexting: mapping risks, protective factors and resilience using the 10 C's psycho-socio-ecological framework

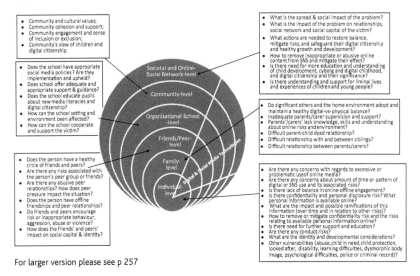

For larger version please see p 257

Depending on the answers to the questions listed in this chapter for each risk typology/category and other relevant questions (also see Figure 6.1), and other related questions, practitioners can develop a fuller view of risks, protective factors and resilience andthis can guide their practice and inform their safeguarding decisions and plans. Furthermore, in speaking with the victim and different stakeholders, and in answering the above questions, practitioners can co-produce an effective safeguarding plan that involves all stakeholders/concerned.

Sexting is not limited to a particular type of activity and can involve a variety of activities, content and media, and therefore there is no silver bullet or single way of doing things. Indeed, each case is unique and different in certain ways and requires a thoughtful and person-centred approach focused on the specific child and their circumstances. However, using the 10 C's psycho-socio-ecological framework can help practitioners flesh out the different risks, protective factors, resilience and safeguarding challenges and opportunities. This model can be used in conjunction with the assessment triangle (see Figure 3.4), and other safeguarding guidelines and procedures, to ensure a holistic approach to safeguarding children and young people.

Depending on the situation, practitioners will encounter different levels of responsiveness from websites and social media platforms, and will experience varying degrees of success in removing inappropriate, indecent or sexually toned images and damaging posts. However, in case of self-produced images (ie, images produced by the young person), it might prove easier and more efficient to remove such content by appealing to copyright rules rather than child abuse, sexual offence or child protection legislation. In the UK, https://www.saferinternet.org.uk/ and the Child Exploitation and Online Protection (CEOP) command can be helpful in removing such content. Furthermore, Queen Mary University in London offers free legal advice for people experiencing revenge porn; this service can be accessed through Queen Mary's 'web enquiry form'. Although as much as possible practitioners should aim to remove all inappropriate sexting content, this does not guarantee full retrieval and removal of such material – the content may have been downloaded by individuals either in its original format or as a screenshot or by other means (for example, replication machines). Hence, it is crucially important that practitioners support children and young people who are negatively affected by sexting to build their resilience and develop their ability to respond resourcefully to residual risks, challenges and effects that may remain indelible in cyberspace or somewhere offline.

Online grooming and child sexual abuse

Luke Sadowski

In 2002, the US Immigration and Customs Enforcement Agency (ICE) placed an online advertisement offering special sex tours with children as young as eight. This was part of a covert US Law Enforcement Agency (LEA) initiative to identify and prosecute sex offenders and paedophiles who were using the internet to abuse children. Luke Sadowski, an 18-year-old trainee school teacher, used the name 'Ben Smith' to reply to the advert and to ask further details and the price for a girl about ten years old to go 'all the way'.

When he realised the advert was US-based, Sadowski replied that he could not travel to the US. Through the US embassy, the ICE contacted New Scotland Yard's (NSY) Paedophile Unit to pursue the operation with Sadowski. However, UK law had yet to appropriately recognise such a crime, and so UK law enforcement agencies were unable to authorise and deploy such covert officers. Nonetheless, NSY used a covert officer to convince Sadowski that his request could be arranged in the UK. On Friday, 4 October 2002, Sadowski, from Bishop's Stortford, Hertfordshire, travelled to a London hotel thinking he was going to meet a nine-year-old girl, telling the covert officer, 'I am not going to mistreat her, not too much, if you know what I mean' (quoted in BBC News, 2003).

Instead, Sadowski met the covert officer and was arrested and charged for inciting '... another to procure a child under 16' and possessing an imitation gun. He was sentenced to 18 months for each offence, with sentences to run consecutively (BBC News, 2003). At the time, he was about to start his placement in a primary school with 5- to 11-year-old pupils. Due to inadequate legislation in the UK at the time, Sadowski did not go on the Sex Offender Register. This became a landmark case that led to the new Sexual Offences Act (SOA) 2003 that addresses some of the difficulties in Sadowski's case, and allows the sentencing of an offender to as much as 14 years in prison. Later on, Sadowski changed his name to 'George Richards'. Fast forward to shortly before 9am on Thursday, 12 September 2013, and Richards attempted to abduct a 10-year-old girl off a footbridge on her way to school. His attempt was thwarted by an off-duty officer. Undeterred, he later acquired an imitation gun and tried to abduct a five-year-old girl off her mother's doorstep. This time he was cornered and arrested by police officers, and subsequently sentenced to life imprisonment. Officers found a kitchen knife, tape and lengths of string in his pocket; he had blackened the windows at his home and fitted high bolts on the doors.

Sadowski's case and its subsequent developments highlight the insidious and persistent nature of sexual offences and the complex, hidden and silent nature of this crime. Today the NSY Paedophile Unit and London Metropolitan Police Service's High Tech Crime Unit conduct regular and continuous covert operations to proactively identify and prosecute online sex offenders, while the latest updates to statutory guidance from the UK Department for Education, *Keeping children safe in education*, which came in to force on 5 September 2016, highlight policy makers' awareness of the need for more specific and effective guidance. A recent CNN article (2017) reported on the techniques used to identify fingerprints from the photograph of a perpetrator's hand, which led to his sentencing to 110 years' imprisonment. Similar approaches and technologies have been used in other instances and by law enforcement agents in the UK and other countries. Interestingly, hackers have used similar techniques, demonstrating the power of technology and how its potential may be used by different agents for very different purposes.

Sexual contact between adults and children is not a new phenomenon. Indeed, it used to be commonplace in certain communities and rural areas (Foucault, 1976/1998; Corby, 1998). For example, 'In July 1925 *The Lancet* carried a report which read: "On Jan. 26th, 1924, 17 girls between 6 and 10 years old, living in an exceptionally well-administered home, were notified as suffering from gonorrhoeal vulvo-vaginitis ..."' (11 July 1925, p 101)' (quoted in Smart, 2000, p 57). There were discussions in the medical literature about outbreaks of venereal diseases in children's homes and children's wards of hospitals and schools. Even 'after the Second World War the dominant medical discourse available to "explain" venereal diseases in children consisted of denial and lack of recognition' (Smart, 2000, p 59). Unfortunately, this is unsurprising given that fathers had to consent to the medical examination of raped children and considering the hegemonic patriarchal values that continue to dominate society (Connell, 1987). Such values define the meaning and significance of childhood, children's rights and child abuse, including child sexual abuse. Indeed, social workers, police officers, therapists, psychiatrists and other professionals and practitioners operate within this context, and are influenced and conditioned by such values.

Digital and online media and social technologies offer many more opportunities for predators, and augment practitioners' challenges in safeguarding children and young people from sexual abuse. Therefore, in this chapter we draw on the 10 C's psycho-socio-ecological model to discuss the dynamics and elements of online grooming and child sexual abuse from a safeguarding perspective. We begin with a brief discussion of child sexual abuse and online grooming and its stages, followed by a structured and systematic examination of risk factors associated with child sexual abuse that make children and young people most vulnerable to online sexual solicitation and abuse. We conclude with some safeguarding considerations and a reflection on the impact of grooming and child sexual abuse.

Defining child sexual abuse

Child sexual abuse (CSA) is a significant problem, and previous research by the Children's Commissioner into child sexual abuse indicates that only 1 in 8 victims of sexual abuse come to the attention of authorities, and that abuse in the family environment counts for two thirds of all child sexual abuse. However, unfortunately, CSA is not a new phenomenon; on the contrary, it has very deep roots, and, depending on the historical timing and methodological tradition, different researchers have defined it differently. Normative definitions are embedded and shaped by social norms and cultural, professional and individual values (Dunphy, 2000), and so MacLeod and Saraga (1988) suggest that in defining grooming and CSA four key elements should be considered, namely:

- betrayal of trust or responsibility
- abuse of power
- inability of children to consent
- violation of another's right.

To combat increasing sexual approaches to children online, SOA 2003 adopts a more proactive approach. Hence, befriending a child on the internet or by other means and meeting or intending to meet the child with the intention of abusing them is recognised as a crime and is punishable by a sentence of up to 10 years' imprisonment. Furthermore, in the UK, Section 67 of the Serious Crime Act 2015 makes it a criminal offence for an adult to send sexually explicit messages to a child under 16 years old.

To be clear, it may be helpful to remember the following mindlines.

- Any non-consensual sexual activity (with or without intercourse) or any non-consensual use of a person's sexuality (for example, images) is always an abuse.
- Any sexual activity or use of a person's sexuality for a 12-year-old or younger is always CSA.
- Any sexual activity or use of sexuality of a young person below the age of 16 by an adult is sexual abuse.
- There is a grey zone in the application of SOA 2003 for young people in the sense that although sexual activity for young people aged 13 years or above but below 16 is illegal, the UK CPS does not pursue and prosecute such sexual activity as long as it occurs between similarly aged young people, and is mutually consensual and non-exploitative.

UK government guidance, *Child safety online: A practical guide for providers of social media and interactive services* (DCMS, 2016), classifies online risks into three categories: content, conduct and contact risks. However, as described in Chapter 3, from a safeguarding perspective, we suggest that practitioners should consider the full range of risks in relation to children's online activities and identities, as described in the 10 C's psycho-socio-ecological model.

Stages of grooming and child sexual abuse

Sexual abuse of children is a complex unique phenomenon, and its dynamics are often quite different from adult sexual abuse.

- Physical force or violence is rarely used in CSA; instead, the perpetrator tries to manipulate the child's trust and hide their abuse.
- In cases of offline/face-to-face abuse, the perpetrator is often known to the child and/or the family; the perpetrator may even be a trusted caregiver.
- CSA often occurs over a period of weeks, months and even years.
- Perpetrators usually engage the child in a process of sexualisation and relationship building that leads to eventual sexual abuse.
- CSA often involves repeated episodes of abuse that become incrementally more invasive over time.

O'Connell (2003) and Winters and Jeglic (2016) divide the online grooming process for CSA into six and four stages respectively, and argue that during each stage a deeper sense of mutual trust is developed, leading to eventual violation of that trust and sexual abuse/exploitation. Here we combine these two conceptualisations of the grooming process for CSA as follows.

Target selection and friendship forming

This stage involves the offender gaining information and getting to know the young person. Offenders select their targets based on the young person's appeal and their preferred characteristics and vulnerabilities. For example, Elliott et al (1995) found that sexual offenders often focus on physical appearance such as being pretty (42 per cent), dressing (27 per cent), or the child being small (18 per cent). More cautious offenders carefully evaluate the young person's vulnerabilities such as emotional neediness, social isolation, low self-confidence and those who respond well to attention from online contacts (Conte et al, 1989). Young people from single-parent families and those with less adult/parental supervision, children from families with domestic violence or parental conflict, children whose parents experience emotional and mental health difficulties or addiction and substance misuse, children experiencing neglect or emotional or mental health difficulties, 'children who will co-operate for a desired reward (such as money, computer games), and children with low self-esteem' (Stanley, 2001, p 14) or high respect for adult status are the most vulnerable and most desirable targets (Olson et al, 2007). Research indicates that for more cautious offenders, target selection and relationship forming is a strategic and well-planned process whose length can vary among offenders; it may also be revisited/re-enacted as need be and depending on the frequency and level of contact. During this stage the offender may request a picture of the child/young person. At this stage, the picture request is to verify they are targeting a child/young person and that the young person is to their liking. The picture also allows physical identification of the child/young person; this is particularly important for offenders who target children in their vicinity, aiming for eventual contact with the child (O'Connell, 2003).

Gaining access, developing trust and relationship forming

This is an extension of the friendship forming stage, but not all offenders engage in this stage. Focusing on the young person's vulnerability, during this stage the offender aims to fill the young person's needs and appear either as the young person's 'best friend' or as a 'father figure' (Lanning, 2010), by taking the time to gain information and to learn about them, asking about their daily experiences, school, life, family etc. This serves the dual purpose of building a relationship and trust while assessing any risks. Isolating the young person and gaining and maintaining access to them is an important objective of this phase. Whereas offline offenders target children in their home environment (for example, their bedroom), or in places children visit such as parks, schools, shopping centres, amusement parks etc, online, offenders target children in chatrooms or where children 'hang out' or seek conversation.

Offenders use a combination of tools and techniques to gain young people's trust, developing and maintaining control over them; these include using gifts, bribes, attention and affection, pornography and indecent images, persuasion, stimulation, entrapment and blackmail, etc. In the UK the Home Office Task

Force (2008, pp 18-19) provides a list of techniques and approaches used by offenders, including:

- gathering personal details, such as name, address, mobile number, name of school and photographs
- offering opportunities for modelling, particularly to young girls
- promising meetings with pop idols or celebrities or offers of merchandise
- offering cheap ticket to sporting or music events
- offering material gifts including electronic games, music or software
- offering virtual gifts, such as rewards, passwords and gaming cheats
- suggesting quick and easy ways to make money
- paying young people to appear naked and perform sexual acts via webcams
- gaining a child's confidence by offering positive attention and encouraging him or her to share any difficulties or problems he or she may have at home and providing a sympathetic and supportive response
- bullying or intimidating behaviour, such as threatening to expose the child by contacting his or her parents to inform them of their child's communications or postings on a social networking site and/or saying they know where the child lives or goes to school
- using webcams to spy and take photographs and movies of victims
- asking sexually themed questions, such as "Do you have a boyfriend?" or "Are you a virgin?"
- asking children or young people to meet offline
- sending sexually themed images to a child, depicting adult content or the abuse of other children
- masquerading as a minor or assuming a false identity to deceive a child
- using schools or hobby sites to gather information about a child's interest, likes and dislikes.

Risk assessment

This is a recursive stage that can be carried out as need be. At this stage the offender assesses relevant risks, evaluating and avoiding the possibility of being detected. There are a number of approaches and techniques to assess risk, ranging from examining the young person's profile and online postings (for example, blog posts or Facebook page) to asking questions such as whether the young person is using a computer or phone, or the location of the computer, and whether others use the same computer, etc.

Exclusivity, emotional dependence and deepening trust

In this stage the grooming sex offender uses the developing relationship with the child (for example, 'best friend' or 'mentor'/'fatherly figure') to create a sense of exclusivity and mutual trust (asking explicitly if the child trusts them), understanding and emotional dependence (for example, 'I understand what you're going through') and shared feeling (for example, 'I feel the same'). The strengthening of the bond between the offender and child is matched by increasing trust, secrecy and exclusivity in the relationship (a 'special relationship' or 'our special secret'). Increasingly separating and isolating the child from peers and significant others, the offender emphasises the importance of mutual trust. The offender cultivates in the child a sense of being loved and valued by the offender in a special way that not even the child's parents can offer. When the offender is known to the family and has access to the family, parents might unknowingly feed into this narrative by praising the 'special relationship' between the offender and the child.

Advancing the sexuality of the relationship

Having created sufficient emotional dependence and trust in the relationship, the offender begins to introduce more intimate questions that may seem innocuous (for example, 'have you ever been kissed?' or 'do you touch yourself?'. These conversations are combined with sexually explicit pictures. At this stage, both the context and content of conversations can evoke curiosity and strong emotions, resulting in 'hot cognition', which makes it difficult for children to think clearly (this obfuscates the offender's intentions, making them vulnerable to impulsive/emotive decision-making); the unfamiliarity of the experience and intensity of emotions make it difficult for the child/young person to maintain control and navigate the situation. In the meantime, the offender uses this opportunity and the child's natural curiosity to manipulate the conversation and the child's stimulation and feelings to gain maximum control over the child and to advance the sexuality of the relationship.

Maintaining control

The experience of sexual abuse can generate varied emotions and reactions in children. Therefore, offenders use secrecy, trust and blame, combined with other strategies, to maintain the relationship and to continue the abuse and the child's silence. Often overwhelmed by feelings of guilt, shame and blame, children find themselves entangled in a web of complex emotions while fearing the threat of the adult ending the relationship and the consequent loss of the emotional and material needs associated with it. The child feels trapped, and is made to believe that exposing the relationship will result in even greater humiliation and rejection by their peers and significant others. This results in a vicious and perverse cycle of self-perpetuating abuse.

It is important to note that these stages offer a conceptual framework for examining offenders' behaviours rather than a rigid linear process. Indeed, most online offenders do not follow these stages in a linear manner, and instead, may revert back to an earlier stage when need be. The following example demonstrates some of the dynamics and complexities of online grooming and sexual abuse.

Nazima's story

Nazima is a 14-year-old Somalian Muslim female who was placed in foster are under a full care order at the age of 13 due to having been sexually abused by her father, who is currently in prison for raping and sexually assaulting

Nazima and her sister, Zadaher (19 years old). Nazima's mother passed away when she was one, and so, apart from Zadaher and her father, Nazima has no family in the UK. Zadaher is married and lives with her husband and their one-year-old daughter.

After her placement in foster care, Nazima started a new life and her academic performance had begun to improve. However, in the past six months Nazima has regularly gone missing, but her social worker (Beth) and the police suspect that the foster carer is not reporting all of the instances in which she is missing from her placement. In one instance, Beth received a police report that Nazima had been picked up by the police after midnight; however, the foster carer had not reported her missing. On that occasion Nazima was wearing make-up with no hijab. Nazima has displayed sexually inappropriate behaviour toward men, and has been referred for individual counselling.

Nazima uses Facebook to socialise and stay connected with her friends. Her profile picture shows her wearing no make-up and a hijab covering her head and part of her face.

Beth asks Nazima about her disappearances, and she says she likes to hang out with her friends, but refuses to identify who they are or where they meet. However, due to the frequency of Nazima's disappearances and the high risk of her experiencing serious harm during these disappearances, on one occasion the police access Nazima's phone and this enables them to see her social media messages. The police uncover that Nazima uses a different social media account under a pseudo-name to keep in touch with Sam. From the messages it seems that Nazima and Sam are in regular contact, and that Sam is sexually abusing, and possibly commercially exploiting Nazima. The police are able to identify that Nazima regularly travels to two cities in the north and north east of England, where she has sex with Sam and Sam's friends.

Given the serious nature of the situation, the next time Nazima disappears the police track her phone and locate her on the train and on her way to her usual destination in the north of England. After her arrival, Nazima takes a taxi from the train station to a hotel, and is followed by undercover officers who intervene and arrest Sam and his friend, who were expecting to have sex with Nazima.

Subsequently, Nazima tells Beth that she met Sam about six months ago in a chatroom for young people. She added that when she first asked Sam how old he was he answered 'not too old, I hope', and then followed that he was 24 (police records show that Sam was 52 – it is common for perpetrators to lie about their age in the first instance, and then to correct their age subsequently, as the relationship progresses). Initially Sam was very supportive of Nazima, and seemed to always be there for her. So they became best friends and eventually met and had sex. On that occasion Sam took some nude photos and videos of Nazima. Nazima explained her ordeal, and how Sam had become increasingly dominating and sexually invasive, and how, after their first few meetings, she had to have sex with Sam and his friends and submit to all kinds of abuse.

Reflection and analysis

We will use the 10 C's psycho-socio-ecological model to assess Nazima's circumstances and offer brief pointers about her story based on the above information. As a practice exercise, you may want to expand on these points and develop a more detailed reflection and analysis of Nazima's story. We should highlight that, as far as possible, the following steps should be carried out in a co-productive and collaborative manner between Beth (the social worker) and Nazima.

Confidentiality and personal disclosure risk

Aside from a discussion with Nazima and other appropriate stakeholders, this requires conducting various internet searches to identify and review any available information about Nazima online, and to take appropriate action to remove any personal or inappropriate information. Social media technologies connect various bits of information about people (for example, name, email address, phone numbers, address, related social media accounts, and online behaviour, etc) therefore, internet searches conducted for safeguarding purposes should go beyond name search and should include a combination of keywords to identify any relevant information. It is also necessary to examine and adjust the security and privacy settings for Nazima's different social media accounts, and to remove any personal disclosure that could be a source of vulnerability (for example, birthday, address, phone numbers, etc).

Context risk

It is important to make a comprehensive list of all of Nazima's software apps and online social media accounts and profiles, and to assess their context-specific risks. Beth and Nazima need to critically discuss how and why Nazima uses a given website or SNS, and the specific risks associated with that SNS, website or app. For example, Snapchat's content, context, structure and type of communication, and the risks associated with it, are different from Facebook or Instagram's content, context, structure and types of communication, and their associated risks. It is important that the choice of social media engagement is relevant and meaningful for Nazima, while mitigating any risk of negative outcomes.

Consonance-dissonance and compatibility risk

Nazima's conservative Facebook profile and interactions may represent part of her identity that she feels is socially expected and acceptable. However, this is not compatible with her offline identity and behaviour (her regular disappearances and sexually inappropriate behaviour when relating to men). In conversation with Nazima, Beth should explore Nazima's preferred self-narrative, and once they have a shared understanding of a healthy preferred self-narrative, Nazima should be supported in achieving it. This includes guiding and supporting Nazima to configure her online profile and social media interactions so that they can contribute towards achieving her preferred self-narrative. Identity development and negotiations are complex, and so this may not be a linear process. However, with shared understanding and open and effective communication, and co-production between Nazima and Beth, they will be able to navigate the different challenges along the way.

Connection and social capital risk

Nazima's choice of whom she connects with and how she manages the relational aspects of her social media account and online identity is essential for enhancing her social capital, and can have an impact on her future opportunities, development and resilience.

Content risk

Nazima has been sexually abused and exposed to inappropriate sexual content. She therefore needs appropriate counselling and support as well as education about gender relationships, and non-exploitative sex and sexually appropriate behaviour based on her own cultural values and context.

Contact risk

Throughout this case there has been a clear risk of virtual and physical contact, and Nazima has suffered significantly due to such contacts. Research suggests that children with previous experience of abuse face a higher risk of future abuse. Therefore, even after resolution of the case, as described above, there is still a risk of future virtual or physical contact for Nazima. To mitigate such a risk, it is essential to enhance Nazima's resilience and awareness of various risks and their consequences, and to ensure she has a healthy and supportive network of friends and peers.

Conduct risk

At times Nazima relates to men, especially older men, in a physical and sexual manner. Re-establishing a healthy sense of self and boundaries requires re-education and continued and targeted support to gradually heal the wounds of the past and to help her along her path to healthy growth. Support groups can play an important role in facilitating Nazima's journey.

Commercial exploitation risk

Nazima is the survivor of commercial CSA that objectifies and dehumanises the individual. Therefore, she is at risk of commercial exploitation, and requires continued support to mitigate this risk. The proposed specialist support and a healthy peer group can help Nazima better manage the effects of her traumatic experiences.

Composite and complex risk

The combination of the above give rise to a number of complex composite and contextual risks and interdependencies. Can you elaborate on the above risks and also identify the composite and complex risks that may affect Nazima?

Mapping onto 10 C's psycho-socio-ecological model

Staksrud and Livingstone (2009) found significant differences in risks and coping strategies across gender, age and socio-cultural settings that point to different styles of risk management among young people. Figure 7.1 lists some of the risks and protective factors in relation to online grooming using the 10 C's psycho-socio-ecological model. In Chapter 4 we applied the 10 C's psycho-socio-ecological model to offer a detailed analysis of online/video games, while in Chapter 5 we offered a non-exhaustive list of questions to help practitioners think about the various risk typologies. To complement that information we offer a brief psycho-socio-ecological analysis relating to Nazima's circumstances.

Having examined the analysis of 10 C's risk typologies, the result of the above risk analysis should be mapped onto the 10 C's psycho-socio-ecological model. Therefore, below are some practice reflections and mindlines in relation to mapping of the 10 C's risk typologies onto the model.

Figure 7.1: Online grooming and child sexual abuse: mapping risks, protective factors and resilience using the 10 C's psycho-socio-ecological model

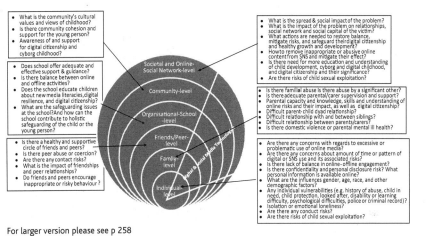

For larger version please see p 258

Individual factors

Gender

Nazima is a girl, and gender influences every aspect of human experience, including grooming and CSA. Livingstone et al (2011a) report that boys use the internet slightly more than girls, and are generally more likely to generate and encounter online risks. However, girls face a significantly higher risk of being approached sexually or becoming the target of grooming or sexual abuse, both online and offline. Girls are also more likely to be affected by risks and experience distress or feel upset due to online content (Livingstone and Haddon, 2009). While taking note of the gender differences in data, it is important to avoid any misconception that boys may not be at risk of sexual abuse, either online or offline, as a significant number of CSA survivors are male (Finkelhor et al, 2000; Wolak et al, 2008). Indeed, due to patriarchal norms and the negative stigmatised identity associated with male victims (Goffman, 1967; Connell, 1987; Butler, 1993), it is likely that sexual abuse of male victims is under-reported (O'Leary and Barber, 200). Furthermore, a Swedish study found that homosexuality and bisexuality are the most significant predictors of a young person (male or female) being approached sexually online (Suseg et al, 2008). Young people who are gay or who are rethinking their sexuality may be especially vulnerable to abuse, as offenders often target these young people, and try to exploit their uncertainties and insecurities.

Age and developmental stage

Research offers differing conclusions as to which age group is at the highest risk of grooming and abuse. However, a large body of literature suggests that adolescents may be at greater risk of online sexual solicitations, grooming and sexual abuse (Quayle et al, 2012), which is understandable due to the greater amount of time and higher level and frequency of online activity and communication by this group (Livingstone et al, 2011a, 2011b; Munro, 2011; Ofcom, 2015). A further explanation may lie in the developmental and behavioural challenges of adolescence, including children's relational and social identity, and the desire for greater social recognition and engagement combined with greater risk-taking behaviour.

Nazima is in the early stages of her adolescence, and adolescence is often characterised by risk taking and impulsive behaviour (Gumbiner, 2003). However, Weithorn and Campbell (1982) found that the cognitive capacity of 14-year-olds resembles that of adults, while Albert and Steinberg (2011) conclude that, compared to adults, adolescents are equally capable of risk perception and assessing their own vulnerabilities to it. Van Duijenvoorde et al (2010) confirm Dahl's (2004) assertion that adolescents tend to make poorer decisions in emotionally charged situations with high emotional arousal (what Dahl, 2004, calls 'hot cognition'), but are capable of good decision-making in less emotional circumstances and when cognitively engaged ('cold cognition'). Therefore, the context of online boundaries and behaviours, as described in Chapter 2, and the emotionally charged nature of the grooming process due to feelings of love and intimacy, combined with young people's poorer decision-making capabilities in emotionally charged situations (Dahl, 2004; van Duijenvoorde et al, 2010), and with other factors (for example, a sense of belonging) help explain why a young person may continue to engage with a sex offender during the grooming process. This highlights the importance of relationship-based practice and of offering an environment that provides acceptance and security, and contains Nazima's fears, anxieties and trauma (an environment that offers 'cold cognition'), to enable Nazima to better process her thoughts and emotions and make better decisions.

Nazima is also experimenting with new identities, and is trying to expand her relationships and social engagement, seeking attention, social acceptance and validation (Megele, 2015); this can make children vulnerable to sexual abuse or exploration (Quayle et al, 2012). The amplification of vulnerabilities online exacerbates the risks of online sexual solicitation, grooming and abuse for young people (Megele and Buzzi, 2018d, 2018e). Hence, it is essential that Nazima has a healthy peer group that helps meet these needs while mitigating the risks of negative outcomes.

Other individual factors

In safeguarding children and young people online, practitioners need to consider the above factors in combination with other personality and identity challenges that have an impact on interpersonal relationships and influence children and young people's vulnerabilities to grooming and sexual abuse. These include factors such as disability, mental health and/or emotional or behavioural difficulties, low self-esteem, poor judgement and decision-making, and susceptibility to persuasion, all of which are associated with people who experience offline or online grooming or sexual abuse (Olson et al, 2007).

Nazima does not have any disability; however, it is worth mentioning that young people with a disability may have a more trusting attitude toward adults due to their interdependence and past experiences with carers, and this may pose additional risks of abuse for this group (Megele and Buzzi, 2018c). Additionally, young people with a learning disability may be less sceptical of others' intentions and may therefore more readily trust a groomer or sexual offender online (Megele and Buzzi, 2018c). Even if they used the internet less frequently and had less exposure to online risks than other children, they may be less likely to recognise such risks or to cope with them effectively. Elliott et al (1995) found that 49 per cent of offenders targeted children who lacked confidence and self-esteem, and another 13 per cent targeted innocent and trusting children.

As discussed in Chapter 3, risks and protective factors associated with a child in a given situation are relative to the context, and are strongly influenced by systemic and ecological factors, which then, in turn, shape the person's resilience. In general, 'Sexual abuse is predicted by, and predictive of, more general child maltreatment and both are predicted by the same family environmental risk factors' (Smallbone et al, 2008, p 135).

Parental and familial factors

Parents, family relationships and culture have a great impact on children and their experiences, risks and resilience. However, Nazima's mother is dead and her father is in prison, and she has no contact with her family. This limits the support she can draw on and increases her vulnerability. Indeed, parental influence goes beyond a parent's role as the protector of their children and influences every aspect of their children's lives. Research shows that although risks of online grooming cannot be simply correlated with the young person's socioeconomic status (Livingstone et al, 2005), parents' level of education is an important protective factor for children, and is inversely correlated with the likelihood of children experiencing online sexual abuse. This means that children with well-educated parents are at lower risk of experiencing online grooming or sexual abuse, and there is higher resilience among these children. Livingstone et al (2011a, 2011b) report that young people of higher socioeconomic background have multiple and greater access to digital devices and the internet, and a diverse range of contacts online and offline, including people they don't know, and are therefore more likely to receive sexual solicitations. Conversely, although young people from low socioeconomic backgrounds are less likely to receive sexual solicitations, they are more affected and upset by such experiences when they occur (Livingstone et al, 2011a, 2011b). This may imply greater resilience towards online risks on the part of young people from higher socioeconomic standing due to greater support structures. Therefore, in safeguarding children and young people, practitioners should consider the complex range of parental capacity and difficulties and familial factors that may have an impact on young people's lives and vulnerability to online grooming and sexual abuse.

Suseg et al (2008) suggest that young people whose families experience financial difficulties are at a higher risk of online sexual abuse. Therefore, the relationship between the socioeconomic status of the young person and risk of online sexual abuse is complex. It is important to use the 10 C's psycho-socio-ecological model in conjunction with the assessment triangle (see Figure 3.4) to ensure a holistic assessment of relevant risks and protective factors that may influence children and young people's experiences and likelihood of their sexual abuse. Unfortunately, many of the psycho-socio-ecological factors at a familial level that can lead to increased risks for children are present in Nazima's family. Can you identify some of these additional factors?

Other risks that may lead to increased likelihood of CSA include lack of family cohesion and sense of belonging (Stith et al, 2009), poor relationship between parents or the parent–child dyad (Jack et al, 2006), and being from single-parent families or other familial challenges (Olson et al, 2007). Discussing family problems online is a significant vulnerability indicator that is targeted by online offenders; such children seek adult attention and validation, and predators tap into this need. From a safeguarding perspective it is important to note that although previous experience of trauma, maltreatment or abuse may increase young people's vulnerabilities, many victims of online grooming may not have experienced trauma or abuse until the grooming began. This means that practitioners need to consider a different and wider range of indicators and family dynamics when assessing risks for this group of young people. However, children whose families face domestic violence, parental conflict, emotional and mental health difficulties, or addiction and substance misuse, or are neglectful, are at higher risk of sexual abuse (Olson et al, 2007).

Once again, we should underline the impact of proactive parenting and refer practitioners to the brief suggestions for restoring the online–offline balance in Chapter 5. Proactive parenting and balancing online and offline activities are not only protective factors; they also offer opportunities for bonding and the transmission of values, and for discussing and explaining potential risks (grooming and other risks) with young people.

Friends and peers

As mentioned in Chapter 3, resilience is a dynamic construct, and the result of individual interaction with their environment, resources and support structures/networks. Therefore, building a healthy and supportive peer group around the child is one of the strongest protective factor for holistic and effective safeguarding, as it enhances the child's social capital, identity and resilience.

Schools (organisational factors)

Schools play a significant role in safeguarding children, ranging from protective measures and preventive policies to enhancing young people's resilience, to educating young people and their parents about digital citizenship and social media and its associated risks and safeguarding measures. Schools can draw on the 10 C's psycho–socio–ecological model to discuss the dimensions, risks and resilience associated with online digital and social media identities, interactions, posts and engagements, including topics such as creating a new online profile or adult supervision and support. These are dynamic risk factors that require close collaboration between social work practitioners and schools to ensure the effective and holistic safeguarding of children.

Community and social vulnerability

Social vulnerabilities such as marginalisation and isolation are significant risk factors and strong indicators of various negative outcomes and victimisations (Olson et al, 2007). Social capital and healthy relationships with a peer group are protective factors for children online. By the same token, emotional loneliness and isolation or an outsider identity and being in the 'out-group' among peers increases risks for children. Isolation also offers a layer of protection for offenders since there is a lower risk of the young person being influenced or warned by their peers – emotional loneliness is an important indicator of social vulnerability. Young people who feel alienated and avoid social interactions or have few or no friends are at higher risk of sexual solicitation, grooming, abuse and exploitation (Suseg et al, 2008). Emotional loneliness and social exclusion are particularly severe as they undermine both the young person's social capital and their resilience.

Practitioners should consider the impact and intersection between other structural and socio-environmental factors that can contribute to vulnerabilities (for example, social disorganisation, environmental violence, poverty, social norms, social stigma and prejudice and community practices) vis-à-vis those that can serve as protective factors (for example, family, school or neighbourhood resources). Social norms and community are a critical element of a supportive and protective environment for children. They can increase children's vulnerability, especially if they lead to discrimination, bias or other divisive or harmful practices. They can also lead to normalisation and social acceptance or under-reporting of abuse (for example, from child labour to familial practices). Conversely, social norms promoting diversity, positive values and protective behaviours play an important role in reducing the risks of negative outcomes and enhancing resilience. Social norms also influence professionals and their practice as well as formal institutions and their governance and accountability (see the earlier cited example from *The Lancet*, 1925).

Therefore, from a safeguarding perspective, it is important to strengthen the social network and support structures (both online and offline) around the young person; these networks and support structures are key for greater resilience. Peer support groups have a crucial impact in enabling young people to meet like-minded peers who can offer validation and mitigate isolation and emotional loneliness. Creating a positive peer group and support structures around the child can enhance resilience and their positive and validating experiences, both online and offline; this is also an important protective factor against risks of virtual or physical contact.

Overall, the internet offers several advantages for sex offenders including the 'universality' of the web that enables offenders to contact anyone, anywhere, anytime, while anonymity allows offenders to create multiple anonymous profiles that veil their real identity. However, anonymity is a double-edged sword as it also enables law enforcement agents to disguise themselves. Furthermore, anonymity can generate a false sense of security for offenders, emboldening them to seek immediate personal gratification such as acquiring and viewing pornography or other forms of sexual gratification (for example, virtual sex, masturbation).

Signs and effects of child sexual abuse

CSA has wide-ranging short- and long-term effects. In the short term children and young people may become withdrawn and avoid peers (for example, not wanting to see friends or go to school or engage in social activities). They may also show emotional difficulties, regressive behaviour such as thumb-sucking, bed-wetting, sleep disturbance, eating problems, behavioural and performance problems.

The long-term effects of CSA include emotional and mental health difficulties, anxiety-related difficulties, low self-worth and low self-esteem, alcohol and substance misuse, insomnia, depression, suicide and suicidal ideation, continued fear and anxiety towards their abuser and people who share similar characteristics, and difficulties with adult relationships and sexual functioning – they may experience traumatic sexualisation, and this may shape their sexuality in developmentally inappropriate and interpersonally dysfunctional manner (Browne and Finkelhor, 1986). CSA survivors may also carry deep-rooted anger towards the abuser(s) and towards themselves for not stopping the abuse, and at other people who failed to protect them. In adult life, this anger may manifest as bitterness. Furthermore, CSA survivors may experience a deep sense of betrayal that may make it difficult to trust other adults, which can, in turn, influence their relationships in adulthood. They may also experience continued feelings of powerlessness, shame, guilt, self-blame and stigmatisation, and are at higher risk of revictimisation and future sexual abuse (Silver and Karakurt, 2014).

These effects also offer hints for the detection of CSA. Below we list some of the behavioural and emotional markers that are correlated with CSA. This list is indicative rather than exhaustive, and is intended to draw attention to some of the more frequent emotions and behaviours that are correlated with CSA. However, although such emotions and behaviours are an indication of negative experiences by children and young people, they do not ascertain

CSA, and may be attributable to other experiences of neglect, abuse or trauma.

CSA has a deep emotional and behavioural impact on children and young people. Therefore, observing these or other similar changes or difficulties in children's behaviour requires appropriate attention and action:

- a sudden change in behaviour and low mood
- emotional withdrawal and loss of interest in a previously enjoyable activity
- avoidance of peers and social activities
- increased risk taking
- missing school
- increased anxiety and becoming more clingy
- sudden bouts of anger or aggressive behaviour
- changes in eating or sleeping habits or problems with eating or sleeping, such as nightmares, bed-wetting or soiled clothes
- obsessive behaviour
- self-harm or suicide
- new unwelcomed behaviour such as smoking, drinking or drug taking.

Other important signs include:

- avoidance or fear of certain people or places or a reluctance to interact with them (this could be a member of the family, a friend or another adult who may be in contact with the child)
- age-inappropriate behaviour including sexual behaviour, promiscuity or use of sexual language
- having physical symptoms such as anal or vaginal pain, unusual discharge or sexually transmitted diseases or pregnancy
- increased and unusual interest in sexuality and sexual topics (for example, asking unusual questions or sexual curiosity)
- age-inappropriate sexual preoccupation or sexual behaviour with peers or adults (for example, sexualised behaviour, showing genitals to peers or adults, touching peers or adults in sexual or inappropriate ways, age-inappropriate friends or partner, use of force or coercion with others to undress or sexually interact with others).

Conclusion

Digital and social media technologies are an integral part of children and young people's lives and identities, but they also offer a myriad of new possibilities for online grooming and sexual abuse. There is a wide range of online resources in relation to grooming and CSA that can help practitioners keep abreast of new challenges and developments in this area. However, the constantly changing digital and social media technologies mean that the dynamics and possibilities for online grooming and sexual abuse are in constant evolution and expansion. Therefore, given the rapid changes in technology and the vast and increasing number of constantly evolving SNSs and social media apps, and their psycho-socio-ecological implications, we suggest that practitioners should have appropriate training in online safeguarding followed by annual refresher workshops in relation to new developments in technology and its implications for the holistic safeguarding of children and young people.

To conclude, each case is unique, and practitioners' responses may vary depending on context, and may involve a combination of approaches ranging from the use of filtering software to digital citizenship education, and from balancing online and offline activities to face-to-face conversations and direct supervision. It is important to remember that CSA is a complex multidimensional phenomenon and requires an equally integrated and multidimensional intervention and response that takes into consideration all the relevant stakeholders (family, friends and peers, school, community, etc). Most importantly, the perception and significance of risks are different between adults and children, and holistic safeguarding requires an understanding of risks and resilience from children's perspective. Therefore, close and effective communication and partnership with children and young people lies at the heart of any effective practice and intervention. This implies appreciating children's curiosity and offering patient and thoughtful support and guidance, while making sure that they are comfortable expressing their ideas and sharing their experiences, that they feel and know that their curiosity is natural and their opinions are valued, that they can share any experience and speak about any topic they feel curious about, and that they are respected, loved and supported at all times.

8

Cyberbullying

Definition of bullying and cyberbullying

Bullying has been defined in a number of ways depending on the author's perspective and methodological background. However, all agree that bullying begins with intent to harm, and becomes more insidious as it is repeated over time.

Perhaps the most common definition of bullying is that of Olweus (1991, 1993, p 9), which states that '... a person is being bullied when he or she is exposed, repeatedly and over time, to negative actions on the part of one or more other persons', while Nansel et al (2001) offer a panoptic definition of bullying as aggressive behaviour or intentional 'harm doing' by a person or group, generally carried out repeatedly and over time, and involving a power differential.

These definitions highlight three important characteristics of bullying: (1) a power difference between the bully and the victim; (2) intent to harm; and (3) repetition over time. Although some argue that a critical, single incident of aggression may be considered bullying (Arora, 1996) repetition over time and power imbalance distinguish bullying from more general aggression (that is, intent to cause harm) (Olweus, 1999). Extending the traditional definition of bullying, Smith et al (2008, p 376) define cyberbullying as 'an aggressive act or behaviour that is carried out using electronic means by a group or an individual repeatedly and over time against another person who cannot easily defend him or herself.' Given the power differential between the bully and the victim, bullying involves the systematic abuse of power (Rigby, 2002), and cyberbullying involves the systematic abuse of power using information and communication technologies (ICT).

There are several types of bullying, including physical and verbal (direct, face-to-face forms of aggression) and indirect and relational bullying. In the 1980s, bullying and aggression were mainly considered as a direct physical or verbal attack. However, in the 1990s this scope was broadened to include indirect aggression (done via a third party), relational aggression aimed at damaging the victim's relationships, and social aggression and social exclusion, or the demand for certain behaviour as a prerequisite for inclusion, aimed at damaging the social status and self-esteem of the victim; this may not always be immediately apparent (for example, when the aggressor starts to spread rumours about the victim; see Underwood, 2002; Monks and Smith, 2006).

Research indicates that relational bullying is more predictive of emotional distress than other forms of bullying (Bauman, 2008). Indeed, there is evidence that social exclusion and damage to one's social capital and identity are among the most frequent and painful of bullying experiences (Mynard et al, 2000), which can lead to post-traumatic stress (PTS). However, relational bullying is not always sufficiently recognised by parents or teachers, and is often considered as the least serious (Yoon and Kerber, 2003; Jacobsen and Bauman, 2007), although in recent years there has been greater recognition of its serious impact. However, in an increasingly digital society, cyberbullying has emerged as a new form of aggression, becoming the most widespread form of bullying.

Differences between offline bullying and cyberbullying

There are substantial overlaps and significant differences between offline and online bullying. Both involve intent to harm and targeted aggression towards the victim, have similar underlying dynamics, and have a significant and similar impact on people experiencing bullying and their lives; these can vary from low self-esteem, isolation and withdrawal to generalised anxiety, depression and suicide. Notwithstanding these similarities, there are significant differences between online and offline bullying. Indeed, the characteristics and features of online context and digital and social media technologies influence the dynamics, process and impact of cyberbullying. These include the following:

Anonymity: Anonymity and fluidity of online identities offers an important distinguishing characteristic of cyberbullying, and serves as a protective veil that increases its appeal and further emboldens perpetrators (Patchin and Hinduja, 2006). However, as discussed in Chapter 2, anonymity is an evolving and complex phenomenon, and one can often find evidence to retrace the source of many online postings. Nevertheless, the illusion of anonymity can result in disinhibition and intensify aggression. The Pew Research Center (2001, cited in Patchin and Hinduja, 2006) states that as early as 2001, 37 per cent of teenagers had said things in an online communication that they would not say in person; this is consistent with Suler's (2004) disinhibition effect (see Chapter 2). Indeed, whereas in offline bullying the victim knows who the bully/bullies are, anonymity of the online bully means the bully could be anyone, within or outside of the victim's peer group. The anonymity of the aggressor undermines interpersonal trust and the victim's sense of personal safety, and generates fundamental insecurity, which leads to a persistent and pervasive fear and sense of insecurity that influences the victim's social and interpersonal relationships.

Power imbalance: This is an important element of bullying that is altered in cyberbullying. In offline bullying, physical stature (size, physical strength or attractiveness) (Atlas and Pepler, 1998) or social standing (wealth or popularity) are usually the main sources of the bully's power. However, neither one of these is necessary in a cyberbullying context. Indeed, although there is no empirical data in this regard, we can plausibly suggest that cyberbullying may be appealing to people experiencing offline bullying as anonymity offers a 'safe' way to retaliate. A cyberbully can be anyone who has a relative position of projected or perceived online power with respect to the victim (Megele and Buzzi, 2018d; see also Chapter 2). Hence, the source of the cyberbully's power could vary widely from technical knowhow to online social capital, to pure virtual and perceptual power (as perceived or imagined by the victim) (for a discussion of power in the online context, see Megele and Buzzi, 2018d).

Universality and transcending time and space: 'Universality' of the web and the ability to contact anyone, anywhere, anytime transcend the boundaries that contain and delimit most communication. This means that as long as someone has access to the internet they can be either the source or recipient of online messages, postings and other forms of communication, and as such they can potentially become the perpetrator or target of cyberbullying. Furthermore, offline bullying is more isolated/contained in the sense that it takes place in 'real time' (Walther, 2007) and requires the co-presence of the bully and the victim; hence, by avoiding such co-presence, the victim can find respite in relative safety (for example, seek refuge in the safety of one's home). However, given the significance and all-permeating nature of online media and the asynchronous nature of online postings, and drawing on the discussion of boundaries in Chapter 2, cyberbullying violates the victim's sense of self and social identity, and in this sense, casts a shadow over every moment of the victim's life and experience. Indeed, in cyberbullying, co-presence with the bully is supplanted by pervasive and invasive virtual permanence (Megele and Buzzi, 2018d, 2018e). This exacerbates and magnifies the aggression and generates a deep sense of vulnerability and helplessness as the victim can experience the aggression as relentless and feel that there is no respite and nowhere that is safe and free from the bully's presence.

Limited cues: A further difference between online and offline bullying is the absence, or substantial reduction, of non-verbal, visual, contextual and social cues. This affects online bullying in two ways: first, it increases the likelihood of misunderstanding the meaning of the message, which can lead to unintended consequences or exacerbate the situation; and second, it allows deindividuation and separation of self from one's behaviour, which means some bullies may not fully appreciate the seriousness and grave impact of their actions for the person experiencing the bullying. The cyberbully is far removed from the victim's experience as they do not have to observe the effect of their actions on the victim. (An exception to this is sadistic bullying where the bully derives pleasure from the other's pain and seeks evidence of the victim's distress.) This reduces the possibility for empathy or remorse in the online world.

Relative permanence and repetition: Although repetition is an important feature of both online and offline bullying, there are new dimensions to repetition of online abuse or aggression. Given the relative permanence of online postings (Megele and Buzzi, 2018d), cyberbullying is inscribed in an online communication/interaction such as an image, video, text message and other online postings, and in effect, the bullying, humiliation, aggression and abuse are repeated each time such a posting is (re)visited/viewed, and remain part of the victim's online self-narrative and identity. Indeed, the bullying, humiliation, aggression and abuse are continued and continuous so long as such posts remain online, and in this sense, cyberbullying leaves an indelible scar (see Chapter 2) on the victim's psyche and identity.

'Shareability', replicability, and virtually unlimited visibility: The shareability, replicability and potential for wide and unlimited visibility are part of the attraction of social media for young people. However, these same qualities exacerbate and magnify the significance and impact of online bullying and abuse. Indeed, at times, online postings of bullying or abuse can go viral, and this can infinitely compound the effects of the bullying, humiliation and abuse. The case of Ghyslain Raza, dubbed 'the Star Wars Kid', whose video was shared over a billion times, is an early example of such a situation (Hawkes, 2016). Shareability also means an image or posting that may seem temporary can be captured (for example, in a screenshot) and shared online; reposted images from Snapchat are a good example of such threats. This is worsened by a common feeling that nothing can be done about such a posting, and even worse, that some people collude with the bully/abuser by further sharing such postings.

Increased frequency and intensity: The triangle of harm (see Chapter 3, Figure 3.5) and routine activity theory (Cohen and Felson, 1979) can help explain the reason for an increase in cyberbullying and its intensity. These suggest that when children and young people are placed in high-risk situations and in close proximity to motivated offenders, and are unsupervised, they face increased risks of experiencing aggression, abuse and cyberbullying. Online media transcend geographical boundaries and offer new, and virtually unlimited, possibilities for self-expression, communication and relationships, and creating new, immediate and permeating proximities. Such proximities offer many more opportunities to motivated offenders. This is exacerbated by digital and social media technologies' capability to project and amplify strengths and vulnerabilities (real, perceived or imagined). Hence, social media and online interactions can project and amplify the actions and perceived 'strengths' of the bully while magnifying the vulnerabilities of the victim. Young people may also use social media unsupervised, and routine activity theory suggests that this lack of supervision removes a protective factor and paves the way for the bully. Therefore, the context of online engagements and social media technologies can facilitate and increase the frequency and intensity of online aggression, abuse and cyberbullying; this is part of the context risk associated with digital and social media (see Chapter 3, and Megele and Buzzi, 2018d).

The role of the bystander

People can play different roles in a bullying situation, although most studies distinguish between three main types of participants: bullies, the victim and bystanders (those witnessing the bullying). The objective of most bullies is to increase their own social capital and influence. In this sense, bullying is a performance and bystanders are its audience; indeed, most bullying occurs in the presence of bystanders (or audience). Therefore, bystanders intensify the impact of bullying as bullying becomes a public humiliation, and the presence of silent bystanders (not to mention those who support and encourage the bully) socially validates the bully and the act of bullying and the power imbalance between the bully and the bullied. Indeed, research (Twemlow et al, 2002) indicates that the number of bystanders observing a bullying situation can be a source of power for the perpetrator. Therefore, the effects of cyberbullying are exponentially increased by the cyber-audience effect (the presence of assumed audiences; Megele, 2014b; see also Chapter 2). Hence, bystanders play a huge role in bullying, and can be a source of power for the bully.

There can also be a blurring of roles in cyberbullying – for example, if a person shares or posts something that was initiated by the bully, do they switch from being a bystander to the bully?

Bystanders can be divided into three categories, namely: (1) those assisting or reinforcing the bully; (b) those defending the victim; or (c) outsiders (for example, ignoring the bullying) (Salmivalli et al, 1996). Nickerson et al (2014) note that bullying and harassment usually occur in the presence of bystanders (Lodge and Frydenberg,

2005), and research suggests that 10-40 per cent of adolescents have experienced cyberbullying (Whittaker and Kowalski, 2015), and approximately 70 per cent of adult internet users have witnessed some form of online harassment (Duggan, 2014). Notwithstanding these figures, and although when asked young people reject bullying and suggest that they would like to help the victim (Lodge and Frydenberg, 2005), less than 20 per cent of bullying witnesses actually intervene (Atlas and Pepler, 1998). Using a two-wave panel study with a six-month time interval and involving 1,412 10- to 13-year-olds, Pabian et al (2016) found that a previous observation of bullying was predictive of a lower empathic responsiveness in the subsequent instance of being a bystander. However, the participants' attitudes toward bullying were not influenced by seeing more cyberbullying. This helps explain the discrepancy between bystanders' intentions and actions. Nonetheless, this discrepancy is significant as research indicates that bystander intervention in support of the victim can help reduce the bullying. This remains an important area for bullying prevention.

The bystander intervention model

Investigating the role of the bystander, Latané and Darley (1970) found four factors that influence bystander intervention: (1) self-awareness – the bystander's action is dependent on the presence of an audience; (2) social cues – the bystander's action is influenced by others' actions or non-actions; (3) blocking – the bystander's action may be prevented by another bystander; and (4) diffusion of responsibility – in the presence of other witnesses, bystanders tend to think that someone else will take action and therefore tend not to intervene in the presence of other witnesses. Bystander action is influenced by audience size (the number of bystanders/witnesses – the larger the audience/number of witnesses, the more likely that the bystander may feel obligated to take action).

Nickerson et al (2014) explain that the bystander intervention model (Latané and Darley, 1970) provides a framework for understanding bystander intervention or lack thereof. This model suggests that there are five sequential prerequisites for bystander intervention, namely, the bystander should: (1) notice the event; (2) interpret the event as an emergency; (3) accept responsibility for an intervention; (4) know how to intervene; and (5) take action. Here we briefly consider the application of these factors in cyberspace and the social media context.

The effect of an online audience vis-à-vis anonymity: Applying the bystander intervention model in online social media settings, it becomes apparent that although social media offers increased visibility to the act of bullying due to social media dissociative anonymity and the deindividuation effect of online media (Suler, 2004), increased online visibility doesn't necessarily lead to positive intervention on the part of witnesses/bystanders.

Social cues, noticing the event and interpreting the event as emergency: Online digital and social media increase the visibility of cyberbullying events and the probability of the bystander noticing cyberbullying or online aggression. However, social cues are either absent or significantly reduced in the online environment and social media interactions, and this reduces the likelihood of bystander intervention. Furthermore, the lack of social cues may result in the misinterpretation of online interactions, and may mean that an observer may not always correctly identify an act of cyberbullying.

Self-awareness and accepting responsibility for intervention: Suler (2004) posits that online deindividuation reduces self-awareness and facilitates distancing one's self from online interactions and events. This reduces the likelihood of bystander intervention or taking responsibility for an intervention. Furthermore, the effect of the cyber-audience (assumed audience) facilitates the diffusion of responsibility in an online environment (see Chapter 2).

Cyberbullying signs and effects

As discussed in Chapter 5, psychosocial difficulties are correlated with problematic internet use, which is then reflected in specific patterns of behaviour (for example, cyberbullying, gambling, pornography) or generalised patterns of behaviour (general use of internet resulting in negative outcomes) (Davis, 2001). This cyclical process can become self-reinforcing and can compound the effects of cyberbullying. Cyberbullying heightens the victim's fears and anxieties and generates feelings of anger, shame, guilt and self-blame that can lead to depression, emotional and mental health difficulties including eating disorders, insomnia, alcohol and substance misuse, suicidal ideation and suicide. However, depression, sadness, hopelessness, powerlessness and trauma symptomology are only some of the psychosocial effects associated with cyberbullying. Cyberbullying can have further devastating and wide-ranging social, psychological, behavioural and psychosomatic effects and can affect children's development. For example, cyberbullying affects the victim's sense of safety and interpersonal trust, which, in turn, affects their relationships and social identity and often leads to isolation, emotional loneliness and withdrawal that aggravates the victim's experience.

It is essential that practitioners pay attention to behavioural and emotional changes in young people, and detect emotional and behavioural markers that may be a consequence of cyberbullying. The following are a few mindlines giving examples of some behavioural and emotional changes that may be indicative of cyberbullying.

The young person experiencing cyberbullying may:

- seem withdrawn, or feel upset or outraged after using the internet or their computer, mobile phone or digital device
- seem anxious when receiving a text, Instant message, email or other message
- avoid discussing or be secretive about online activities and mobile phone use
- spend much more or much less time texting, gaming or using social media
- withdraw from family, friends and activities they previously enjoyed
- avoid peers and social occasions
- not want to go to school and/or avoid meeting friends and school mates, or avoid specific classes or group activities
- have many new phone numbers, texts or email addresses showing up on their mobile phone, laptop or tablet
- avoid previously enjoyable social situations
- have an unexpected deterioration of academic performance

- show a change in mood, behaviour, appetite or sleep (difficulty sleeping)
- show signs of low mood or low self-confidence and low self-esteem.

An examination of individual behaviours, attitudes and beliefs towards aggression can help provide a better understanding of the role of aggression and normative thinking in bullying, both online and offline. Human aggression has been classified into many dichotomous typologies, and one such classification is proactive versus reactive. From a safeguarding perspective, proactive/instrumental aggression is premeditated, goal-oriented and motivated by internal desires (for example, domination), while reactive/hostile/expressive aggression is reflexive and a response to external/social stimuli that are perceived as aversive or a threat. Proactive aggression has been linked to offline/face-to-face bullying (Davis, 2001), and this relationship can be extended to cyberbullying.

Cyberbullying and the law

Although there is no specific 'cyberbullying law' in the UK, there are a number of different legislations that may be used to combat cyberbullying. For example, the Defamation Act 2013 makes the website host responsible for removing defamatory material posted on their website. Different websites and SNSs have different ways for reporting inappropriate or abusive material, and practitioners should use the appropriate channel to report such material. For example, YouTube members can report inappropriate content by using the option 'Flag content as inappropriate' that appears under every video, while Facebook users can report inappropriate material by clicking on the 'Report' option/link that appears on each page on Facebook, or by emailing abuse@facebook.com (see www.facebook.com/safety). Section 127 of the Communication Act 2003 makes it an offence to send an electronic message that is grossly offensive or of an indecent, obscene or menacing character. The Protection from Harassment Act 1997 covers repeated bullying amounting to harassment, while Section 154 of the Criminal Justice and Public Order Act 1994 covers all forms of harassment including textual/written messages. Finally, the Malicious Communications Act 1988 makes it an offence to send a communication with the intention to cause harm, distress or anxiety, although intent may be difficult to prove. Furthermore, there are several policy and guidance documents relating to cyberbullying, including the Department for Education's (2014) Guidance: Preventing bullying series, which includes *Advice for parents and carers on cyber bullying* and links to resources, and the Anti-bullying Alliance (2013) which offers guidance about *Cyberbullying and children and young people with SEN and disabilities*; as well as publications by CEOP, Childline, Childnet, NSPCC, Thinkuknow, UK Safer Internet Centre, and others.

It may be helpful to note that although social workers cannot confiscate or search children's mobile phones, the Education Act 2011 allows teachers, under certain circumstances, to look for, identify and delete inappropriate images or data from pupils' electronic devices such as mobile phones. Finally, practitioners may also consult the Crown Prosecution Service's (CPS, 2013) guidelines on prosecuting cases involving communications sent via social media.

To elaborate on the multidimensional, complex and interlinked dynamics of cyberbullying, let us examine an example using the 10 C's psycho-socio-ecological model.

Shane's story

After years of relentless bullying, Shane, aged 15, took his own life. Shane was sensitive and kind, with an easy-going nature. "He always tried so hard to make everyone happy", says his mum, Sarah. She believes it was this tendency that made him an easy target for bullies. Shane endured years of torment and abuse until one day he did the exact thing his tormentors wanted: "What do you want me to do? Kill myself?" "Yeah, kill yourself."

Sarah cannot recall exactly when or why the bullying started, but she remembers that it started with small things a few years back, and then escalated. She first noticed that Shane was no longer invited to parties and started to become isolated. It then progressed to name calling and insults that extended to online harassment and abuse. At the time of his death he was being cyberbullied by people he had never met and who didn't know him. At the age of 11 he had started to self-harm with a razor blade, and to hide the wounds he started to wear long-sleeve tops all year round. Shane had spoken about suicide before, but always told Sarah not to worry as he wasn't brave enough.

Shane was the youngest of four children; he had two older brothers (aged 18 and 19) and one older sister (aged 21). The family had a comfortable life, and Shane attended a private independent school. Shane was a handsome boy with an easy and open smile but, due to continued abuse, by the time of his death he no longer smiled, and his confidence was so low that he shied away from having his photograph taken. But the most disturbing experience was when the bullies told him to take his own life: "Why don't you just kill yourself?"

Two years earlier, Sarah had noticed that the abuse was particularly intense and worried about his wellbeing, and therefore stopped all his access to social media. But not having access to online platforms only made Shane more worried, isolated, unhappy and desperate to make friends. Shane would get up in the middle of the night to access the family computer in the living room and read the abusive messages that were posted about him online. His family couldn't understand why he would seek out those messages. When asked about it, he had told his mother that he needed to know what people were saying about him.

On two occasions Sarah had discussed the matter with Shane's teacher and head teacher, but by that time the abuse was mainly online and being carried out anonymously. Therefore, the school referred the matter to the police, but indicated that there was no evidence that the abuse was coming from Shane's peers. The police had talked with Sarah and Shane and had concluded that there was insufficient evidence to take action against the cyberbullies. Shane was not referred to children's services as both the school and the police felt that he was supported by his parents, and there were no indications of parenting issues or problems.

Sarah tried to reach out to the other mothers but nothing seemed to help. At one point she wrote to the bullies in Shane's school asking them to desist and to leave him alone. But the bullies wrote back to her saying how they were offended by her letter as they were Shane's friends and cared about their friendship. Shane was ostracised and shunned every day at school but always pretended that everything was okay. Shane become chameleon-like in order to try and fit in. He styled his hair and wore fashionable clothing, but that was just more reason for the bullies to target him. He tried different personas hoping to fit in, but was labelled as trying too hard. His parents encouraged him to 'just be' himself, but he would say: "I can't do that, I've tried being Shane and everybody hates Shane." The cyberbullying continued, and although the atmosphere at home was very stressful, everyone tried to be positive, and as the years went by, the bullying became a normalised part of their lives. Everyone tried to stay positive, but there was always an undercurrent of stress. Shane started to see a psychotherapist and that helped. The family discussed moving Shane to a new school, but by then the bullying was primarily online. When he eventually did move to a different school, the online abuse followed him and targeted his new friends, so he was soon isolated again.

Someone would post a message calling him a 'dirty dick' on BlackBerry Messenger, then someone would re-post it and add expletives and post it on ASK.fm, Facebook, Twitter, Instagram, YouTube and so on. But the most damaging posts were when people encouraged him to kill himself. For example, one of the conversations started with an anonymous posting: 'Shane trying hard to be somebody when everyone knows he is a no body', and from there it went into how ugly and worthless he was, how no one could bear to be around him because he was so unpopular, followed by expletives. Shane posted: 'What do you want me to do? Kill myself?' And he received replies such as 'Yea, slit your wrists pussy'; 'Hang yourself'; 'Slit your throat and video it'; 'Yeah, slit your wrist and hang yourself in your room so your mum can find you.'

Shane printed and kept all the abusive messages he had received in a box that he kept on the top shelf in his wardrobe. Sarah had encouraged him to throw them away, but he was insistent that they were evidence. However, in his last week, Shane threw away all of the abusive and bullying messages he had kept in his box, except one. At the time, Sarah viewed this as a positive step and "thought he was over his obsession and was finally ready to let go of those hateful messages and move on with life."

The day before killing himself, he blocked his family from his social media accounts and posted just one word, 'Sorry', on Instagram, Facebook and Twitter. That evening Shane was relaxed, talking and joking with his family.

He told his family that he was sorry for all the troubles and difficulties in the past years, and agreed with them that he just needed to be positive and have a new start. Everyone interpreted that positively, and his mum cried and hugged him, telling him it was like finding her lost son. His dad, an engineer of Asian heritage, was often away on business trips, but that evening he was at home and patted Shane on the shoulder saying, "Good to have you back son." For once there seemed to be no tension in the room, and everyone was relaxed and had a good time.

The following day, Shane laid the only bullying message that he had kept on his pillow. Then he slit both his wrists and walked to the chair he had put in the middle of his room and climbed onto it. He put the noose he had prepared around his neck and kicked off the chair from beneath his feet. Later that day Sarah found Shane's hanging body in his room. The message on his pillow read: 'What do you want me to do? Kill myself?' 'Yeah, slit your wrist and hang yourself in your room so your mum can find you.'

Reflection and analysis

Experiences of rejection and cyberbullying are very distressing and can be relentless and overwhelming. Therefore, in consultation and agreement with someone experiencing bullying similar to Shane, it is essential to establish immediate safeguarding measures to protect him and to mitigate the negative effects and outcomes of cyberbullying. We will use the 10 C's psycho-socio-ecological model for examining Shane's story.

Confidentiality and personal disclosure risk

Shane's bullying began offline and was extended online. The original bullies were Shane's classmates and peers, and this means that at least the initial cyberbullies knew Shane, but could hide behind online anonymity and therefore Shane didn't know them. This exacerbates the power imbalance in cyberbullying. However, even after changing his school, Shane's social media posts were accessible to the cyberbullies. Indeed, although Shane changed his school, the cyberbullies continued their harassment, and began targeting Shane's new friends in his new school until he was eventually isolated once again. When children are moved to a new school due to cyberbullying, it is important to agree and establish a comprehensive plan for their protection. This may include unplugging from technology and offering opportunities for new activities and meeting new people. Furthermore, even without moving school, in consultation with young people, agreeing digital-free zones in the home can help create a respite by separating the young person from the persecutory messages of cyberbullies. Agreeing digital-free times can also help break the link between the cyberbully and the victim (for example, digital-free time before sleeping); if appropriate this can be extended to digital-free days (for example, digital-free Sundays). These approaches can be accompanied by family activities that reinforce familial interactions and bonding. Finally, device curfews before sleeping and overnight can help restore the victim's sense of separation from the cyberbully and cyberbullying messages.

Content risk

Shane clearly suffered from content risk, and there was a continuous posting of abusive and bullying messages online. Shane's family didn't fully appreciate the significance of social media for Shane, and the importance of engaging in critical and open conversation with Shane to gain a better understanding of his experiences and to arrive at possible alternatives to address the cyberbullying and to mitigate its risks and effects. Unilateral measures about young people's use of social media can lead to covert access and can create unexpected repercussions, as demonstrated by Shane waking up in the middle of the night to use the family computer to check his social media accounts and the cyberbullies' messages/posts about him (see also the case of Tallulah in Chapter 1). Furthermore, Shane was right to print and collect the bullying messages and, as he told Sarah, they should be kept as evidence. Below are a few mindlines in relation to cyberbullying.

It is important to explain to children and young people to take screenshots and save the evidence of cyberbullying and to report cyberbullies and their inappropriate and aggressive messages. However, let cyberbullies know that their behaviour or messages are inappropriate and report them with evidence, but don't engage in an online discussion with them, and don't try to answer every message no matter how tempting, inappropriate, hurtful or untrue they may be. Instead:

- save the evidence of cyberbullying;
- report the cyberbully and their behaviour and posts/messages; and
- block the cyberbully and their posts/messages (block mobile phone numbers, email addresses, social media accounts and other forms of online communication).

Cyberbullying is rarely a one-off incident; it is usually a repeated and relentless attack over time. Therefore, people experiencing bullying should be as relentless as the cyberbullies, taking screenshots and saving evidence, and documenting and reporting each instance of cyberbullying. This includes reporting cyberbullies and their behaviours and posts to the police and to the ISP as well as SNSs or other websites used by the cyberbully. Depending on the type of message/posts and severity of the situation, the behaviour of the cyberbully may warrant criminal charges.

After saving the cyberbully's message/post (documenting the evidence of cyberbullying), when possible, remove the abusive cyberbullying messages/posts and offer alternative positive and validating experiences for the young person. Positive and supportive messages and experiences can help the young person cope with the impact of negative messages/posts and experiences of cyberbullying. This should not be construed as acceptance of cyberbullying; cyberbullying is never justified and should not be accepted – it should be challenged and stopped in an appropriate manner. However, this approach can help the young person and reduce their dwelling on the negative cyberbullying messages while recognising their feelings and experience, offering the space and understanding to unpack them.

One of the tactics used by cyberbullies is to create fake social media accounts in the name of the person they want to bully, and then post inappropriate content under that account and engage in derogatory and defamatory conversations that undermine the victim. In this sense, the cyberbully hijacks the identity of the victim and uses it to damage the reputation and identity of the victim. Such behaviours are very hard to block or challenge as it is difficult to prove that the account concerned is a fake account; it could be considered as having the same name but a different owner. However, the police may be able to help retrace such accounts to an IP address and locate the person operating the account. Also Shane's social worker or the police could have contacted the relevant SNSs and websites to remove the defamatory and abusive information about Shane, although at times this can be a lengthy, difficult and frustrating process. There are also a number of charities and organisations that are dedicated to challenging bullying and that could help in supporting people experiencing bullying like Shane.

Context risk

Shane used Twitter, Facebook and Instagram, and it is important to consider the specific risks associated with each of these platforms, and to support young people to adjust the privacy setting for each of their social media accounts to block out the bullies and ensure that their posts are only seen by their friends and followers. Apps used by Facebook friends can access one's Facebook data. Therefore, aside from other privacy settings, it is important to edit the 'Apps others use' setting to ensure that the apps used by young people's Facebook friends cannot access their data.

Consumption risk

Social media is an important part of young people's lives, and social media posts from cyberbullies were at the top of Shane's mind. This should be recognised by parents and any practitioner supporting people experiencing bullying. Shane should have been introduced to offline activities and peers to establish a better balance between his online and offline activities. Furthermore, blocking his access to social media proved counter-productive. Therefore, he should be allowed to access his SNS accounts but should be supported (for example, through co-viewing or co-surfing and appropriate online support).

Consonance-dissonance and compatibility risk

Social media is an integral part of young people's social identity and a primary tool for maintaining their relationships. Shane continued to experiment with different identities and adjusted his online and offline behaviour and appearance in order to 'fit in', although his attempts were rejected by his peers. This is deeply damaging for the person's identity, self-esteem, confidence and emotional and mental wellbeing. Shane presented dissonant and conflicting identities online and between online and offline; such dissonance and incompatibility is usually a reflection/indication of underlying difficulties and needs to be explored with the young person. Also, when need be, it is important that young people experiencing bullying are referred to and supported by specialist counselling and psychological services. Such support can help address issues relating to self-worth and self-efficacy and can support the young person's overall psychological wellbeing; it can also improve coping, relaxation, self-soothing and stress management capabilities. However, resilience should never be construed as acceptance of aggression or abuse. Therefore, Shane also needed support to reconfigure his online presence and identity.

The relentless name calling, abuse and bullying severely damaged Shane's confidence and made him the most hated boy in his school, and the cyberbullying followed him even when he moved to a different school. This is a very difficult experience, and such young people need therapy and extended support to ensure their safety, healthy development and wellbeing.

Offering positive validation and enhancing the person's sense of self-worth and self-efficacy are strong protective factors against a number of negative outcomes including negative thoughts and negative information-processing patterns, low mood and depression, emotional loneliness and isolation, and self-harming behaviour. Therefore, it is important to create opportunities for positive and validating experiences for people experiencing bullying. These could range from engagement in peer groups within one's local community to attending extra classes, activities or workshops (for example, an art class, painting workshop). Group therapy for young people with experiences of bullying can also be helpful. This will enable them to meet other young people of a similar age and with similar experiences, including survivors of cyberbullying. Such support groups help reduce the sense of isolation, reaffirming that they are not alone and are not 'the problem' or 'at fault', that it is the cyberbully who is the aggressor and the source of problem and who must change his/her behaviour.

Connection and social capital risk

Shane was connected with his classmates and peers online; however, many of these people had been abusive towards him, either bullying him offline or had been complicit in bullying through their actions or inactions. In such cases, it is important to have an open conversation about the person's existing online digital presence/identity and relationships, and to review and reconfigure their online connections and relationships. By disconnecting from his classmates (for example, unfollowing them on Twitter or unfriending them on Facebook) and setting appropriate privacy settings (for example, protecting his tweets or setting his default privacy/sharing option to friends on Facebook; checking his activity log to view all his Facebook posts and things he was tagged in; limiting the send friend requests and 'who can look me up' options; limiting the audience for his Timeline and not allowing search engines to link to it), Shane would have been able to better protect himself and his social media accounts and postings from the cyberbullies, as this information would no longer be accessible or visible to them. Although such changes might not stop cyberbullies and their posts, to some extent these changes could influence and protect the young person's online digital identity.

Contact risk

Although Shane was isolated in his new school and suffered from cyberbullying, he was no longer in face-to-face contact with the bullies from his previous school, that is, the bullying was focused online. In such cases, it is important to report cyberbullies to the relevant SNS and to block them and cut their every line of access or communication with the young person. There are also various organisations and resources that may be able to support the process and the young person.

At one point Sarah wrote to the bullies in Shane's school asking them to desist and to leave Shane alone. But the bullies wrote back to her saying how they were offended by her letter as they were Shane's friends and cared about their friendship. This highlights the perverse and complex dynamics of bullying, and that any action or communication can be distorted and should therefore be thoughtfully considered and reviewed.

Most of the cyberbullying was carried out using anonymous accounts. As described earlier, this amplifies the impact of cyberbullying and undermines the person's interpersonal trust, generating fundamental and constant insecurities. Furthermore, as described in Chapter 2, the unbounded nature of cyberspace combined with the effects of solipsistic introjections and dissociative imagination create a form of 'solipsistic presence' and 'virtual sociality' that is experienced as constant, continuous and all-permeating; this heightens and aggravates the experience and impact of abuse.

Aside from the use of the Tor (see Chapter 2), there is no full-proof anonymity on social media. Hence, even if the accounts are anonymous, the police may be able to track and retrace the location and identity of the person behind the account. However, from a safeguarding perspective, it is important to engage people experiencing cyberbullying in healthy and supportive offline activities with peers and away from online social media. It may also be advisable to set up new anonymous and private accounts for the individual to enable them to develop new and healthy online friendships. This is part of protecting individuals' digital rights and supporting their digital resilience and citizenship. As digital citizenship is fundamental to young people's development and future opportunities, as far as possible the actions and aggression of cyberbullies should not result in cyber-exclusion and the loss of the young person's digital rights and opportunities.

Using an anonymous account with appropriate privacy settings, and creating a new healthy circle of friends around Shane and away from the old circle of acquaintances (for example, by building new friendships away from his school and old group) could offer a cautious new beginning and a reconfigured and safer online identity for Shane.

Most cyberbullies seek social attention and validation; indeed, most bullying takes place in the presence of an audience/bystanders. Therefore, while it is important to save the evidence of cyberbullying (for example, take screenshots and printouts of the abusive messages and save them) and to report cyberbullies, it is equally important not to acknowledge the cyberbullies' messages and posts, and not to engage with them or seek validation or acceptance from them in any way. Instead, it is best to block their access by blocking and reporting their phone numbers, email addresses, online accounts and other sources of online communication and contact.

It is also essential to support and enhance the young person's confidence, and to ensure that the young person engages in activities they enjoy and are supported to maintain positive relationships and healthy friendships and peer groups with like-minded individuals and based on shared interests – for example, engaging the young person in a youth group, book club, peer support group, sporting or hobby group and other communities of interest. This can protect the young person from isolation and mitigate emotional loneliness and feelings of shame, guilt or self-blame.

Conduct risk

Although research indicates that people who have experienced bullying, either online or offline, have a higher likelihood of cyberbullying others, there was low probability of conduct risk in relation to Shane becoming a bully. However, the main conduct risk for Shane was the risk of self-harm and suicide. Shane needed immediate and effective support, and the cyberbullies needed, and need, immediate intervention and appropriate action and re-education.

As mentioned in Chapter 2, dissociative anonymity and the disinhibiting effect of online media result in reduced empathy on the part of cyberbullies, while the illusion of anonymity further emboldens cyberbullies and amplifies conduct risks. Furthermore, anonymity moderates the audience effect and reduces the likelihood of bystander action/intervention in favour of the victim.

Commercial exploitation risk

There were no significant commercial exploitation risks for Shane.

Composite and complex risks

There were a number of composite and complex risks that affected Shane, ranging from his self-harm to his family situation and their difficulty in understanding Shane's experience. Therefore, drawing on Shane's story, a number of mindlines are set out below that may be helpful when dealing with cyberbullying.

Shane's father is from an Asian heritage and the family live in a small, predominantly white, town in the UK. Several online messages refer to Shane as a 'black rat' and 'black cunt', and other racist and racially abusive expletives. Therefore, these attacks could be considered a hate crime.

Normative beliefs are culturally based; they refer to cognitions about the acceptability of a behaviour and regulate individual behaviour (Huesmann and Guerra, 1997). Young people with normative beliefs that endorse aggression perceive bullying and aggression as acceptable behaviours. This is exacerbated by online anonymity that can result in deindividuation, reducing self-awareness and self-regulation and influencing mentalisation and the probability of considering the consequences of one's behaviour from others' perspectives. The limitations of non-verbal, contextual and social cues combined with deindividuation and solipsism can increase interpersonal misunderstanding and facilitate the activation of normative beliefs that support aggression, resulting in more proactive/instrumental aggression online (Werner et al, 2010).

Schools and practitioners should educate and support young people so they can understand that cyberbullies are sad, frustrated and disturbed individuals trying to deal with their own fears and sense of inadequacy by projecting those fears and inadequacies on to others. When the bullying target internalises the projections of a cyberbully, the two form the self-reinforcing and psychosocially damaging bully–victim dyad. By raising young people's awareness and understanding of such dynamics, and through effective engagement and support and though targeted interventions, practitioners can disrupt/break the behavioural cycles that perpetuate the cycle of cyberbullying.

Shane's mother indicates that he tried to please everyone, and she believes this contributed to his victimisation. Indeed, research indicates that individual vulnerabilities can increase both the likelihood and effects of adverse experiences for individuals, and can lead to 'digital predation'. However, from a safeguarding perspective, while practitioners should consider individual vulnerabilities, they should be mindful that this thinking doesn't lead to implicit or explicit victim blaming; the perpetrator is fully responsible for the aggression, abuse and cyberbullying, and their effects and consequences.

Research indicates that people experiencing bullying have a higher likelihood of becoming cyberbullies. However, enhancing young people's self-awareness, emotional capacity, reflective thinking and perspective-taking are important protective factors that mitigate individual vulnerabilities, support their growth and encourage positive behaviour, hence mitigating the risk of people who experience bullying becoming cyberbullies themselves.

Open dialogue and discussion with young people about their positive and negative online experiences can enhance the practitioner's professional relationship and understanding of the young person's strengths, challenges and lived experience. For example, discussing cyberbullying and enhancing young people's awareness and understanding of why and how it occurs and its associated effects and risks of negative outcomes, as well as how to report cyberbullying or inappropriate posts on websites or SNSs, have been shown to have a positive effect on reducing cyberbullying. Other relevant and helpful topics could include discussing netiquette, digital citizenship and internet safety, etc.

School can play a significant role in prevention, protection and remedial action in relation to cyberbullying. Therefore, it is important that schools have a proactive stance toward digital citizenship and online risks of positive and negative outcomes for children including problems such as cyberbullying. It is essential that appropriate training and education in relation to digital citizenship is embedded in the school curricula. Looking at Shane's story, although referral to the police was an appropriate action, the role and support from other important stakeholders and support organisations is not clear. Given the complex and multidimensional nature of bullying (either online and offline), it is essential to involve the school and for the school to proactively investigate and support the young person. Furthermore, involvement of social workers and children's services can ensure more effective and holistic coordination and safeguarding of children while other non-governmental organisations can provide invaluable support, advice and engagement for the young people and their families.

From a safeguarding perspective, the combined and coordinated effort by all stakeholders is essential for the protection of children. However, at times, when the bullying is primarily online and by anonymous individuals/accounts, it may be unclear whether the cyberbullies are from the same school or not and, in the absence of such evidence, a school may want to protect both their pupils and their reputation by distancing themselves from the situation. However, in such cases prevention is usually the best protection for both the pupils and the school. Indeed, there are many ways in which a school can play a significant role in the protection of children. For example, the school should have and proactively implement an anti-bullying policy; or as part of their digital citizenship classes, schools could invite psychologists to discuss the impact of cyberbullying and engage pupils in exercises that explore its effects and sensitise children and enhance their empathy; or they could invite the police to speak with pupils about bullying/cyberbullying and its ramifications as a criminal offense, etc.

Both the school and the police felt that Shane was supported by his family, and in the absence of any parental concerns, they decided not to refer Shane's case to children's services. Although we cannot know with certainty if referring Shane to children's services could have prevented his death, it is important to adopt a more holistic approach to the safeguarding of children and note that local government's involvement is not limited to cases of parenting concerns and could involve various services within the council that can help support children and their families. Children's services should be engaged when children's development and wellbeing are adversely affected, and this was the case for Shane. Hence, given the multifaceted and complex nature and impact of cyberbullying, it is essential that there is an integrated and strong, multiprofessional and multiagency team around the child that is able to meet their needs and ensure their healthy development and growth. Indeed, safeguarding children and young people, both online and offline, is everyone's responsibility.

Parents influence their children's media consumption, and a good parent–child relationship and parental supervision are important protective factors that have a significant impact on young people's behaviour and online experiences. Indeed, Ybarra and Mitchell (2004), using a nationally representative sample (n=1501, aged between 10 and 17), found that 44 per cent of aggressors/bullies reported having a very poor emotional bond with their caregivers versus 16 per cent reporting strong emotional bonds. Conversely, 19 per cent of non-aggressors/non-bullies reported having a very poor emotional bond with their caregivers versus 32 per cent reporting strong emotional bonds. Furthermore, lacking caregiver supervision was correlated with an 84 per cent higher likelihood of reporting aggressive or bullying online behaviour. Therefore, as we have highlighted repeatedly, a strong parent–child relationship and a healthy circle of online and offline friends are perhaps the two most important protective factors for effective safeguarding and the healthy development of children and young people. However, as demonstrated in this example, a number of factors can influence and complicate the family dynamics and relationships, and these need to be carefully considered by practitioners.

Notwithstanding parental goodwill, given the rapid changes in technology, many parents may misunderstand or feel they do not have the knowledge, experience or ability to teach and guide their children about digital citizenship and social media technologies. Shane's parents did not understand the dynamics of cyberbullying and misunderstood Shane's actions. For example, they didn't understand why Shane was collecting screenshots and printouts of the online messages. Even after Shane had explained that he was collecting evidence of cyberbullying, his parents remained sceptical, and continued to encourage him to throw those messages away.

Most importantly, cyberbullying, cyber-aggression and cyber-abuse are all-permeating and affect the whole family, and this can result in composite and complex risks that can overwhelm individuals' emotional and mentalising capacity, and complicate the family dynamics and relationships. This can influence parental capacity and prevent parents from noticing or acknowledging the painful dynamics of cyberbullying and their children's concerns, thoughts, emotions and experiences. For example, when Shane 'reassured' his mother that he was not brave enough to take his own life, his mother didn't seem to appreciate the significance of that communication, and that Shane's statement was reflective of his state of mind and an indicator of contemplating suicide. Shane was depicting suicide as a desirable outcome and himself as weak and not courageous enough to achieve that outcome. Figure 8.1 show the transposition of some of the relevant risks using the 10 C's psycho–socio–ecological–model.

Figure 8.1: Cyberbullying: mapping risks, protective factors and resilience, using the 10 C's psycho-socio-ecological model

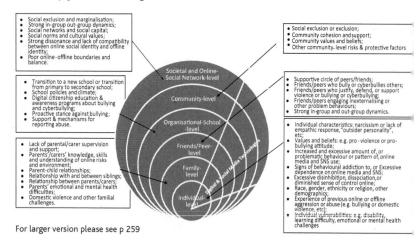

For larger version please see p 259

In his last week, Shane threw away the evidence he had gathered over the years – an indication of him giving up hope. But the prevailing anxiety in the family didn't allow this to be explored between his parents and Shane, while a day before killing himself Shane blocked his family on his social media accounts and posted 'Sorry' on Twitter, Facebook and Instagram. This was Shane giving 'hope' one last chance until the next day, and hoping somehow someone would notice, listen and show concern and change his circumstances. But none of his tormentors and peers seemed to care; Shane and his pains, needs and experiences had become invisible to them, and Shane had become the reservoir for the projection of their own problems, fears and inadequacies.

In his last night with his family, Shane was relaxed as he did not have to worry about the bullies any longer, for all was going to end the following day. This highlights the importance of paying attention to mental, behavioural and emotional changes in young people, and exploring such changes (dissonant and incompatible behaviours or moods) with them to understand their thoughts, motivations and perspective, and to ensure they feel heard and understood. Indeed, suicide prevention can often be as simple as taking the time to notice and to lend an empathetic ear that offers containment for the person's emotions and anxieties. In such critical moments, feeling connected and understood can make a crucial difference that can keep the candle of hope and life burning.

9

Cybercrime, online offending and youth justice

Cyberspace, and the challenges of cybercrime

While cybercrime is a relatively recent phenomenon that has evolved and will continue to evolve with changing technologies, and therefore defies a precise definition, it refers to '... any activity occurring online which has intended negative consequences for others ...' (Kirwan and Power, 2012, p 2). Hence, cybercrime refers to a range of offences, and as defined by US Department of Justice, cybercrime broadly encompasses three categories of offences:

1. Crimes in which the computer or computer network is the target of the criminal activity (for example, hacking, malware and Distributed Denial-of-Service (DDoS) attacks)
2. Existing offences where the computer is a tool used to commit the crime (for example, child pornography, harassment, cyber-fraud, criminal copyright violations, etc.)
3. Crimes in which the use of the computer is an incidental aspect of the commission of the crime but may afford evidence of it (for example, SMS messages relating to a crime).

The ransomware attack in 2017 across different countries is an example of such cybercrime (CNN, 13 May).

Drawing on the discussion of boundaries and differences between online and offline environments (see Chapter 2), below we highlight some of the differences that facilitate cybercrime, hinder its detection and augment its effects:

Networked society: the nature of the networked society and increasing use of social media, cloud computing and other similar services means that data and communication may be routed through different time zones and jurisdictions before reaching their destination. This makes tracing of data and communications difficult, time-sensitive and subject to different legal frameworks.

Scale: From a criminological perspective, the sheer number of people using digital and social media technologies represents a pool of potential offenders and victims, and the shareability and replicability of online data exacerbates and amplifies the audience effect and the potential impact of online events and behaviours, and crimes.

Accessibility and online community: Digital devices and 24-hour access to the internet are widespread and readily available to both offenders and victims. For activities that are beyond a person's knowledge or skill level, cyberspace offers ready access to individuals who can either offer those skills and do the job or teach you how to do it. This is very helpful when used positively, but it also means that offenders, who might otherwise have been isolated, are able to find like-minded individuals and form online groups or create communities that facilitate the commissioning, planning and execution of criminal activity.

Anonymity and multiple identities: Anonymity, combined with ease of creating a new online identity and possibility of maintaining multiple identities, offers great advantages for offenders. From the use of disposable phones to opening a new email account that can offer a basic false identity, to the use of a proxy server, false IP addresses or use of Tor, or anonymous emailers, etc, cyberspace can offer different levels of false identity with varying degrees of sophistication. Encryption technology and various software that can remove traces of digital evidence are readily available to all users. This makes it much more difficult for law enforcement authorities to detect criminal activity and to obtain and use such digital evidence.

Tor and the 'dark web': The so-called 'dark web' refers to the encrypted network of hidden websites (about 30,000 sites) and untraceable activities that exist between Tor servers. Tor stands for 'The Onion Router', which transmits messages through multiple Tor servers and therefore, hides the original sender's Internet

Protocol (IP) address, with onion-like layers of multiple IP addresses, which makes it difficult to retrace/identify the original sender. Tor was created in the mid-1990s by the US military as a means of anonymous communication between intelligence agents. Today, however, it is used for all sorts of anonymous communication, ranging from government intelligence to espionage and from drugs to paedophilia. But it is also used for positive privacy purposes, for example, it is used by the 'Anonymous' network, and activists claim that Tor is our last and best hope for privacy and free speech in a world of surveillance, where every computer, individual, post, activity, communication and interaction is recorded, logged and monitored. The Chinese government attempted to block access to Tor but failed, as Tor project introduced secret 'bridges' (entrance nodes) to Tor that are very difficult to block.

Portability and transferability: Digital technologies offer unprecedented means of data storage, replication and transferability at increasing speeds and with decreasing costs, creating new forms of theft, fraud and offending opportunities, ranging from sexting data, online sexual abuse and pornography to espionage. The convergence of computing and communication technologies has made this process a seamless one, with the ability to take a digital image with a mobile phone and then to upload it to a website within seconds. The volume of sensitive data that is now stored electronically makes the devices themselves vulnerable to attack.

Global reach and unlimited audience: Offenders can reach anyone, anywhere, anytime, invading personal spaces as long as there is an internet connection. Indeed, whereas new technologies and computer networks transcend private and public as well as geographic and national boundaries, legislation and crime detection and prosecution are bounded by territorial limits and restricted to the jurisdiction where the offence occurred. This provides virtually infinite opportunities for offenders, while complicating and challenging law enforcement efforts.

Social media and cyber-offending

As mentioned in previous chapters, social media is an integral part of young people's identity, and identity development is a central task in adolescence, accompanied by developing sexuality and romantic attachments. However, social media has been used to inflict harm on self (for example, cyber-suicide) or others (for example, cyberbullying and harassment), and sites such as Facebook, Twitter, Instagram, Snapchat and ASK.fm have provided unmonitored and uncensored environments that can expose young people to age-inappropriate, harmful and unlawful activities or violent content and behaviour. This has motivated an increasing number of studies examining how social media and the internet facilitate crime and violence. For example, Hinduja and Patchin (2013) examined a random sample of 4,441 10- to 18-year-olds from 37 school districts in the US, and found that 20 per cent of the participants had been cyberbullied and 20 per cent had cyberbullied others at some point in their life. Young people who behave aggressively online are more likely to think of violence against their peers as normative behaviour (Hinduja and Patchin, 2013), and there is abundant evidence that frequent exposure to online aggression has negative psychosocial effects on children and young people. Therefore, effective prevention and intervention strategies require a comprehensive understanding of the types of aggression online, and their implications and associated risk and protective factors.

Having examined several forms of online risks and behaviours (for example, sexting, cyberbullying, sexual abuse, etc) and their impact, and having considered cybercrime in general, in the remainder of this chapter we explore three of the more common examples of cyber-harm and online offending as reported by research and empirical evidence, namely:

1. cyber-harm: online communities that promote negative behaviours;
2. aggression in online romantic relationships and cyber-stalking; and
3. gang aggression and violence.

Cyber-harm, anti-social and pro-harm online communities

Online communities of young people can form around a common interest and offer opportunities for engaging with like-minded people. Such communities can be a rich source of support, identity development and learning. However, there are also communities that promote anti-social and pro-harm behaviour, fraud, violence or other forms of cyber-harm, cyber-abuse and offences, or motivate their members to engage in criminal activity. Studies have revealed that some young people engage in risky behaviours online, and this can be in relation to one or more of the online risks discussed in previous chapters. For example, young girls who have internalised norms that place a high value on female sexuality may reflect this in their online profile or behaviour (Baumeister and Vohs, 2004). Given the magnifying effect of online posts combined with lack of social cues and the brevity of most online profiles, emphasis on one's sexuality can be misconstrued and may attract unwanted attention from cyberbullies or sex offenders, leading to virtual, physical or sexual abuse (Mitchell et al, 2007) or dating violence.

Pro-ana and pro-mia sites/communities promote eating disorders, provide tips on how to become 'better' anorexics and challenge and 'trigger' their readers and members to become 'better anorexics'. These sites/communities usually state that they are for people who have an eating disorder and include a disclaimer along the lines of, 'If you do not have an eating disorder then it is better for you if you do not develop one'. These sites/communities are the antithesis of recovery. They encourage pride and a sense of belonging to a community, and offer tips to amplify the eating disorder, celebrating it as a form of perfection, superiority, empowerment and liberation achieved through self-control and the 'power of will over body'. Many use provocative language to challenge their reader, 'if you can't handle it, leave'. These sites/communities and their followers present themselves as the 'elite' that have adopted a 'superior lifestyle' rejecting 'weakness' and the conventional 'weak' values. They claim that they promote self-control and not self-harm, and that they make most people's desire/dream to be thin a reality. Regardless of their claims, however, eating disorders are a mental health challenge and are self-destructive, and extreme eating disorders cause serious self-harm and are life-threatening.

The framing of people with eating disorders as liberated rebels or activists leads to complex problems that usually exacerbate the person's difficulties. Through a combination of encouragement, challenges, tips, support and community cohesion, these sites/communities lead their followers/members to ever more extreme forms of eating disorders and make recovery much more difficult and complex. It is essential that young people understand that eating disorders are a serious mental health challenge and can be life-threatening.

Pro-ana and pro-mia sites/communities represent an extreme and distorted version of societal values and as such, challenge us to reflect and re-examine our own dichotomous thinking and values about nutrition, diet, health and beauty. They are the reveal and the extreme version of some of society's delusions, attitudes, preconceptions and discriminations about nutrition, weight and beauty and their association with the 'good' and the 'superior'.

Another example are self-harm and cyber-suicide sites/communities that promote self-directed forms of violence. Although the definitions of cyber-suicide may vary, they all include use of the internet and social media to communicate suicide or suicidal ideations. Cash et al (2013) examined 1,038 publicly available postings on MySpace, and found that young people communicated suicidal thoughts including various forms of suicide as a response to negative experiences with personal relationships, substance misuse or mental health difficulties. They concluded that such online postings could be an expression of pain and help-seeking behaviour, and to cope with difficult experiences in their lives. Cyber-suicide websites teach young people about different ways of ending their life and connect them with others who have already tried doing so, encouraging them to emulate the experience. People susceptible to suicide often suffer deep emotional loneliness and are challenged by difficult thoughts and emotions. Social media and cyber-suicide offer such young people a sense of visibility in their invisibility.

Conversely, research (Ruder et al, 2011) has shown that as individuals communicate their intention and suicidal ideations in various ways before actually doing so, an empathic ear and positive and empathic interventions and support from online communities or others can serve as a protective factor, and may help deter them from ending their lives. In this sense, social media offer an important opportunity for intervention and support for young people.

There are many other harmful sites/communities such as those that encourage the making or consumption of harmful substances, including medication (for example, homemade Valium, etc).

Aggression in online romantic relationships and cyber-stalking

Aggression in online romantic relationships such as dating violence is a significant public health concern among young people and is associated with emotional and mental health difficulties and future involvement in intimate partner violence (Gomez, 2011). Research shows increasing use of technology (for example, text messages, emails and social media) for sending aggressive messages among young people aimed at controlling one's partner (Draucker and Martsolf, 2010). Although aggression in online romantic relationships and dating violence are relatively widespread and can lead to serious negative long-term effects, many young people do not report it due to fear or stigma. 'The 2013 national youth risk behaviour survey' (Vagi et al, 2015) by the Centers for Disease Control and Prevention in the US found that 10 per cent of high school students reported physical victimisation and 10 per cent reported sexual victimisation from a dating partner during the 12 months prior to the survey. During adolescence, as young people become more aware of their sexuality, they explore and learn new skills that form the basis of their adult relationships. This is a crucial time for learning about healthy relationships and preventing couple aggression, dating violence and abusive partnerships. Awareness programmes and support to enhance young people's problem-solving and relationship skills can help mitigate risks of dating violence, abusive partnerships and other risky behaviour such as alcohol and substance misuse or sexual exploitation risks. Practitioners should also work with parents and carers to ensure they are able to support young people and to help them avoid dating violence and abusive partnerships.

Abusive relationships can lead to cyber-stalking and repeated abuse, threats and other malicious behaviour. Cyber-stalking can include threats of violence and may escalate into physical or sexual abuse/violence. It can feel like a perfect storm and may involve defamation and spreading lies about the person (for example, 'Steve has HIV'), sharing of personal or sensitive information (for example, posting or sharing a person's nude or sexually explicit images, home address, birthday, national insurance or social security number), or hacking and technological attacks (for example, unauthorised access or shutting down a person's social media account). Although anyone may become a victim or perpetrator of cyber-stalking, research suggests that girls comprise the majority of victims, and domestic violence survivors face a higher risk of experiencing cyber-stalking. Cyber-stalking has a profound psycho-socio-ecological effect and can lead to strong feelings of self-blame. Therefore, like other forms of partner violence, it is important to ensure that young people understand that cyber-stalking can happen to anyone and that it is not their fault, that cyber-stalking is about power in a relationship, intimidation and establishing control.

Safeguarding young people experiencing cyber-stalking can be complex, and practitioners can use the 10 C's psycho-socio-ecological model for a systematic assessment of relevant risks and protective factors. Additionally, if the young person is experiencing cyber-stalking and receiving unwanted contact or solicitations, below are some mindlines and initial points to consider.

- Evaluate the situation and, if appropriate, make it clear to the cyber-stalker that the person does not wish to be contacted and that future contacts will be reported to the police. It is important to document this communication (for example, take screenshots and save them).
- Remove the young person from the risky, conflictual or threatening situation or if necessary, from a given online space. This means that at times it may be necessary to close and remove the young person's social media account and online profile. However, online digital presence, posts and activities are an integral part of young people's identity, and the loss of such an identity may aggravate the situation and contribute to tragic outcomes, as described in the case of Tallulah (see Chapter 1). Therefore, it is essential that any such actions are decided and carried out with the agreement and in consultation with the young person.

- Save evidence of all communication with the cyber-stalker including any messages, online postings or other asynchronous or interactive communication. Make sure not to edit any of the messages and instead take screenshots and print screens and save them.
- Unpublish abusive posts on your blog or website rather than deleting them.
- Document and keep a record of all communication with all stakeholders regarding the situation; make sure to back up all the evidence and information on a separate device (for example, memory stick or similar device). Both from a legal and personal safety perspective, it is crucial to be able to evidence the cyber-aggression, abuse, stalking or bullying.
- Block the aggressor/cyber-stalker/cyberbully and filter their messages (block their mobile phone numbers, email addresses, social media accounts and other forms of communication).
- If the cyber-stalker is publishing inappropriate or harmful information about the young person on other websites, make a complaint and report them to the moderator or the person who can take action on the specific website; explain that this is part of ongoing online harassment, and ask that they remove the offensive post and block the harasser.
- In agreement with the young person, discuss the situation with their family, and if appropriate, with their friends, and seek their support and coordinated action – their collaboration can be critical and invaluable in supporting the victim. Also ensure they understand and use appropriate privacy settings on their own social media account and do not share any personal information about the victim.
- Engage all professionals, institutions and stakeholders who can help safeguard and support the young person (for example, teachers and the school).

Gang aggression and violence in the digital age

At their most basic level and from a social network perspective, gangs can be thought of as social networks of individuals who come together in a time and place/space enacting a collective identity narrative. Therefore, gang activity can be seen as a collective activity aimed at reasserting and promoting (that is, producing and preforming) a collective culture and identity (that is, the gang's culture and identity). Traditionally street gangs had clear geographic territories and closely identified with and were defined by their neighbourhood (or 'turf'), and communities and neighbourhoods were formed and maintained on the basis of physical proximity or cultural values. Indeed, as suggested by Papachristos and colleagues (2013, p 419), 'urban ethnographies highlight the significance of the "neighbourhood" for group formation, meaning-making, and patterns of behaviour in communities'. Gangs are important occupiers of such spaces and are woven into the 'fabric of many communities in multiple, complex, and, at times, conflicting ways' and play a dual role as protectors and perpetrators within neighbourhoods; this can sustain or undermine the social organisations within the neighbourhood. However, SNSs offer new opportunities and have added a new dimension to gang identity, culture and activities, and although there is no agreement about the terminology, gang activities on social media have been referred to in different ways including 'gang banging' or 'cyber banging'; as noted by Patton and colleagues (2013, p 54), 'Gang members carry guns and twitter accounts.'

Gangs and gang members occupy both online and offline spaces and use social media to project and promote their culture and identity, conduct business, communicate and coordinate their activities, and recruit new gang members (National Gang Intelligence Center, 2009). However, whereas offline the gang's influence (that is, turf) is closely tied to neighbourhood and delimited by geography, the fluidity of cyberspace doesn't pose such geographic boundaries or physical demarcations online. The absence of such territorial boundaries extends the reach and influence of gangs beyond their geographic territories, and increases the risk of conflict and exacerbation of violence between gangs. Hence, in vying for dominance and promoting their identity, gang members use social media such as Twitter, Facebook, YouTube and others to exchange dares and insults or to make threats of violence; these practices are ways of asserting the gang's online 'turf' and identity. Gangs' online identities and activities add a new layer of complexity and present significant risks and new challenges for young people and safeguarding practitioners.

Notwithstanding its importance, the study of gang-related activities on social media is a relatively new area of research, and until recently gang aggression and presence on social media was conceived as a form of cyberbullying. But offline violence that follows gang threats online (for example, at times gang activities online lead to victimisation, crime and even loss of life or homicide offline) suggests that this may be a distinct phenomenon (Patton et al, 2013). Indeed, addressing the challenges of gang violence and protecting children from gangs is a complex multiagency issue, and partnership working and information sharing are essential in dealing with young people's involvement in gang-related activities and harm.

Gangs assert and promote their culture and identity through various means, ranging from social media postings and dares to physical violence, rape and sexual abuse, which can involve people outside and inside the gang. Problems involving gangs or relating to gang involvement are often complex and can entrap individuals, families and communities in a vicious cycle of negative consequences. We will apply the 10 C's psycho-socio-ecological model to Rea's story below, in order to explain some of these complexities.

Rea's story

Rea is a 14-year-old black British female who lives with her mother and two younger siblings (a four-year-old sister and eight-year-old brother) in a council flat in London. Last month Rea posted a few pictures of herself in her bra on Facebook, and this attracted a lot of attention, including from one of the boys (Marco) who is known to be in a gang and who lives on the same estate as Rea. Since she posted the pictures she has been receiving 'likes' from boys who are known to be part of a gang. She initially enjoyed the new-found attention and posted more pictures of her daily activities and 'hanging out' with friends, including pictures of herself with her cousin. But some of the gang members have started posting 'dick pictures' and sexual comments that have unnerved Rea. Her friends tell Rea to relax and enjoy the added 'street cred'. But Rea doesn't know what to do and who to talk to, and doesn't want to speak with her mother about the situation. Two weeks later, Rea is making her way back home from school when Marco makes a sexually explicit comment about her Facebook page. A couple of days later, Rea is walking back from the local shop when Marco stops her in the alleyway behind the store and tries to force himself on her. Rea shouts for help and a woman from a window looking on to the alley shouts, "I am calling the police if you don't let her go." Marco pushes Rea to the ground and runs out of the alley. Two days later Rea is raped by four gang members on her way back from a party. She suffers multiple bruises on her face and body and a cut on her right hand. The day after the incident, Alex visits Rea at her home. Alex is a tall, white, 14-year-old slim Polish male with an athletic built and is one of the younger gang members. He used to go to primary school with Rea and lives a block away from her. He has always liked Rea but was too shy to approach her. Rea's mother opens the door and asks what he wants and why he is there. Alex apologises to Rea's mother for what had happened and says that he was not there and asks if he could see Rea. Alex gives Rea a flower he picked up from a neighbour's pot, and speaks with Rea.

The following day, due to continued bleeding from the cut on her hand, Rea goes to A&E (the Accident & Emergency department of a hospital) with her mother. She receives five stitches for her cut, but refuses to discuss the incident. She is referred to social services. The case is assigned to Isabel who visits Rea the following day. But Rea's mother insists that the cut was accidental and the incident was consensual, and asks Isabel not to visit them. Isabel refers the case to the police. She also refers Rea for a full medical check, but Rea and her mother refuse to engage. Isabel also refers Rea for counselling, but she refuses to go to any sessions. In the coming days Alex visits Rea every day and they become good friends. After a few days later Rea returns to school. Rea was performing well in school; however, since the incident, her school attendance and academic performance have suffered. About a week later Alex comes to visit Rea and tells Rea and her mother that Rea needs to leave immediately as Marco and his boys plan to target Rea again, to make sure she doesn't speak to the police about what happened. Rea and her mother are terrified. Rea packs her bag and Alex accompanies her to her cousin's. During the next few days Marco becomes increasingly upset and obsessed about finding Rea. Using Rea's and her cousin's Facebook postings and their geolocation, one of the gang members is able to locate Rea's cousin. Marco and three other gang members decide to follow Rea's cousin home from school with the hope of finding Rea.

Reflection and analysis

We'll apply the 10 C's psycho-socio-ecological model to briefly examine the different risks, protective factors and resiliencies in this case.

Confidentiality and personal disclosure risks

Rea's postings on her Facebook attracted the attention of local gang members, and the continued interaction between Rea and the gang members escalated the situation. One of the gang members used the geolocation information from Rea and her cousin's Facebook posting to find Rea. Both the privacy settings and the content of a posting can reveal information that may be compromising.

Context risk

After the rape, Rea stopped using Facebook and is not using any social media platform at the moment. However, should she start using social media in the future, appropriate context risk should then be considered in relation to that specific platform.

Consumption risk

Since the rape, Rea has stopped using Facebook. Therefore there is no immediate or specific consumption risk at present.

Consonance-dissonance and compatibility risk

Although Rea's Facebook page attracted the local gang members' attention and resulted in eventual significant harm, her online identity was compatible with her offline identity and development as a young person.

Connection and social capital risk

Rea is a 'friend' with gang members and other 'strangers' on Facebook, and this presented/presents connection risks that exacerbated/exacerbate the situation. Furthermore, the initial 'likes' and comments on her Facebook page were interpreted as increased social capital and encouraged Rea to post more pictures of herself. Indeed, even when she started to feel uncomfortable about the comments and pictures posted on her page by gang members, her friends were telling her to 'relax and enjoy the added "street cred"' (a colloquial term for social capital). This suggests that in spite of the inappropriate nature of the postings and the added risks, Rea's peers considered the interactions as added popularity and increased social capital. The interpretation of added attention as increased social capital and positive is reflective of the dynamics of value attribution in the attentional economy of cyberspace, and represents an important and frequent challenge in safeguarding children and young people online. Therefore, Rea needs support and guidance to reconfigure her identity and to develop her social capital in a more balanced manner.

Content risk

Rea is not currently using her Facebook account. Therefore there are no immediate content risks at this time. Nonetheless, after securing Rea's safety it is important that she is supported to enhance her understanding of content risks and their associated negative effects.

Contact risk

Virtual: Rea has had virtual contact with local gang members, leading to physical contact. Rea needs support to reconfigure her online relationships and identity, avoiding further virtual and physical contact with the gang members.

Physical: Rea has had physical contact with local gang members. She was raped by four gang members and is at high risk of re-victimisation by Marco and other gang members who are actively searching for her. She needs urgent protection and support by the police and social workers to ensure her safety and the safety of her family. Rea has a close friendship and relationship with Alex who is one of the gang members, and so far this relationship has served as a protective factor for Rea. However, the relationship between Alex and Rea can be a source of risk for one or both of them, and this can occur in a number of ways. For example, Alex could be at risk of significant harm from Marco and other gang members for his relationship with Rea and for protecting Rea as this may be seen as lacking loyalty and betraying other gang members' trust.

Conduct risks

There is a high risk that without effective support Rea may be drawn into gang activities. It is important to mention that Alex is a young and new gang member, and is at risk of further gang involvement and violence. He is also at risk of serious harm with possible threat to his life should Marco or other gang members discover his involvement with Rea or his protective actions and role in Rea's disappearance.

Furthermore, Alex's actions and behaviour demonstrate how gang members can toggle 'between social positions as regular citizens and gang bangers, neighbours and adversaries' (Papachristos et al, 2013, p. 419) This gives rise to a number of composite and complex risks, protective factors and resiliencies. Hence, in working with gang members and young people at risk of gang involvement, practitioners should consider the meaning or rewards derived from gang participation vis-à-vis other aspects of the young person's life; these may include a sense of belonging, social validation, social status or economic rewards. Understanding the meaning and significance of gang involvement from the young person's perspective will enable the practitioner to tailor interventions and ensure more effective and person-centred safeguarding provisions.

Commercial exploitation risk

Rea and Alex are both at risk of commercial exploitation by the gang; for example, they may be commercially and sexually exploited by the gang, or asked to do/carry out actions/tasks that would generate remuneration or financial benefit for the gang; they may also be remunerated for such actions.

Composite and complex risk

The use of geolocation information by gang members to locate Rea is an example of how gangs use and leverage online space and information to support their activities and to assert their territory and dominance. This adds a new layer of complexity and safeguarding challenges.

Alex's story demonstrates that children who harm others are both victims and perpetrators. Indeed, an important challenge for practitioners is to address both the needs and risks for children at risk of gang involvement or violence. Such young people usually have significant needs themselves, and although they are held responsible for their actions and harmful consequences, they themselves are vulnerable. Therefore, practitioners have a responsibility to promote their wellbeing while safeguarding them from further harm to themselves and others. Thinking about these young people as only offenders or only victims fails to recognise the complex and cyclical nature of the victim–offender dynamic, and how that influences the lives of young people (Victim Support, 2007).

For a comprehensive view of the situation, these risks should be transposed and considered within the context of the psycho-socio-ecological model (Figure 9.1 offers an overview of some of the relevant risks). Practitioners can use this information as a point of departure and modify/add the relevant risks (of negative and positive outcomes), needs, rights, protective factors, resiliencies and other relevant considerations to complement the assessment triangle and ensure an accurate, holistic and person-centred picture, analysis and assessment of the situation. Considering the close relationship between street gangs and their neighbourhood/community and the impact of social media on sense of proximity and the definition, formation and operation of communities, we include a brief reflection about the impact of the convergence between digital and urban spaces.

Mapping onto the 10 C's psycho-socio-ecological model

Having examined the 10 C's risk typologies, these should be juxtaposed and mapped onto the 10 C's psycho-socio-ecological model, and below are two brief mindlines in relation to mapping of risk typologies at community and social network levels.

Community level

Many street gangs strongly identify with their neighbourhood or ethnicity, and are often named after them, and often gang dynamics and conflicts reflect/amplify larger community dynamics and conflicts. Hence, awareness of such dynamics and conflicts is important in the effective safeguarding of children and young people. However, the changing meaning of proximity, neighbourhood and community present new challenges for both gangs and their neighbourhoods and communities.

Social network level

At their most basic level, gangs are social networks of individuals who come together in a time and space to engage in collective activities and produce a collective identity. However, digital and social media extend the reach and amplify the influence of gangs while offering a myriad of new and vast opportunities

Figure 9.1: Cybercrime, online offending and youth justice: mapping risks, protective factors and resilience using the 10 C's psycho-socio-ecological model

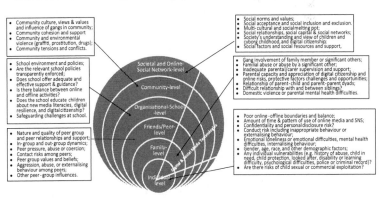

For larger version please see p 260

for communication, coordination, identity expressions, cultural symbolisms, gang business and activities, power and aggression. Hence, digital and social media add a new dimension and a further layer of complexity and sophistication to gangs and gang-related activity and on multiple levels.

Furthermore, gangs' zone of influence, or turf, can be thought of as the space defined by geographies of neighbourhood, symbolisms and memories that shape and reflect the gang's identity, culture and activities. The gang's turf serves a dual role – on the one hand, it dominates the neighbourhood and entraps young people, while on the other, it 'protects' the neighbourhood and provides a transitional space for young people's journey into adulthood. Although the gang's turf is usually well defined by the boundaries of the gang's neighbourhood or other geographic boundaries, given its fundamental value and importance for the gang, turf is often a source of gang violence. This problem is intensified online – whereas offline/in the physical world, strict territorial boundaries between gangs limit encounters between their members, in the online environment gang members may encounter each other all the time. Indeed, the fluidity of online boundaries leads to increasing conflict, aggression and violence within and between gangs. Such online conflicts are reflected in dares, insults and threats of violence by and between gangs as ways of asserting the gang's online 'turf' and identity that can lead to offline violence.

This analysis has been focused on Rea; however, the same should be carried out for Alex.

A reflection on the role of youth justice

Youth crime and violence have captured the attention of a fearful public, creating a moral panic with the tendency to believe that today's youth are more dangerous and prone to violence than any previous generation. Our reference to moral panic is not meant to say that the young people who engage in serious crimes do not represent a danger to themselves and society; on the contrary, it is meant to emphasise the urgent need to avoid moral panic and to engage with the challenge of young people's involvement in violence and criminal activities in an effective and restorative manner. Moral panic promotes labelling and dichotomies that further alienate young people rather than engaging them.

Bandura (1979) and Akers (1990) argue that through socialisation and direct or indirect exposure young people learn to use violence as a method for resolving interpersonal conflicts, managing frustration or obtaining rewards that are perceived as deserved but not otherwise obtainable. Further research suggests that media contribute to normalising and desensitising young people to violence and promoting its congruence with everyday goals.

Structural functionalist theories think of youth culture in terms of intergenerational conflict and as a reaction and opposition to intergenerational values. However, theories built on the concept of 'subcultures' highlight the class differences in shaping youth culture and its relationship to criminal behaviour. In other words, young people from a lower socioeconomic background face reduced opportunities for success due to social class. As they become aware of this divide, they experience increasing frustration that leads to a rejection of dominant societal goals and ideology (Cohen, 1955). In this sense the creation of a subculture represents the struggle against what is perceived as unattainable societal ideals.

Functional theories argue that the separation and categorisation of young people into different subcultures is a reflection of intergenerational conflict between young people's desire for change and struggle against intergenerational values vis-à-vis society's attempt to protect and perpetuate the status quo (Cohen, 1955). Traditionally young people have held little economic or political power, and their voices and experiences have had limited influence in shaping policies affecting their lives and development. Instead, they have been thought about and categorised from an adult-centric perspective, with those who do not conform being labelled and excluded. However, social media offer important opportunities for engaging young people and capturing their views, imagination and experiences (for example, crowdsourcing, hacktivism, etc). Therefore, given young people's seamless engagement with digital and social media technologies, it is incumbent on practitioners to be able to intervene, engage and support young people online; research has shown that the positive engagement of young people is the most effective protective and preventive strategy in combating crime and violence.

Notwithstanding its potential for engaging young people, traditionally the law has tried to protect the general public by removing and isolating the perpetrators of crime and violence. However, new affordances of social media technologies offer new dimensions of criminal activity and add a new layer of sophistication and complexity to detection, monitoring and restorative intervention for cybercrime. In a networked society, it is increasingly difficult to separate individuals from their network of people and resources that support their activities. In this context, the Foucauldian (1979) analysis offers a critical perspective for understanding youth crime and young people's behaviour, and safeguarding young people from harm to themselves and society. Foucault (1980) argues that power operates to control the actions of both the individual and the collective, and that the control of 'deviance' and assertion of social norms are embodied in the very processes of identifying, observing, classifying and monitoring the 'deviant' (Sawicki, 1991, p 39), to create Foucault's (1979) 'docile' bodies.

However, the emergence of social technologies and new forms of institutions and activities in cyberspace has challenged the traditional conceptions of institutions and approaches to crime and offending behaviour, offering opportunities and challenges that can transform the content and context of offending as well as youth justice practice and policy.

For example, the traditional response to youth offending has been through institutional and social control with the intention to define, monitor and manage behaviours. Having created dichotomies of behaviour into normal and abnormal and acceptable and unacceptable, the social institutions of education and the law were charged with defining and repressing and managing those behaviours. This approach was founded on a panoptic notion of authority (Foucault, 1979). However, new technologies have significantly transformed the notion of authority online, and its implications in relation to crime and cybercrime. Indeed, the absence of an observable authority figure combined with anonymity and disinhibition effect of cyberspace in a seemingly hierarchy-free context can lower the normative and psychological barriers for engaging in 'undesirable', anti-social or criminal activity. Indeed, with the increasing dilution of hierarchy and authority, perhaps one of the greatest challenges for society in general and for social work and safeguarding practice in particular may be their ability to resist the culture of hierarchy, social surveillance, punishment and control and instead to promote and emphasise a culture of heterarchy, values, rewards and collective growth.

10

Online radicalisation

Defining radicalisation

Governments often use the word 'radicalisation' in consonance
with violent extremism. However, looking at the historical context,
radicalism has often led to progress and has usually been distinct
from extremism. Whereas both radicalism and extremism are distant
form mainstream politics, radicalism is usually open-minded, while
extremism is usually closed-minded, and justifies the use of violence
for achieving its objectives. Notwithstanding this historical context,
today 'radicalisation refers to an increase in and/or reinforcing
of extremism in the thinking, sentiments, and/or behaviour of
individuals and/or groups of individuals' (Mandel, 2008, p 19).

The UK government defines extremism as:

> vocal or active opposition to fundamental British values,
> including democracy, the rule of law, individual liberty
> and mutual respect and tolerance of different faiths and
> beliefs. We also include in our definition of extremism
> calls for the death of members of our armed forces,
> whether in this country or overseas. (HM Government,
> 2016, p 2)

The process of radicalisation is complex and there are a number
of models for describing the stages of radicalisation. For example,
Mandel suggests a four-step process: pre-radicalisation, self-
identification, indoctrination and 'jihadisation'. However, as
suggested by Mandel, this model fails to consider 'the psychological,
organisational and social processes and drivers that lead people into
radicalisation process' (2008, p 19).

Government strategies for addressing radicalisation

Different countries have adopted different approaches to addressing radicalisation. For example, the Aarhus model in Denmark offers specific counselling and mentoring services for those who have been radicalised. This model also includes an exit programme designed as micro-level interventions for those who support extremism and are prepared to carry out violent acts (instead of imprisonment, for example, the programme offers opportunities for employment to those who wish to leave extremist organisations). The Aarhus model has an important focus on the rehabilitation of fighters returning from Syria. This model involves all the relevant stakeholders, that is, parents, family network, social workers, teachers and all others who can provide support and safeguard the young people at risk of radicalisation. The effectiveness of this model has been due to its co-productive approach and recognition that the process of radicalisation is different for each individual. Most importantly, this model focuses on creating trust between authorities and the social environment in which the extremists operate.

'Prevent' is part of the UK government's overall strategy for counter-extremism and terrorism ('CONTEST'). The Prevent strategy, published in 2011, aims to reduce the threat of radicalisation and terrorism in the UK through early intervention, to prevent 'people from becoming terrorists or supporting terrorism'. The Prevent strategy has three main objectives:

- respond to the ideological challenge of terrorism and the threat we face from those who promote it;
- prevent people from being drawn into terrorism and ensure that they are given appropriate advice and support; and
- work with sectors and institutions where there are risks of radicalisation that we need to address. (Prevent, 2015, p 5)

The Channel process operationalises the Prevent strategy, and is an early intervention and multi-agency process that is part of the UK government's strategy to address the risk of radicalisation. Channel works in a similar way to existing safeguarding partnerships, and is designed to safeguard vulnerable people from being drawn into violent extremist and terrorist activities.

Factors influencing radicalisation

The Youth Justice Board (YJB, 2012, pp 21-3) offers a systematic review of literature to identify the processes of radicalisation among young people and 'the availability and effectiveness of interventions to prevent Islamic radicalisation and violent extremism'. The YJB (2012) proceeds to list seven attitudinal and four behavioural indications as 'signs that indicate the crossing, or imminent crossing, of the threshold of radicalisation', namely, emotional vulnerability and state of distress including a sense of cultural displacement or alienation; political and social dissatisfaction and disillusionment; experience of personal victimisation and identification with the suffering of Muslims globally (the Ummah or 'community', referring to the community of Muslims bound together by religion); acceptability of violence against the state and its symbols; gaining reward from membership of the group; perception of personal marginalisation; and other 'non-religious' behaviours and attitudes. The YJB (2012) also lists four behavioural characteristics indicative of radicalisation: having contact with people with similar challenges and experiences; or being involved with terrorism; having contact or travelling to extremist networks overseas; or having a serious criminal record, etc.

The European Commission's Radicalisation Awareness Network (RAN) offers a list of push-and-pull factors that influence the process of radicalisation, and states:

> The radicalisation mechanisms are a product of interplay between push- and pull-factors within individuals. It is important to recognise that there are different degrees and speeds of radicalisation.
>
> The push-factors involve: social, political and economic grievances; a sense of injustice and discrimination; personal crisis and tragedies; frustration; alienation; a fascination with violence; searching for answers to the meaning of life; an identity crisis; social exclusion;

alienation; marginalisation; disappointment with democratic processes; polarisation, etc.

The pull-factors are a personal quest, a sense of belonging to a cause, ideology or social network; power and control; a sense of loyalty and commitment; a sense of excitement and adventure; a romanticised view of ideology and cause; the possibility of heroism, personal redemption, etc. (RAN, 2016)

Bhui et al (2014) examined a cross-sectional survey of a representative population sample of men and women aged 18–45, of Muslim heritage and recruited by quota sampling by age, gender, working status, in two English cities, and found that only 2.4 per cent of participants showed some sympathy for violent protest and terrorist acts. They found no association between anxiety and depressive symptoms, adverse life events and socio-political attitudes. Sympathy for violent protest and terrorism was more likely among younger people (under 20) and those born in the UK, participants who spoke English at home, and those in full-time education rather than employment. Interestingly, Bhui and colleagues did not find a correlation with poverty; instead, higher earners (£75,000) were more likely to express sympathy for violent protest and terrorism.

Taarnby (2003) argues that five motivational parameters drive radicalisation, namely, religious, social, cultural, political and psychological factors. The combination of one or more of these parameters contributes toward radicalisation. The UK government guidance for the assessment of vulnerability offers a list of engagement factors or psychological vulnerabilities ('psychological hooks') that may attract an individual toward radicalisation (for an explanation of the concept of 'psychological hook', see Megele, 2015). 'They include needs, susceptibilities, motivations and contextual influences and together map the individual pathway into terrorism' (HM Government, 2012, p 2).

Therefore, in the remainder of this chapter, we use the 10 C's psycho-socio-ecological model to examine an example of intervention in the case of radicalisation and its associated risks, protective factors, resilience and challenges.

Suraya's story

Suraya is a 14-year-old British girl with mixed heritage. Her father, Ahmed, is 40 years old and works in the local post office. Ahmed is Egyptian and has lived in the UK since he was 22. Suraya's mother, Sandra, is a 36-year-old housewife. Fatima, Suraya's only sibling, is nine years old.

Two months ago children's services received a referral from Fatima's school due to Fatima's poor attendance, and that when she attends school, she presents as dishevelled and seems unable to concentrate. The school's attempts to sit with the parents to discuss the issues had not resulted in any improvements. The case is assigned to Natasha, who visits Fatima in her school and is able to speak with both Fatima and her teacher separately. Later the same day, Natasha calls Fatima's mother, Sandra, and makes an appointment to visit Fatima at home the following day.

The following day, Natasha goes to Fatima's home. The home is chaotic and untidy and Sandra has a bruise beside her left eye. Natasha introduces herself and asks Sandra if she is okay. Sandra suffers from a depressive mood but says that she is fine and refers to her bruise, adding that she fell. Natasha suspects domestic violence and asks about the parents' relationship, explaining that there are various ways of supporting Sandra. But Sandra insists that there is no domestic violence involved. Natasha asks about Fatima and her routine. Sandra explains that she is unhappy with her situation and that she would leave Ahmed if he had no children. She acknowledged that recently she had not been able to attend to Fatima as she would have wanted. She adds that Suraya used to help her look after Fatima, but in the last few months she has been spending all her time in her room and on her computer. Natasha asks about the quality of the relationship between Fatima and Suraya, and about their friends at school, and Sandra explains that Suraya and Fatima are each other's best friends but are isolated and don't have any friends at school.

After speaking with Sandra, Natasha asks to speak with Fatima and Suraya separately. Natasha speaks with Fatima and then goes to Suraya's room to speak with her. Suraya invites her in. Suraya seems aloof and distant from the rest of family. In contrast to the rest of the house, Suraya's room is spotless and in perfect order. Natasha sits on the chair by the door while Suraya sits at the edge of her bed. Natasha asks Suraya about her school and her friends and Suraya says school is okay and happily speaks about her friends. Natasha asks Suraya if her friends are from her school and how often she sees them. Suraya explains that her friends are online and not from her school. Natasha is concerned about the idealised nature of Suraya's stories and asks if Suraya knows where her friends live. She adds that she has been thinking about leaving the UK, and wondered what Suraya thought of it. Natasha is shocked by Suraya's animated response explaining how the UK was a terrible place to live and delivering a speech about equality, justice and Islam, and encouraging Natasha to leave the UK. Suraya's speech sounds scripted and is concerning. Therefore, Natasha says that she has not had much time to think about a suitable place, when she is interrupted by Suraya, saying, "You should go to Syria. Let me show you" and she opens up her laptop to show Natasha the images of life in Syria with people living in palaces with beautiful gardens and leading wonderful lives. She adds that Natasha should go there, and says that soon she will go there too. Natasha asks Suraya to explain, and Suraya says that she has been saving money for her flight, and that Massoud, one of her online friends, told her that he might be able to help her with some of the cost. So one day she will leave school and not come back. She adds that she would send for Fatima once she is settled in Syria, and asks Natasha not to tell her parents about her intentions. Noting the urgency and seriousness of the situation, Natasha tells Suraya that she will come back to talk to her again, and leaves Suraya's room.

Natasha immediately contacts her manager and informs her about the situation. Her manager raises Natasha's concerns to the head of safeguarding who is also the chair of the Channel Panel within the local authority. That afternoon there is an emergency strategy meeting to discuss Suraya's case and the case is referred to the Channel Panel. It is also agreed that as a safeguarding measure the police should confiscate Suraya's passport. After the strategy meeting Natasha calls the parents and they agree to meet the following day. The following morning Natasha is with the parents when the police come over to collect Suraya's passport and computer for investigation. The parents are distraught but in full agreement for the police to confiscate Suraya's passport and her computer for investigation. Later the same day Natasha revisits the home together with a support worker, Ali, from a charity, to speak with Suraya. Suraya has just returned from school and is upset about the developments. Ali tells Suraya that he is from Syria and explains about his own ordeal of escape from Syria and the devastation and bloodshed caused by ISIS. He explains that once Suraya reaches Syria her passport will be taken from her and she will become a slave of ISIS. Ali then show Suraya pictures and videos of devastation in Syria including the videos of a young person retelling her own powerful and touching story of escaping ISIS, and how in the process her parents sacrificed their lives to enable him and his sister to continue on their journey, and how his sister died during the arduous journey. The conversation, pictures and videos influence Suraya and she is perplexed but feels despondent and upset. Natasha refers Suraya for individual counselling, and during the next few weeks Suraya feels increasingly deflated as she recognises the lies she has been told by her online 'friends' (that is, the radicalisers).

Subsequently, it becomes apparent that during the past few months Suraya has been introduced to various video speeches and other extremist content that has influenced her views. Furthermore, on a couple of occasions Suraya had left school early to meet Massoud, one of her online 'friends', who had then taken her to a meeting with two elders and an imam (religious leader). Suraya recalls that Massoud had come a long way with his car just to pick her up and take her to the meeting, and this had made her feel special. At these meetings they had all prayed together and had discussed the privilege and duties associated with being part of the global Muslim Ummah. They had also watched images of Muslim brothers and sisters being tortured. The elders and imam had described how the media was being manipulated by the government and suppressing the truth about the tortures and struggle of their brothers and sisters. Suraya was moved by the discussion and had passionately wanted to tell others about the 'truth' of what was happening to her Muslim brothers and sisters. However, the imam had told her that he could see the fire in her, but was afraid that others were too corrupted by the system and did not have the eyes of conscience to see the truth. But he was going to give Suraya a chance to discover the truth for herself. Therefore, Suraya was given a pack of leaflets and was told that she could distribute those to her classmates in order to raise their awareness. She was also told what to say to her classmates about the leaflet. At the end of that meeting the imam had warned her once again to prepare herself for her classmates' rejection and refusal to see the 'truth'.

The following day Suraya tried to distribute the leaflets and discuss the issues, raising her classmates' awareness. However, no one seemed to be interested and instead she was ridiculed. She feels rejected, hurt and angry. The following week, she met Massoud during school and he took her to the same meeting. Again, they prayed together, and then the imam asked Suraya about the leaflets and the reaction from her friends. She answered that the imam was right and no one was interested. The imam told her not to worry and explained that he was expecting this outcome. Then he went on to describe the difference between her and her peers, and that by recognising her obligation toward the Ummah she had found the light while others remained in darkness. They then watched further videos of their Muslim brothers and sisters' struggles. One video showed a man being burnt alive, and this made Suraya cry. The imam told Suraya that it was her guilt and shame that had made her cry, and that she was being given the chance to start again and become who she really was.

Reflection and analysis

We will again apply the 10 C's psycho-socio-ecological model to examine the relevant risks and protective factors in this case, and for brevity, we focus the discussion on safeguarding Suraya. However, there are a number of other related challenges and safeguarding issues (for example, domestic violence and the parents' relationship, the mother's emotional and mental health, and safeguarding Fatima's wellbeing) that need to be considered but are not included in the following analysis.

Context risk

Suraya uses Facebook and Twitter, and Natasha and Suraya need to consider Suraya's reason for choosing these platforms and what she likes or dislikes about them, how she is using them and what that signifies for her and the specific risks associated with each of them.

Confidentiality and personal disclosure risk

Suraya has shared personal information about herself including her address, school and other details with the group of radicalisers online. This is a source of concern. But more importantly she considers the radicalisers her friends, and this poses the risk of further personal disclosures. Therefore, it is essential to ensure that Suraya understands the risks with this group and with such personal disclosures.

Natasha and Suraya need to discuss the importance of privacy settings and effective management of personal information; Suraya may need training to develop a more balanced and critical approach to information sharing. Suraya's profile and privacy settings for Twitter and Facebook also need to be reviewed.

Consonance-dissonance and compatibility risk

Suraya's online identity is compatible with her offline identity and her stage of development as an adolescent. However, discussing her online identity and posts may reveal aspects of her desired or preferred self-narrative. An understanding of such self-narratives is essential for effective safeguarding.

Suraya is in the early stages of adolescence, and in her journey to self-discovery and identity development she is questioning and experimenting with her identity and values. This offers fertile ground for assimilation of new ideas and values. Indeed, young people's energy and capacity for adaptation and learning are strong positive factors that, with appropriate support and exposure to positive opportunities, can serve as protective factors and offer significant potential for their growth and development. However, when exposed to negative and violent ideologies, the same malleability and adaptive capacity can be a vulnerability that is often exploited by radicalisers to redirect their beliefs and energy toward violent and extremist ideologies. Therefore, Suraya needs targeted, consistent and continuous support and guidance to ensure that she is able and empowered to develop her capabilities, values and identity in a safe, positive and healthy manner.

Consumption risk

Suraya spends most of her time in her room and on social media. Therefore, she should be incentivised to balance her online and offline engagement; this is an important protective factor.

As Suraya comes to recognise the lies she has been told by the radicalisers and understands their motives and, with Natasha's help, unfriends and blocks them, she begins to feel isolated once again.

Therefore, it is important to ensure she has the opportunity to meet and socialise with like-minded young people, and to develop a healthy group of friends and peer relationships (online and offline). To this end, supported by Natasha, Suraya participates in a Twitter chat, and this allows her to meet and connect with a few positive Twitter users; she is looking forward to joining the next chat.

Connection and social capital risk

What is the spread, effect and urgency of the problem? Although at this time it is only Suraya who is affected by her online connection with the radicaliser group, this is a very serious and urgent situation. Suraya is facing significant risks that require immediate action and safeguarding intervention. Therefore, it is important to review Suraya's connections and online and offline relationships and social capital, and any risk associated with them.

Who are Suraya's face-to-face friends? What are the characteristics of her peer network? Suraya is isolated and marginalised offline. She has tried to fit in but has been rejected by her peers and has withdrawn, and instead has engaged with the online group of radicalisers. Therefore, Natasha refers Suraya to group counselling for children of families with domestic violence. This enables Suraya to meet other young people who share similar family experiences. This is helpful to make Suraya understand that she is not alone, and to enable her to discuss and find a way forward for herself.

What are Suraya's family relations and circumstances? Suraya has a poor family relationship and doesn't consider her family as a source of support. Furthermore, there seem to be indications of domestic violence in the family as well as other challenges including her mother's depressive mood and emotional and mental health.

What is Suraya's social capital and support network? What are the risks and proactive factors associated with this network? Suraya doesn't have a reliable support network and has very low social capital. Although initially she considered the radicalisers as her friends, this group poses a significant risk to Suraya's wellbeing.

What is Suraya's online network? Are there any specific risks or resiliencies associated with this network? Although Suraya is connected with some of her schoolmates, she is marginalised and not accepted by her peers. Therefore, Suraya primarily communicates with the small group of online connections who are trying to radicalise her, and this has exposed her to extremist material and radicalised her views.

Suraya needs a healthy and positive circle of friends and peers online and offline. She is passionate about women's issues and social justice and equality, and so, to improve Suraya's social connections and social capital, Natasha contacts the local office of a national charity that supports women experiencing domestic violence, for Suraya to volunteer with them. This enables Suraya to meet new people and to develop new friendships, enhancing her social network and social capital.

Content risk

Suraya was exposed to false information (for example, false depictions of life in Syria) and online content that has influenced her views and beliefs. Suraya has also been introduced to videos of torture including the video of a man being burnt alive. These are highly traumatic experiences and 'exposed to these images over and over again, the viewer may internalize the message, becoming frustrated and enraged over the enormous injustice he perceives to be occurring' (Cilluffo et al, 2007, p 7). This can result in young people self-identifying with such extremist views and their increasing indoctrination. Indeed, the emotional impact of these images and the vicarious trauma inflicted on the psyche of young people combined with the 'simple but seemingly compelling message: Islam is under attack and young Muslims have a personal duty to fight in the defence of the Ummah' (Cilluffo et al, 2007, p 7) are easy to internalise and indoctrinate the mind of young people, transforming the individual from sympathiser to supporter, and paving the way for radicalisers to further manipulate the young person's curiosity, malleability, frustration, anger and energy toward extremist violence. Hence, Suraya is referred for individual counselling. She is also supported by a mentor from a specialist organisation dedicated to supporting people at risk of radicalisation. Although initially Suraya considered the radicalisers as her friends, as a result of these interventions, she has now blocked them on her social media accounts, and has made her accounts private, reducing the content risk.

Contact risk

Suraya had had virtual and physical contact with the radicalisers; however, she has subsequently realised their intentions and strategy, and has 'unfriended' and blocked them. She has also made her social media accounts private.

Suraya had face-to-face meeting with the radicalisers, and these meetings deeply influenced her. Therefore, in the initial stages of supporting Suraya, Natasha worked collaboratively with the school to better support Suraya, and to monitor her attendance and ensure she does not leave school during school time. However, since then, Suraya has progressed well and has cut all contact with the radicalisers. Suraya's individual and group therapy sessions combined with her engagement with the local charity have created a positive circle of friends, resources and activities around her, and have enhanced her social capital and resilience, and therefore serve as important protective factors against the risk of future radicalisation.

Conduct risk

Natasha's timely discovery of Suraya's intention prevented her further radicalisation and mitigated any conduct risk. In the meantime, the police searched Suraya's computer for information and evidence of criminal activity/conduct and for tracing the radicalisers. Suraya's current activities and social engagements and social network are protective factors against future radicalisation and conduct risk.

Commercial exploitation risk

There has been no remuneration or commercial exploitation at this stage, although there were clear risks of possible future exploitation and extortion. Also, the police confiscated and searched Suraya's computer for possible evidence of commercial exploitation.

Composite and complex risks

There are a number of composite and complex risks in this case, and we present a few examples below.

Cultural factors play a critical role in radicalisation. Children from immigrant families often cannot identify or connect with their parents' beliefs or the local peer culture. This challenges young people's sense of purpose and personal significance, and creates an unstable sense of cultural identity. Radicalisers exploit this instability, aiming to lead targeted individuals into dissociative states coupled with the creation of a new identity and the transformation of individual beliefs and thought processes in line with radical ideologies and extremist violence (Daly and Gerwehr, 2006, p 86).

Radicalisers often amplify their victims' negative emotions and thoughts, and then use splitting to promote in-group similarities and cohesion and to emphasise out-group differences and conflict. For example, Suraya's meeting with the elders and the imam posed composite and complex risks. In that meeting, Suraya was not only introduced to new content risk and the traumatic experience of watching torture and the live burning of a man, the imam's interpretation was also aimed at amplifying Suraya's pain and distorting her crying and natural reaction to the traumatic experience of watching the video as her sense of guilt and shame for her inaction. This redirects Suraya's frustrations and anger toward herself as guilt and shame, which is then used to create a sense of mutual understanding and responsibility between 'us' (that is, in-group cohesion) against others/'them' who do not understand (out-group difference). This sense of frustration and anger is harnessed by radicalisers and eventually directed externally as displaced anger toward the presumed 'oppressors' in the form of extreme violence and terrorism. Another example of a similar dynamic is her distribution of leaflets at school. Through this activity, the radicalisers not only exploited Suraya to promote their message, knowing that most people would not be interested in their message, they also prepared Suraya by labelling her classmates as others who "did not have the eyes of conscience to see the truth". The denigration and disparagement of others as ignorant, incapable or unworthy serves a dual purpose: first, it shields Suraya from her peers by pre-emptively dismissing their views and reactions as ignorant, wrong and unworthy; and second, it reinforces the differences and divisions between 'us' who understand versus 'them' who do not.

Sageman's (2007, p 1) research about Islamist extremism shows that these individuals are 'idealistic young people, who seek glory and thrills by trying to build a Utopia', while Susan Neiman argues that jihadists are idealists 'rising above the extant mire of consumerism and Western Decadence'. Hence, 'if the yearning for idealism drives people to fundamentalism, they could be satisfied by other kinds of idealism as well' (Black, 2009).

This highlights the need for active listening and engaging victims of radicalisation and extremism in open and critical dialogue, ensuring that they are respected and feel enabled to express their ideas openly. It is through splitting, labelling, close and oppressive division and suppression of open dialogue and alternative views that radicalisers spread their destructive and extremist ideologies. Indeed, the most powerful antidote for radicalisation is to provide exactly the opposite environment by offering an inclusive, non-judgemental, open and empowering environment that celebrates diversity, promotes multiplicity of ideas and encourages free expression and mindful dialogue with respectful challenge.

Suraya's volunteering with the charity has given her a new insight into domestic violence, and this has enhanced her empathy and understanding for her mother, and has improved the relationship between them, having a positive impact.

The seriousness of Suraya's involvement with extremist groups was a wake-up call for her mother. Suraya's volunteering with the local charity and Natasha's effective intervention and support have encouraged Sandra to participate in the local charity's domestic violence peer support group, and to seek separation from Ahmed. This has improved Sandra's emotional health and low mood and her relationship with Suraya and Fatima. Also Suraya's performance at school has improved and, with her support, Fatima's school attendance and performance have recovered.

Personal significance is an important motivational force that is exploited by radicalisers. Sympathising with jihad and jihadist movements offers young people the opportunity to develop a religious and political subjectivity that offers a strong and higher purpose with a sense of validation and liberating agency. As suggested by Kruglanski et al (2014, p 80) 'The road to radicalisation beings with arousal of the quest for significance ...', and this was evident in Suraya's case. However, her involvement with the local charity has enabled her to redirect her energy and passion for social justice and making a difference in people's lives to helping women in her community. This has offered Suraya a sense of validation and personal significance, and has strengthened her resilience; these serve as important protective factors against the risk of recidivism and extremist violence.

Some considerations about mapping the 10 C's psycho-socio-ecological model

As stated in previous chapters, the above risk typologies should be considered in conjunction with the assessment triangle (see Figure 3.4) and transposed onto the 10 C's psycho-socio-ecological model. Below are a few considerations in relation to the factors that may lead to terrorism and extremist violence at different levels of the 10 C's psycho-socio-ecological model.

Individual level

This involves identity challenges, alienation and lack of integration, marginalisation, discrimination, oppression, relative deprivation, rejection and lack of validation, humiliation and stigmatisation, injustice and other similar factors, leading to moral outrage and feelings of anger and revenge.

Community level

This is comprised of a radical milieu that is supportive of, or even complicit in, the use of violence for the attainment of political power. Such milieu is often composed of individuals with shared experiences, challenges and vulnerabilities on an individual level, and serves as a rallying point for the formation and mobilisation of young people in line with extremist ideologies.

Societal and social network level

It is important to highlight the role of government, society, politics and policy including party politics in creating and perpetuating today's challenges. The increasing socioeconomic inequality and decreasing social mobility over the past four decades has been accompanied by increasing bifurcation and harsh political divisions and a culture of conflict and confrontations. This has culminated in the rise of populist and extremist politics that is eroding the fabric of society and the foundations of civil rights and democracy. Such an environment offers fertile ground for increasing conflict of cultures and mobilisation and the radicalisation of the disenfranchised and discontented, some of which might involve young people and extremist violence. These difficulties offer cause for pause and reflection, and highlight the need for a critical dialogue and a more inclusive politics dedicated to greater equality and social justice (Figure 10.1 offers an overview of some of the relevant risks).

Figure 10.1: Radicalisation: mapping risks, protective factors and resilience using the 10 C's psycho-socio-ecological model

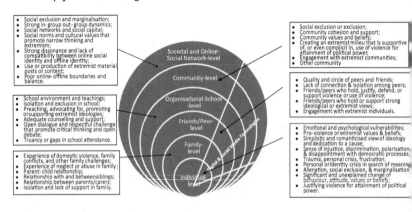

For larger version please see p 261

Some mindlines and practice reflections for preventing radicalisation

Recognising and working with uncertainty and complexity

Radicalisation is a complex process, and profiling individuals based on their characteristics has proved to result in too many false positives and false negatives. Instead, profiling of dimensions, processes and pathways to radicalisation seems to offer a more effective approach to identifying people vulnerable to risk of radicalisation. This approach also offers alternatives for de-radicalisation. The Prevent and CONTEST strategies are accompanied by various guidance drawing on psychological and behavioural studies to offer a range of behavioural indicators to guide practice. However, notwithstanding the proactive value of such guidance, it is important to avoid implicit notions of 'radicalisation' or 'terrorism' as knowable and governable through reductionist and simplistic conceptions of risk and human behaviour. Radicalisation knowledge provides a counterfactual to radicalisation and extremist violence as it makes the future actionable in the present (Heath-Kelly, 2012). However, risk assessment is a reflective exercise in pondered probabilities, and a probabilistic assumption about future outcomes is always indicative rather than deterministic. Therefore, the conscious awareness of the indicative nature of such information and its contextual application in ways that are mindful of complexity and respectful of the uniqueness of human experience spells the difference between effective evidence-informed relationship-based practice driven by professional knowledge and curiosity vis-à-vis labelling and discrimination. However, social workers and safeguarding practitioners are acutely aware of the unknowability of risk and uncertainty in practice, and their approach to the risk of radicalisation and extremist violence should be no different than any other serious risk in practice.

Stanley and Guru (2015) suggest that practitioners should avoid simplistic notions of risk based on behaviourist approaches. Indeed, the 10 C's psycho-socio-ecological model offers a systematic approach to deconstructing risk (of positive and negative outcomes), needs, rights, protective factors and resiliencies for holistic, humanistic and empowering approaches to risk assessments and positive risk taking.

While psychological, behavioural and attitudinal factors provide a useful list of indicators, it is important to note that risks are relative and dynamic, and vulnerabilities and protective factors do not operate in isolation. Indeed, often a single factor cannot adequately explain a given positive or negative outcome. It is rather the balance of vulnerabilities, strengths, resiliencies and their interplay with a host of contextual factors that determine the outcome of a given situation. Furthermore, the dynamic and relative nature of these factors implies that often the balance between them and the significance of each factor may vary over time, depending on the stage of radicalisation. For example, research suggests that although individual vulnerabilities may play an important role in the initial stages of radicalisation, group dynamics and group influence become increasingly more significant over time; once a person moves from intention to action and toward belonging to a terrorist group, group dynamics (or a sense of belonging and group influence, in the case of individuals who self-radicalise and act alone) and ideological control become the dominant drivers for their radicalisation and extremism; indeed, each individual's path to radicalisation and extremism 'will reflect a dynamic, though highly personalised, process of incremental assimilation and accommodation' (Horgan, 2008, p 85). The 10 C's psycho-socio-ecological model enables practitioners to develop a situated and person-centred understanding of the individual and the psychological, social, and ecological factors influencing the individual's experience, actions, and decisions. This allows practitioners to plan for and ensure the effective and holistic safeguarding of children and young people.

Healthy childhood and relationship

A healthy childhood and strengthening children's social networks and surrounding them with a circle of healthy relationships can offer significant protection against radicalisation and extremism. Strengthening family bonds and tapping into extended family for support can also enhance children's sense of belonging and resilience. Children may feel decisions are being imposed on them and may feel under pressure from all sides (family, friends and peers, teachers, society, etc). Radicalisers accentuate these feelings and emotions, and tap into young people's needs and vulnerabilities to achieve their own destructive and violent objectives. Therefore, it is crucially important to engage young people in a developmentally appropriate dialogue and acknowledge their voice and desires. Indeed, often the most effective interventions involve adequate recognition of children's voices combined with the opportunity for their active engagement and self-realisation that rechannel young people's passion and energy toward positive and constructive networks and activities that empower and enable them to develop a strong, healthy and positive sense of self.

Offering dialogue and challenging extremist ideas

Radicalisers use labelling and promote division and a 'clash of cultures' rather than inclusive and open discussion. Therefore, it is important that practitioners do not mirror the divisive approaches of radicalisers, avoid labelling and ensure an inclusive engagement and dialogue. Indeed, when a person is radicalised, one of the most important factors that can help take the person away from the path of radicalisation is establishing an effective dialogue that engages the young person and then challenges their views in a mindful and developmentally appropriate manner. It is important to note that it is not necessary to agree with the young person in order to maintain the dialogue; instead, it may be more appropriate to maintain an open and mindful curiosity without reaffirming/validating extremist ideas. For example, one could say 'that is interesting', but then challenge the young person by asking them to elaborate their idea, or by questioning and offering an alternative (for example, '… but have you considered …').

Maintaining dialogue and expanding young people's minds

In conversation with young people on the path to radicalisation, practitioners should not reaffirm the negative or extremist views that they may express; instead, it is important to affirm their self-worth and individual qualities. This allows for keeping them connected and in dialogue while slowly and progressively working with them to critically unpack their views and their ramifications. Indeed, often all that is needed is to open up young people's minds and to offer a wider perspective that expands their horizon of possibilities and that enables them to see and consider different options and alternative pathways for self-realisation. Equipped with a more critical perspective and horizon of possibilities, young people usually choose more positive alternatives when they come to realise that many of their desires and the opportunities they seek can be achieved in positive ways and without putting themselves at risk and in harm's way.

Apply observational skills and the principles and values of social work

It is important that safeguarding interventions are targeted, timely and proportionate. Although this may seem particularly complex in cases of radicalisation, evidence suggests that signs of radicalisation often stand out, and what is needed is good observational skill to identify the change in young people. Indeed, although practitioners may not be fully familiar with the dynamics and complexities of radicalisation, to intervene effectively, they are not being asked to draw on expertise and resources that they don't have or experiences they don't possess. Instead they need the sensitivity and observational skills 'to observe and see the other and their needs and vulnerabilities and to notice when they need help or are changing in ways that may be concerning' (Megele and Buzzi, 2018c), and to act in empowering ways and apply the fundamental values and principles of the profession to safeguard the person's wellbeing and support their growth and development.

Concerted approach

In the online realm, there are many overt and covert modalities and triggers that can lead an individual's journey toward extremism and possible violent atrocities. For example, the online anonymity and disinhibition effect mean that online, the individual may not feel the social, ethical, moral and cultural obligations that guide their thoughts and behaviours offline. This can lead to dissociative states and experiences that make the individual vulnerable to exploitation by extremist radicalisers, leading young people's natural curiosity into the dark path of violence and terrorism. Therefore, traditional enforcement strategies of targeting specific groups or individuals are not adequate for addressing this challenge. Last year, Google revealed plans to redirect extremist-related searches to anti-radicalisation links. Although such initiatives represent an important step in the right direction, there is an urgent need for a strong and effective counter-narrative and comprehensive and coordinated action that encompasses all the five motivational drivers of radicalisation and terrorism (Taarnby, 2003), and that involves individuals and stakeholders on all levels. Such actions and counter-narrative should be co-produced and should proactively involve the influential and charismatic leaders from communities to open up a credible dialogue and to meaningfully engage and interact with young people at risk of radicalisation. This should be combined with urgent government and policy action to address the profound and increasing social injustice and socioeconomic and cultural inequalities in society.

11

The future of technology and its safeguarding implications

Social media and the societal landscape are in rapid evolution, and there is much confusion ranging from uncritical advocacy and promotion of disruptive digital and social media technologies to the fears and moral panic around the use of SNS in general and children's or practitioners' use of SNSs in particular. However, such divergent reactions to the novelty and transformative power of technology are neither new nor supported by evidence. Indeed, often the moral panic and fears about technology and change are the projection of individual and collective anxieties and lack of familiarity with digital and social media technologies. A lack of critical perspective can lead to misinformed and unhelpful claims such as 'social media should not or cannot be taught', or that it is 'common sense', and other similar views. This simplistic thinking and these reductionist ideas are at best misinformed and unhelpful, and fail to appreciate the intricacies and significant differences between the online and offline environments, and the liminal (that is simultaneously online and offline) nature of human subjectivity and lived experience.

As changes in technology create new opportunities, they also generate new risks and ethical challenges. Indeed, technology has an impact on and transforms every aspect and notion in people's lives including the very meaning of childhood, parenting, friendships, relationships, education, work, play, leisure, privacy, identity, equality and the very notion of humanness. In previous chapters we used the 10 C's psycho-socio-ecological model as a model for holistic assessment and safeguarding, and applied this model in analysing and unpacking various practice case examples and their different dimensions and challenges. In this concluding chapter we briefly highlight examples of some of the salient trends in technology, and some of their applications and implications for safeguarding children and young people.

Evolution of the web

The evolution of the web is one of the most important trends impacting human life and experience. However, most conversations about social media and the web tend to refer to Web 2.0 when Web 3.0 is already here, and the development of Web 4.0 is well under way. Changes in web technologies have significant and far-reaching implications for services and safeguarding; Table 11.1 presents some of the differences between Web 1.0, Web 2.0 and Web 3.0. However, the evolution of the web already extends beyond Web 3.0, so let us briefly consider the evolution of the web, from Web 1.0 to 5.0.

Web 1.0 was the web of content and documents, and as a one-way read-only web it was information-focused and built around home pages and content accumulation and ownership. Its data and content were mainly text and pictures organised in directories while its user engagement was counted and evaluated based on page views. Britannica Online was an example of Web 1.0.

Web 2.0 is the web of communication and people, or the social web, and with mostly two-way read-write capabilities, it is interactive and community-focused. Built around blogs, Wikis, SNSs and mashups, its user focus is around sharing content and content circulation rather than only accumulation, while its content and data are user-generated organised based on tagging and hashtags. A web of widgets, videos, and live streaming, Web 2.0 is interactive and social. Examples of Web 2.0 are SNSs and Wikipedia.

Web 3.0 is the web of context and data, and is focused on the individual and personalisation. Have you had the experience of Googling something and having Google suggest an alternative search word or question? And have you noticed how, at times, Google seems to have the right answer even if you ask the wrong question? Google uses hundreds of different specialised software including artificial intelligence (AI) systems to come up with its search results. Google search is an example of Web 3.0 or semantic web. Web 3.0 is built around Life Streams and offers contextual content and its data organisation is built around user behaviour and evaluated based on user engagement. Web 3.0 is also known as the 'Internet of Things', as it offers the possibility of connecting all devices. With Web 3.0 everything from your cooker, to your coffee maker, toaster, light bulb, car keys, phones and computers and other gadgets will have microchips, sensors and an IP address and will stream data to services that can improve over time by using that data. This will render such devices more responsive and allow us to interact with them through touch or voice command. It also allows central and remote control of each gadget or service. These capabilities will transform health and social care as they enable more sophisticated and effective e-interventions and e-care.

Web 4.0 is the web of thoughts, AI and direct brain link, and is still in the making but should be with us in the next decade. Web 4.0 is the intelligent web that offers read-write-execution concurrency (that means systems will be able to recognise stimuli, gather the relevant data to make an informed decision, decide an appropriate response or course of action, and then execute that decision), and interfaces and interacts with its user in multiple ways including through natural language (normal speaking). It makes extensive use of AI and natural language and information about the user to receive, process and execute, often predictively, and in this sense it is much like an intelligent, live, personal assistant. This will lead to the automation of most processes including many caring, supporting and safeguarding tasks and responsibilities. It will also result in significant displacement of jobs that will affect many individuals and families. Virtual assistants such as Alexa, Cortana, Google Now and Siri are examples of Web 4.0 apps. In future these apps will be able to do everything from managing diaries and organising schedules to responding to emails, booking restaurants, events and travel, making business plans and providing business support, answering questions and offering information and decision support; such systems can also offer active listening and serve as a loyal companion. Robots and apps can also help children with their development or serve as their personal assistant and protect them; they can also support and assist parents/adults including those who experience Alzheimer's, dementia or other challenges. In the future, apps and specialised technologies will also help practitioners in carrying out assessments and developing effective safeguarding plans, and supporting, guiding and supervising practitioners and more.

Table 11.1: Evolution and impact of Web 1.0, Web 2.0, Web 3.0 and Web 4.0

Web evolution	Web 1.0	Web 2.0	Web 3.0	Web 4.0
Use of data	Mainly read-only	Widely read-write	Portable and personal	AI and personal assistants
The main focus of postings	Information focus	Community focus	Person and data focus	Read-write-execute concurrency
Known as	Web of content	Web of communication	Web of context	Web of thoughts and direct brain link
Organisational perspective	Home page	Blogs, wikis, SNS, mashups	Life stream / waves	AI automation
Change in web content	Owning content	Sharing content	Contextualising content	Merging of content and application
Software focus	One-way communication	Interactive web of sharing	Smart apps	intelligent & cognitive capabilities
Interface with users	Web forms	Web apps	Smart apps	AI and human-oid interface
Organisation of data	Directories	Tagging and hashtag	User behaviour	Behavioural profiles and thought maps.
Measure of activity	Page views	Cost per click	User engagement	Thought sharing and connecting with
Example of software	Britannica Online	Wikipedia	The Semantic Web	Alexa, Cortana, Google Now, Siri
Impact on privacy	Limited non-interactive data mostly private until shared	Postings are 'social' and interactive that can be made private	Surveillance culture and virtual absence of privacy, technology registers every action, consumption, location and behaviour.	Profiling users' behaviour, personality, digital body language including actions and lack of action, mood, etc
Impact on identity	Identity understood as mostly offline	Liminal (online and offline) narratives and identity	Multiple data points online and offline that create detailed user profiles *	Predictive capability to assess and interact based on person's needs, thoughts, emotions and behaviour

Web evolution	Web 1.0	Web 2.0	Web 3.0	Web 4.0
Impact on behaviour and thinking	Increasing reliance on digital in everyday life	The Web is an integral part of people's lives and identity	Smart devices and wearables extend individual control and capabilities	Use of androids and robotics; cybernetics enable use and absorption of technoogy as extension of human body
Impact on children	Relatively limited impact on childhood and children	Increasing and widespread use of tech and emergence of cyborg childhood	Children are born digital and raised social, increasing use of tech in childcare	Technology and AI guide parenting, use of robotics for surrogate parenting
Impact on young people	Relatively limited impact	Changing communication and transformation of identity, relationships and social capital	Indispensible for young people's learning, development, identity and digital citizenship	Virtual and global are refocused on physical and local in productive ways
Impact on parenting	Little use of web in parenting	Increasingly challenged by technology and its impact on children and childhood	Use of apps to assist parenting, including ability for surveillance to monitor and block children's activity	Use of intelligent and predictive technology to support and facilitate parenting and surrogate parenting
Impact on local government	New channel for non-interactive information sharing	Interactive information sharing, crowd sourcing and collective decision making	Co-production of practice and e-governance and public behavioural modification	Collective governance, advanced behavioural management
Impact on health and social care	Increased use of email and other private channels for interprofessional working and information sharing	Use of online communities, support groups, online therapy and interactive communication	Use of wearables and assistive technology for e-support, e-meetings, e-interventions and co-production of services	Predictive and intelligent, person-centred and person-led support and intervention

Web evolution	Web 1.0	Web 2.0	Web 3.0	Web 4.0
Impact on safeguarding practice	Increased use of email and other private channels for interprofessional working and information sharing	New safeguarding risks and opportunities, digital safeguarding and need for holistic safeguarding	Integrated safeguarding and innovative use of data points and apps, e-support and e-interventions	Predictive safeguarding, use of machine learning to identify and remove abusive content and behaviour

Web 5.0 is the web of emotions and is expected to be the open-link intelligent and emotional web that uses neurotechnology to perceive and interact with human emotions including changes in facial expression and so on. An example is www.wefeelfine.org, which maps the emotions of people (with headphones, users will interact with content that interacts with their emotions or changes in facial recognition). Especially designed avatars and apps are already helping people who experience emotional or mental health difficulties better manage their feelings and difficult experiences. In the future these may be used to provide a personalised, contextual and emotionally appropriate interface. Hence, your phone or television or wearable devices and others will recognise your mood and will be able to react in supportive and soothing ways, alleviating everyday stress or mental health distress.

These changes offer new possibilities and ways of integrating the web into our lives; however, they also entail significant transformation of boundaries, behaviours and extend our consciousness and sense of self. This is the essence of cyborg identity with the inseparable and seamless merging of human and machine into an extended idea of humanness. This merging of human and machine occurs on multiple levels and goes beyond physical (bionics). Indeed, some of the most powerful, transformative, and disruptive impacts of social media technologies transcend the physical and are non-physical, for example, for many people the answer to many questions is just a 'Google' away, which means Google search is weaved into our everyday thinking and living, not to mention services such as Alexa, Cortana, Google Now or Siri. In effect, these technologies are an extension of human thinking and consciousness, and represent distributed cognition. This means that our thinking about and understanding of safeguarding are also influenced, extended and transformed by these technologies. For example, similar to parental control software that is used to block access to harmful or age-inappropriate websites for children, AI assistants will be able to provide much more dynamic and sophisticated supervision and protection for children which may mitigate many of current safeguarding challenges such as sexting, online grooming for child sexual abuse or radicalisation.

Digital and biotechnological convergence

One of the most important impacts and continuing trends in social technologies is the increasing digital and technological convergence between content, context, contact, connection and behaviour. These changes will result in continued shifts in boundaries with their ethical and practical implications for the definition of professional roles, boundaries and the safeguarding of data and privacy. The increasing data sharing, behavioural analysis, user profiling and other ways of learning and understanding the user will dominate access to services and will result in substantial transformation of the very notion of privacy, and with digital devices becoming our virtual and individual assistants, there will be little if anything about anyone that will not be available to Google, Facebook, Microsoft or other major platforms or providers of online services. This is a significant change as access to most services, including basic services, will require sharing of detailed personal and behavioural data which results in continued dilution of individual privacy and its increasing displacement and replacement by new forms and notions of privacy and trust. Hence, we need a much more proactive and creative notion of privacy, confidentiality, trust and professionalism as well as their correlates and derivatives.

Furthermore, digital convergence and the transformation of boundaries poses new and immediate challenges for safeguarding practice. For example, technology enables parents of adopted or looked after children to be able to retrace and contact their children online and often in an unsupervised manner. Indeed, as acknowledged by Justice McFarlane (2017, p 17) '… the erosion of the hitherto impermeable seal around the adoptive placement created by social media' requires a new approach and mindset and remains one of the most urgent and important challenges for adoption and fostering services.

Social networking sites and apps

Continued changes in SNSs and social media will lead to different and new forms of engagement, sociality, friendship and co-production. For example, the *Wall Street Journal* (Mims, 2017) reports that 'generation Z' (those born between the mid-1990s and early 2000) prefer 'live chilling' to 'hanging out' in person. Apps such as Houseparty allow live chat for up to eight users per chatroom, and if more people join the chat, just like a real party, it will just spill over to a second room. To get the chat going, when a Houseparty user logs on to the app and starts a chat, the other users connected to them get a push, and soon enough join the chat. Young people use the app for a variety of purposes, from discussing class projects or collaboratively doing their homework, to just 'hanging out' and chatting with friends.

However, SNSs can also be used in damaging ways. For example, the spread of false news and 'fake news' websites and the manipulative use of SNSs combined with behavioural data analytics allow micro-targeting and influencing of audiences, and such tactics can be coordinated to produce large-scale shifts in opinion or behaviour; by supplanting informed-choice with dis-informed- or misinformed-choice, these developments undermine the foundations of democracy. These developments are encapsulated in the *Oxford Dictionary*'s Word of the Year for 2016, 'post-truth', an adjective defined as 'relating to or denoting circumstances in which objective facts are less influential in shaping public opinion than appeals to emotion and personal belief'. Such manipulations of information and SNSs combined with marketing techniques have been used to hide individuals, organisations and governments' inadequacies, and to promote division, discrimination and exclusionary policies that will result in increasing inequality and marginalisation. This highlights the need for greater digital knowledge, skills and capabilities and the art of curation.

Privacy rights and trade-offs

SNSs and digital and social media technologies and apps offer a myriad of information, services and possibilities. However, content posted on SNSs remain a part of the SNS data even if deleted and no longer visible online. Furthermore, face recognition software can tag and connect images with the person's online behaviour, interactions, posts and usage patterns. This generates a detailed personal and behavioural profile and history of the individual that can then be used to provide them with a personalised experience. As mentioned in Chapter 6 there are no free apps; instead accessing and using apps and online services is a trade-off between what they offer and an individual's information and privacy. It is advisable that practitioners and young people check the list of apps, SNSs and websites on their phones, and consider how often they use a given app or SNS and whether any services they receive from an app are worth the data and privacy that they give up and share with that app, SNS, website or company.

An example of such a privacy trade-off and its challenges is the landmark case of the 18-year-old Austrian woman who sued her parents for posting what she argued were embarrassing photos of her on Facebook without her consent. She noted that since 2009, her parents had posted about 500 photos of her on Facebook, including photos of potty training and changing her nappies. Her parents continued to share these photos with their 700 online friends despite her repeated requests for them to remove the photos. Her father argued that, "It's a nice family album that's been well received by our Facebook friends", and that he had the right to publish the photos because he took them.

Although this is a landmark case it is not unique. Indeed, foreseeing, such an ethical dilemma, the French authorities have warned parents that under that country's privacy legislation parents could face up to a year in prison and a fine of €45,000 (£35,000) if convicted of posting/sharing intimate details of the private lives of others – including their own children – without their consent. This means breaching children's rights to privacy can lead to future complications and legal liabilities for parents. These challenges have led to the idea that children should have the right to request for removal of their photos from the web (*The Telegraph*, 28 July 2015) and that SNS companies should remind their users about their responsibility and liabilities when posting images of others, especially children. We should mention that an European Union Court of Justice rulingbased on the European Union's 1995 Data Protection Directive, grants the right to be forgotten to all individuals who are resident in the European Union (for details see EU Court of Justice, 13 May 2014).

The main challenge and the heart of the dilemma in relation to digital and social media technologies is that our technological abilities to reproduce, manage, manipulate and bundle/remix images and data are rapidly changing and far outpace our capability to examine and understand their implications or to agree about how that ability should be used; this creates a cultural and ethical gap and a significant and evolving challenge for all concerned.

Wearable technology

In the same manner that mobile technologies have changed our habits and behaviour and today offer an infinite range of services and opportunities as well as risks and challenges, wearable technology will offer seamless support and services, and will lead to further merging of humans and technology, reshaping and redefining everyday life and the very meaning of life and death and humanness. Offering new cures and support systems, new possibilities and hopes as well as new challenges, wearable technologies will have an impact on both the services and the people who access services, and transform social work and safeguarding practice. For example, in February 2017 eSight announced the release of its new headset that utilises a combination of liquid lens, optical prisms and high-resolution display to enhance legally blind people's ability to see. While this implies that children with visual impairment may benefit from such technologies, it also raises the question as to whether such technologies would be supported by public funding and made available to all children based on need or whether such solutions would become another source of inequality in society.

Wearables can also help safeguard and support children in numerous other ways, for example, they can help autistic children to avoid emotional or stimulation overload. Periods of stimulation overload are unique to each person and the inexperience and challenges of childhood can make such experiences particularly difficult for autistic children. New wearable devices such as reveal (a wearable band) can monitor various bodily data such as heart rate, temperature and sweat levels to predictively report increase in anxiety and stress levels that may lead to a situation of emotional or stimulation overload (*Forbes*, 14 June 2016). Reveal is an example of how electrodermal and autonomic nervous system activity (this is the nervous system that acts unconsciously and regulates many of the body function) can be monitored to preventively support children and young people who experience emotional overload or sensitivities.

Digital and social technologies in health

Digital and social technologies have had a significant impact in healthcare. For example, AI, 3D printing, robotics, big data, combined with life sciences have led to significant advances in new genetics, medical imaging, bio-engineering and other developments, and are bringing about a host of transformations across industries and services. For example, in 2015, the US Food and Drug Administration (FDA) approved the first 3D-printed prescription drug. With the increasing refinement of the material used in 3D printing, it can now produce medical and surgical instruments including devices to be implanted in patients. This will have a transformative impact in healthcare by delivering such instruments and devices based on demand and flexibly, rapidly and cheaply to any destination, from remote communities to the space shuttle. A Gartner study predicts that by 2019, 3D printing will be a central tool for about one-third of surgical procedures involving prosthetic and implanted devices, and about 10 per cent of people in the developed world will be living with 3D-printed items on or in their bodies.

Virtual and augmented reality

Increasing use of virtual and augmented reality will influence self-expression, communication and our sense of self and relationships, and will transform health and social care practice and services. Augmented reality is in use from online/video games such as in Pokémon (see Chapter 4) to SNSs such as Snapchat (see the example of Snapstreak in Chapter 1); and as we described in Chapter 4, movement-based games such as Pokémon or Wii are transforming the nature of gaming. Online/video games, simulation and teaching/training systems and surgical procedures make use of augmented and virtual reality. For example, virtual reality is used to facilitate and accelerate physical therapy and rehabilitation, learning new skills and behavioural change for children and adults in a safer, more accessible and convenient manner, while stereoscopic systems generate a 3D visual representation of a section of the body to facilitate intricate neurosurgeries and retinal micro-surgery. These technologies combined with robotics will enable professionals, including doctors, to carry out e-interventions including remote operations or remote drug administration (where pre-established doses of drug are implanted with a chip under patient's skin and the doctor is able to release the drug into the body via remote signal) and so on.

Robots and artificial intelligence

In Japan, from hotels (*The Guardian*, 16 July 2015) to banks (*The Guardian*, 4 February 2015) are using humanoid (human-like) robots for a variety of tasks, and it is expected that the 2020 Olympics in Japan will make extensive use of robotics for assisting tourists and visitors to the country. Furthermore, in the future, robots may become children's companions or be used to look after them (*The Guardian*, 29 September 2016). AI is perhaps the most significant technological development of all times, with its rapidly expanding use. From scientific problem-solving, to playing games to complex decision-making systems in business, from vehicle navigation systems to space exploration, from call centres to customer service and relationship management systems, and from personal companions to employee evaluation and selection, AI systems are providing individuals and companies with an increasing number of information and services. For example, predictive analysis and machine learning are being used in different industries including medicine to more accurately interpret patients' data, while robots can be used from factories to homes to carry out routine as well as specialised tasks. A 'CBS 60 minute' programme suggested that AI could identify evidence-based therapies for 30 per cent of cancer patients that were not identified by their oncologists; in this sense the AI system outperformed the specialist doctors. In future these systems may be used in assessments to identify risks or develop holistic safeguarding plans. Autonomous self-driving cars are another example of the application of these technologies, and will eventually offer mobility to people who, either due to age or other challenges, are unable to drive and are dependent on others for their mobility; for example, such cars can be used to take children to school, community events or medical appointments, and so on when their parents are unable to do so. AI is also being used in combination with image recognition technology to help detect indecent images of children online.

Notwithstanding its great positive potential, one of the most urgent social care and social policy challenges created by AI is its potential for displacement of human labour at all levels and across all sectors; The World Bank's (2016) study indicates that 57% of jobs across Organization for Economic Cooperation and Development (OECD) nations are vulnerable to replacement within the next 20 years. We have seen how the use of machinery in farms transformed farming and resulted in the industrialisation of farming, or how robots in factories replaced millions of blue-collar workers. Although those effects were limited to specific sectors of economy and allowed transition of workers from one industry to another – for example from farming to manufacturing – the impact of AI is much greater and runs simultaneously across all sectors of the economy and society, leaving workers with no alternative employment. Such a dramatic change requires a new conception of work and an innovative system of retribution that values human contribution in a different and more creative manner, in order to avoid a catastrophic social division and paralysis. Therefore, while AI offers the greatest potential transformation of industry, economy and society, it also entails the greatest risk and challenge for ensuring that developments in technology and their disruptive effects do not become exclusionary, resulting in greater social inequity and inequality.

Examples of some SmartGlass applications in practice

Google, ODG, Snap, Sony, Vuzix and others are examples of SmartGlass technology that offer a range of possibilities and can potentially serve as a virtual assistant, providing vast contextual information, support and services. Benefits of SmartGlass applications include the following:

- *Team work:* SmartGlass enables virtual presence and supports team working. For example, in a home visit, practitioners may need the input of another professional (for example, the health worker, psychologist or other professionals). With SmartGlass, these professionals can livestream into the home visit to provide the necessary support or contribute towards decision-making and to meet the needs of people who access services in a more timely and holistic manner. This can lead to new services and new ways of working with greater quality and efficiency; however, this may also result in reduction of face-to-face support and contact.
- *Overcoming language barriers:* Smart technologies can provide simultaneous translation and help practitioners overcome language barriers. This can enhance practitioners' rapport and understanding of people's needs and preferences.
- *Empowerment and better selection of services:* Smart technologies can also offer a range of information and support that enhance autonomy and informed decision-making on the part of people who access services. These can vary from information about people's rights to services to offering comparison of alternative services including the pros and cons and qualitative ratings associated with each. This enables informed decision-making based on one's own preference.
- *Monitoring and support:* SmartGlass can also enable people to make informed choices and to develop and maintain healthy habits with information about food labels, nutritional values and whether a given food is compatible with one's dietary needs or any health conditions. It can also provide health tips, recipes and step-by-step how-to guides, or serve as a personal health or fitness tracker to monitor one's activities and support people to maintain their preferred health or dietary objectives. It can deliver medication and medical information or health warnings,

give advice on personal safety and help people with visual, auditory and physical disabilities (for example, eSight).

- *e-Interventions and enhancing care:* With people's consent, SmartGlass and smart technologies can monitor (for example, people's heart rate, blood pressure or any other relevant information) and share relevant information with professionals or others who support children or adults. This enables timely support and intervention. Furthermore, it also allows e-interventions by enabling professionals to intervene remotely either to resolve a given situation or to support the person (for example, in emergencies) until the arrival of appropriate professionals or support staff. Furthermore, the possibilities for enhanced communication and virtual visits mean people can reach practitioners (for example, for a virtual visit between two scheduled home visits) or for virtual visits to or by their families and friends. This means hospitalisation or changing home will not result in isolation and loss of contact with family and friends. Such services can enhance care for children and adults.
- *Safeguarding children and young people:* SmartGlass and smart technologies can help safeguard children and young people. For example, these technologies can alert parents when children need their attention or support.

On the negative side, smart technologies can be used, and are being used by parents, carers and schools, both overtly and covertly, as a means of surveillance and to locate children or monitor their activities(Leaton and Phippen, 2017). Indeed, there is wide range of surveillance software that is marketed under the umbrella of safeguarding children and young people including:

- *Filtering and access control software:* these kinds of software enable parents/carers or organisations to restrict access to the internet and web content with either blocking specific online websites (URLs) or blocking any online content that contains specific words (for example, pornography). However, such software can easily result in excessive and oppressive blocking of web content. For example, blocking phrases such as 'sexual violence' can block many websites that present sexual violence or sexually violent images; however, it will also block content from websites that discuss or offer advice about sexual violence.

- *Location tracking and control:* enables parents/carers to track the location of the phone/device or to receive an alert when the phone/device is in proximity of or in a given area.
- *Monitoring and interception software:* such software allows tracking and monitoring of SMS and email messages and other communications; these systems either log all such activities or deliver a copy of the message or communication to the parent/carer. Parents/carers can combine this monitoring system with filtering capability based on a word list, to receive alerts every time their child uses a word from that list; for example, inappropriate words or profanities.
- *Remote control of devices:* this enables parents/carers to remotely disable the device or a given functionality on the device (for example block all calls). This technology can help block a lost phone as well as blocking children's phones as a punishment.

These devices have given rise to a culture of surveillance among parents, carers and at times schools (Leaton and Phippen, 2017). Limitations, and at times the futility, of such systems aside, there are a number of significant concerns with such systems:

- Children can often circumvent such software and its restrictions;
- The use of such software can undermine the child's integrity, self-esteem, identity and human rights;
- Such systems fail to recognise the dynamic and contextual nature of risks and protective factors and can lull parents/carers into a false sense of security;
- Most importantly, such systems undermine the two most important pillars of effective safeguarding of children and young people, namely: an informed, effective and engaged guardianship and supervision, and a strong bond and trusting relationship between the child and their guardian (parents, carers or professionals).

As we have seen throughout this book, every new technology that affects the way we process information, communicate, think, behave or relate to others also poses new risks and ethical challenges. Therefore, smart technologies generate new risks and raise important questions about authenticity, privacy, boundaries and personal and professional identities and relationships.

If you are interested in the use of technology in practice or in services, we provide case studies, numerous examples and detailed discussion and examination of the impact of social technologies in health and social care practice and services in our upcoming book, *Using social technology in health and social care provision: Strategies for implementation and good practice* (Megele and Buzzi, 2018e).

Social work and its mission

Safeguarding lies at the heart of social work, and social work is a relationship-based and embodied practice that operates at the sharp end of society's fears, anxieties and traumas, and in an in-between space straddling and bridging people's private and public lives, personal and professional domains, and subjectivities and objective statuses (Megele, 2015). Therefore, the impact of technology and the transformations of communications, relationships, communities, societies and cultures have significant implications for social work, social care and safeguarding professions and professionals. In an increasingly digital society, where digital and social media technologies are inextricably embedded and weaved into the lives, experiences and identities of children and young people, digital knowledge and skills, access to digital and social media resources, and digital citizenship are integral part of, and play a significant role in, children and young people's healthy growth and development and future life opportunities and outcomes. Indeed, these should be part of every child's digital rights. Therefore, it is essential that social workers and safeguarding practitioners have a nuanced and sophisticated understanding of online risks, needs, rights, protective factors and resilience and their ramifications over time, and are able to ensure holistic assessments and safeguarding of children and young people.

This book and the 10 C's psycho-socio-ecological model is the fruit of the authors' years of experience, work and research, and we hope it will support and equip social work, social care and safeguarding practitioners with a holistic, structured and analytical approach to assessments and safeguarding of children and young people.

This book is part of a trilogy of books namely:

1. *Safeguarding Children and Young People Online*;
2. *Safeguarding Adults Online*;
3. *Safeguarding Mental Health Service Users Online*.

As we have noted earlier, given the fluidity and ease of accessibility of digital and social media technologies, repressive and restrictive approaches to safeguarding can lead to false compliance and covert behaviour and should be used only as a last resort. It is only through appropriate education, open conversation and positive engagement and support that children and young people can be empowered and enabled to develop their own developmentally and contextually appropriate understanding and understandable code of ethics, appreciation and solution for safeguarding challenges, and resilient responses to possible risks of harm while leveraging the positive potential and online opportunities of the cyworld to enhance their digital citizenship.

Just a few decades ago the popular conception was that children were incapable of expressing their views, and even scholars such as Anna Freud thought that due to their insufficient ego, small children and infants could not mourn. Reflecting back, just a few decades ago, teachers smoked in classrooms; children received physical punishment for missing homework; and at best, their views were considered irrelevant and hence, practitioners did not seek children's views. As unthinkable as these may seem today, it was unthinkable back then to imagine today's appreciation of childhood and children's identity or to consider listening to children's voices and preferences, much less to co-produce safeguarding plans with children. These are significant changes and reflect society's ability to grow and adapt and learn to think about and value children and childhood in less adult-centric manner. By the same token, today's digital and social media technologies offer disruptive opportunities and challenges that are impacting every phase of our lived experience and transforming our notions of human activity and relationships and this may be discomforting on various levels. However, reflecting on childhood and technology, it is evident that most of twenty first century children live better and safer lives than their parents and enjoy better health, education and social care than their parents and have a level of understanding and sophistication that far exceeds their preceding generations. Notwithstanding these positive developments, there seems to be much greater concerns about their safeguarding among their parents and professionals. This is perhaps attributable to the significant sophistication and increased complexity of our cultures, societies, lives and experience.

The rapid changes in technology do not allow society to digest its impact and this creates uncertainty and complexity that is often the source of anxiety for parents and practitioners alike. However, it is important to remember that children and young people are not naïve or passive consumers of technology. To the contrary, research indicates that they have the capacity to develop their own code of behaviour that is relevant to and understandable by themselves and their peers (Leaton Gray and Phippen, 2017; Livingstone, 2012). Although such norms of behaviour may not always be sufficient or may not consider the full repercussions of a given action, they are accepted and understandable to young people. Therefore, what is needed is a developmentally-appropriate dialogue to engage young people and to create mutual understanding, support and guidance to assist them in their developmental journey of becoming increasingly autonomous social actors.

It is essential that parents and practitioners recognise the complexity of technologies, society and social relationships and their associated uncertainty and that they are able to contain their anxiety, bear the uncertainty and defend complexity to avoid simplistic solutions to the nuanced and complex challenges in society. Technological solutions and innovations are the source of enormous good in society; however, an over reliance on technology to resolve what are fundamentally social and humane challenges would only lead to an increasing culture of surveillance that undermines the very humanity and relationships we are trying to protect.

Perhaps the most significant impact of digital and social media technologies is the change in mindset and in our ways of seeing, sensing, relating and being. In our observational studies, we have seen children lead the way in this area, everyday examples of which include children swiping a television screen to change the television channel or swiping a bunch of mail and wondering why the envelopes do not open. Such behaviours are reflective of the new ways in which they think about and relate to objects and their environment and offer us a window into their mind and the shape of things come; after all it is today's children that will shape tomorrow's technology, society and practice. At this juncture, the direction of travel is irreversible and the speed of change ever augmenting; therefore, it is incumbent on parents and practitioners to develop a reflective and critical understanding of these developments and their associated risks and opportunities if we are to remain relevant and able to safeguard children and young people both online and offline. It is only through a critical appreciation of technology that we can have any hope of maintaining its ethical relevance and maximise its unbounded potential to serve humanity.

Notwithstanding their positive potential, changes in technology exceed our ability to process their impact, understand their implications and agree about their use and this poses a significant and increasing cultural and ethical gap as a result of which technology is today driving society and defining humanity rather than other way around. Hence, it is urgent that policy makers, employers, practitioners, people who access services and others, collectively pause for reflection to consider the impact of new technologies in everyday lives, remembering that only when technologies are able to support and promote human life and humane values, and are used to reduce the gap between the political leaders and the richest and most powerful vis-à-vis the most vulnerable in our societies can we argue that technology is once again at the service of society and humanity and not vice versa (Megele and Buzzi, 2018e).

Figure 4.1: Play and online/video games: mapping risks, protective factors and resilience using the 10 C's psycho-socio-ecological model

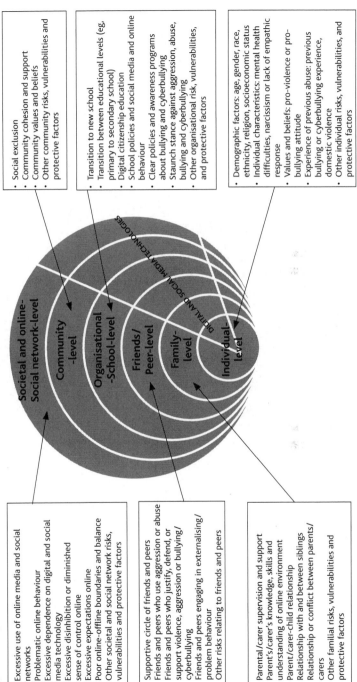

- Social exclusion
- Community cohesion and support
- Community values and beliefs
- Other community risks, vulnerabilities and protective factors

- Transition to new school
- Transition between educational levels (eg, primary to secondary school)
- Digital citizenship education
- School policies and social media and online behaviour
- Clear policies and awareness programs about bullying and cyberbullying
- Staunch stance against aggression, abuse, bullying and cyberbullying
- Other organisational risk, vulnerabilities, and protective factors

- Demographic factors: age, gender, race, ethnicity, religion, socioeconomic status
- Individual characteristics: mental health difficulties, narcissism or lack of empathic response
- Values and beliefs: pro-violence or pro-bullying attitude
- Experience of previous abuse: previous bullying or cyberbullying experience, domestic violence
- Other individual risks, vulnerabilities, and protective factors

Societal and online-Social network-level
Community-level
Organisational-School-level
Friends/Peer-level
Family-level
Individual-level
DIGITAL AND SOCIAL MEDIA TECHNOLOGIES

- Excessive use of online media and social networks
- Problematic online behaviour
- Excessive dependence on digital and social media technology
- Excessive disinhibition or diminished sense of control online
- Excessive expectations online
- Poor online–offline boundaries and balance
- Other societal and social network risks, vulnerabilities and protective factors

- Supportive circle of friends and peers
- Friends and peers who use aggression or abuse
- Friends and peers who justify, defend, or support violence, aggression or bullying/cyberbullying
- Friends and peers engaging in externalising/problem behaviour
- Other risks relating to friends and peers

- Parental/carer supervision and support
- Parent's/carer's knowledge, skills and understanding of online environment
- Parent/carer-child relationship
- Relationship with and between siblings
- Relationship or conflict between parents/carers
- Other familial risks, vulnerabilities and protective factors

Figure 5.1: 'Internet addiction': mapping risks, protective factors and resilience using the 10 C's psycho-socio-ecological model

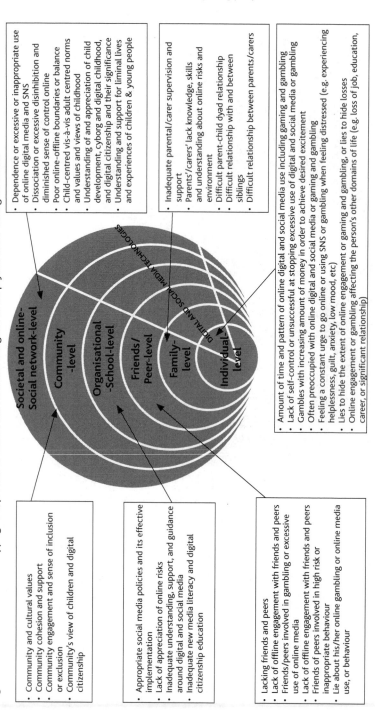

Figure 6.1: Sexting: mapping risks, protective factors and resilience using the 10 C's psycho-socio-ecological framework

- What is the spread & social impact of the problem?
- What is the impact of the problem on relationships, social network and social capital of the victim?
- What actions are needed to restore balance, mitigate risks, and safeguard their digital citizenship and healthy growth and development?
- How to remove inappropriate or abusive online content from SNS and mitigate their effect?
- Is there need for more education and understanding of child development, cyborg and digital childhood, and digital citizenship and their significance?
- Is there understanding and support for liminal lives and experiences of children and young people?

- Do significant others and the home environment adopt and maintain a healthy digital-vs-physical balance?
- Inadequate parental/carer supervision and support?
- Parents'/carers' lack knowledge, skills and understanding about online risks and environment?
- Difficult parent-child dyad relationship?
- Difficult relationship with and between siblings?
- Difficult relationship between parents/carers?

- Are there any concerns with regards to excessive or problematic use of online media?
- Are there any concerns about amount of time or pattern of digital or SNS use and its associated risks?
- Is there lack of balance in online-offline engagement?
- Is there confidentiality and personal disclosure risk? What personal information is available online?
- What are the impact and possible ramifications of this information (over time and in relation to other risks)?
- How to remove or mitigate confidentiality risk and the risks relating to available personal information online?
- Is there need for further support and education?
- Are there any conduct risks?
- What are the identity and developmental considerations?
- Other vulnerabilities (abuse, child in need, child protection, looked after, disability, learning difficulties, dysmorphic body image, psychological difficulties, police or criminal record)?

- Community and cultural values
- Community cohesion and support
- Community engagement and Sense of inclusion or exclusion
- Community's view of children and digital citizenship

- Does the school have appropriate social media policies? Are they implementation and upheld?
- Does school offer adequate and appropriate support & guidance?
- Does the school educate pupils about new media literacies and digital citizenship?
- How can the school setting and environment been affected?
- How can the school cooperate and support the victim?

- Does the person have a healthy circle of friends and peers?
- Are there any risks associated with the person's peer group or friends?
- Are there any abusive peer relationships? How does peer pressure impact the situation?
- Does the person have offline friendships and peer relationships?
- Do friends and peers encourage risk or inappropriate behaviour, aggression, abuse or violence?
- How does the friends' and peers' impact on social capital & identity?

257

Figure 7.1: Online grooming and child sexual abuse: mapping risks, protective factors and resilience using the 10 C's psycho-socio-ecological model

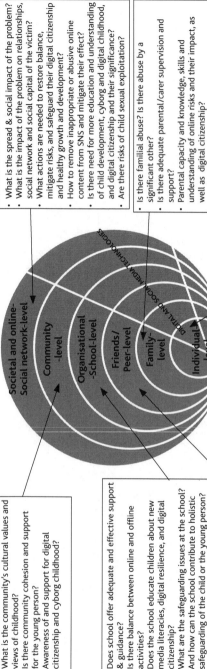

Figure 8.1: Cyberbullying: mapping risks, protective factors and resilience, using the 10 C's psycho-socio-ecological model

Societal and online-Social network-level
- Social exclusion or exclusion
- Community cohesion and support
- Community values and beliefs
- Other community-level risks & protective factors

- Supportive circle of peers/friends
- Friends/peers who bully or cyberbully others
- Friends/peers who justify, defend, or support violence or bullying or cyberbullying
- Friends/peers engaging in externalising or other problem behaviours
- Strong in-group and out-group dynamics

- Individual characteristics: narcissism or lack of empathic response, "outsider personality", etc.
- Values and beliefs: e.g. pro-violence or pro-bullying attitude
- Increased and excessive amount of, or problematic behaviour or pattern of, online media and SNS use
- Signs of behavioural addiction to, or Excessive dependence on online media and SNS
- Excessive disinhibition, dissociation, or diminished sense of control online
- Race, gender, ethnicity or religion, other demographics
- Experience of previous online or offline aggression or abuse (e.g. bullying or domestic violence, etc)
- Individual vulnerabilities: e.g. disability, learning difficulty, emotional or mental health challenges

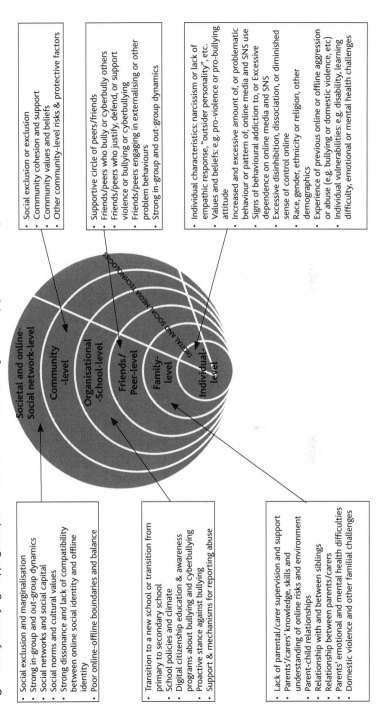

- Social exclusion and marginalisation
- Strong in-group and out-group dynamics
- Social networks and social capital
- Social norms and cultural values
- Strong dissonance and lack of compatibility between online social identity and offline identity
- Poor online-offline boundaries and balance

- Transition to a new school or transition from primary to secondary school
- School policies and climate
- Digital citizenship education & awareness programs about bullying and cyberbullying
- Proactive stance against bullying
- Support & mechanisms for reporting abuse

- Lack of parental/carer supervision and support
- Parents'/carers' knowledge, skills and understanding of online risks and environment
- Parent-child relationships
- Relationship with and between siblings
- Relationship between parents/carers
- Parents' emotional and mental health difficulties
- Domestic violence and other familial challenges

Figure 9.1: Cybercrime, online offending and youth justice: mapping risks, protective factors and resilience using the 10 C's psycho-socio-ecological model

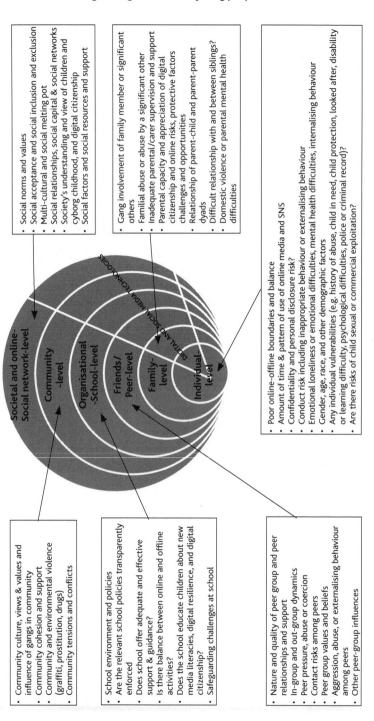

- Social norms and values
- Social acceptance and social inclusion and exclusion
- Multi-cultural and social melting pot
- Social relationships, social capital & social networks
- Society's understanding and view of children and cyborg childhood, and digital citizenship
- Social factors and social resources and support

- Gang involvement of family member or significant others
- Familial abuse or abuse by a significant other
- Inadequate parental/carer supervision and support
- Parental capacity and appreciation of digital citizenship and online risks, protective factors challenges and opportunities
- Relationship of parent-child and parent-parent dyads
- Difficult relationship with and between siblings?
- Domestic violence or parental mental health difficulties

- Poor online-offline boundaries and balance
- Amount of time & pattern of use of online media and SNS
- Confidentiality and personal disclosure risk?
- Conduct risk including inappropriate behaviour or externalising behaviour
- Emotional loneliness or emotional difficulties, mental health difficulties, internalising behaviour
- Gender, age, race, and other demographic factors
- Any individual vulnerabilities (e.g. history of abuse, child in need, child protection, looked after, disability or learning difficulty, psychological difficulties, police or criminal record)?
- Are there risks of child sexual or commercial exploitation?

- Community culture, views & values and influence of gangs in community
- Community cohesion and support
- Community and environmental violence (graffiti, prostitution, drugs)
- Community tensions and conflicts

- School environment and policies
- Are the relevant school policies transparently enforced
- Does school offer adequate and effective support & guidance?
- Is there balance between online and offline activities?
- Does the school educate children about new media literacies, digital resilience, and digital citizenship?
- Safeguarding challenges at school

- Nature and quality of peer group and peer relationships and support
- In-group and out-group dynamics
- Peer pressure, abuse or coercion
- Contact risks among peers
- Peer group values and beliefs
- Aggression, abuse, or externalising behaviour among peers
- Other peer-group influences

Figure 10.1: Radicalisation: mapping risks, protective factors and resilience using the 10 C's psycho-socio-ecological model

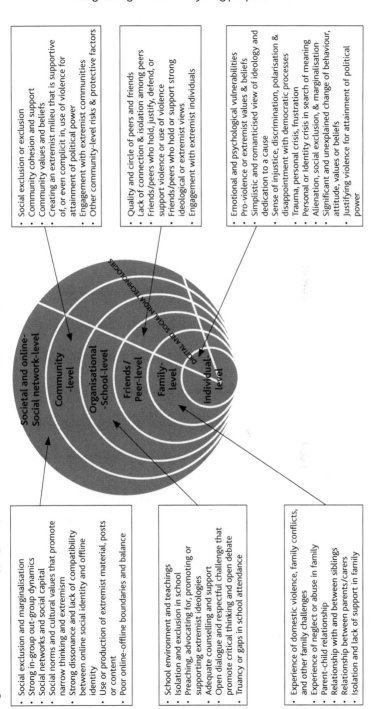

References

Aboujaoude, E., Koran, L.M., Gamel, N., Large, M.D. and Serpe, R.T. (2006) 'Potential markers for problematic internet use: A telephone survey of 2,513 adults on the CNS spectrum', *The Journal of Neuropsychiatric Medicine*, vol 11, no 10, pp 750-5.

Adler, A. (1992 [1931]) *What life could mean to you* (translated by C. Brett), Oxford: Oneworld.

Akers, R. (1990) 'Rational choice, deterrence, and social learning theories in criminology: The path not taken', *Journal of Criminal Law and Criminology*, vol 88, pp 653-76.

Albert, D. and Steinberg, L. (2011) 'Judgement and decision making in adolescence', *Journal of Research on Adolescence*, vol 21, pp 211-24.

Anderson, C.A. (2004) 'An update on the effects of playing violent video games', *Journal of Adolescence*, vol 27, pp 113-22.

Anderson, C.A. and Bushman, B.J. (2001) 'Effects of violent video games on aggressive behavior, aggressive cognition, aggressive affect, physiological arousal and prosocial behavior: A meta-analysis', *Psychological Science*, vol 12, pp 353-9.

Anderson, C.A. and Bushman, B.J. (2002) 'Human aggression', *Annual Review of Psychology*, vol 52, pp 27-51.

Anderson, C.A. and Murphy, C. (2003) 'Violent video games and aggressive behavior in young women', *Aggressive Behavior*, vol 29, pp 423-9.

Anderson, C.A., Gentile, D. and Dill, K. (2012) 'Prosocial, antisocial, and other effects of recreational video games', in D. Singer and J. Singer (eds) *Handbook of children and the media* (2nd edn) (pp 249-72), Thousand Oaks, CA: Sage.

Anderson, C.A., Shibuya, A., Ihori, N., Swing, E.L., Bushman, B.J., Sakamoto, A. and Saleem, M. (2010) 'Violent video game effects on aggression, empathy, and prosocial behavior in eastern and western countries: A meta-analytic review', *Psychological Bulletin*, vol 136, pp 151-73 (http://dx.doi.org/10.1037/a0018251).

Anderson, K.J. (2001) 'Internet use among college students: An exploratory study', *Journal of American College Health*, vol 50, no 1, pp 21-6.

APA (American Psychiatric Association) (2000) *Diagnostic and Statistical Manual of Mental Disorders* (4th edn), Arlington, VA: American Psychiatric Publishing.

APA (2013) *Diagnostic and Statistical Manual of Mental Disorders* (5th edn), Arlington, VA: American Psychiatric Publishing.

Arendt, H. (2000). The Portable Hannah Arendt. Ed. Peter Baehr. New York: Penguin.

Arora, C. (1996) Defining bullying: Towards a clearer general understanding and more effective intervention strategies. *School Psychology International*, 17, 317–329.

Atlas, R.S. and Pepler, D.J. (1998) 'Observations of bullying in the classroom', *The Journal of Educational Research*, vol 92, pp 86-99.

Bakhtin, M. (1984) *Problems of Dostoevsky's poetics* (edited and translated by Caryl Emerson), Minneapolis, MN: University of Minnesota Press.

Bandura, A. (1973) *Aggression: A social learning analysis*, Englewood Cliffs, NJ: Prentice Hall.

Bandura, A. (1979) 'The social learning perspective: Mechanisms of aggression', in H. Toch (ed) *Psychology of crime and criminal justice*, New York: Holt, Rinehart & Winston, pp 198–236.

Bandura, A. (1983) 'Psychological mechanisms of aggression', in R.G. Geen and E. Donnerstein (eds) *Aggression: Theoretical and empirical reviews* (pp 1-40), New York: Academic Press.

Bauman, S. (2008) 'Effects of gender, grade, and acculturation on overt and relational victimisation and depression in Mexican American elementary school students', *Journal of Early Adolescence*, vol 28, pp 528-54.

Baumeister, R. and Vohs, K. (2004) 'Sexual economics: Sex as female resource for social exchange in heterosexual interactions', *Personality and Social Psychology Review*, vol 8, pp 339-63.

BBC News (2003) 'Student jailed after child sex sting', 11 August (http://news.bbc.co.uk/1/hi/uk/3141803.stm).

Beard, K. and Wolf, E. (2001) 'Modification in the proposed diagnostic criteria for internet addiction', *CyberPsychology & Behavior*, vol 4, no 3, pp 377-83.

Berkowitz, T., Schaeffer, M.W. and Maloney, E.A. (2015) 'Math at home adds up to achievement in school', *Science*, vol 350, no 6257, pp 196-8.

Bhui, K., Warfa, N. and Jones, E. (2014) 'Is violent radicalisation associated with poverty, migration, poor self-reported health and common mental disorders?', *PLoS ONE*, vol 9, no 3.

Bielik, P. (2012) 'Integration and adaptation of motivational factors into software systems', in M. Barla, M. Šimko and J. Tvarozek (eds) *Personalized web – Science, technologies and engineering*, Proceedings of the 11th Spring 2012 PeWe Workshop, Modra, Piesok, Slovakia, 1 April (pp 31-2), Bratislava: Nakladateľstvo.

Billieux, J., Thorens, G., Khazaal, Y., Zullino, D., Achab, S. and van der Linden, M. (2015) 'Problematic involvement in online games: A cluster analytic approach', *Computers in Human Behavior*, vol 43, pp 242-50.

Black, T. (2009) 'We want to determine the world, not be determined', *Spiked Magazine*, 31 July (www.spiked-online.com/review_of_books/article/7214#.WJ-bu_mLTIU).

boyd, d. (2008) 'Taken out of context: American teen sociality in network publics', PhD thesis (www.danah.org/papers/TakenOutOfContext.pdf).

Bronfenbrenner, U. (1977) 'Toward an experimental ecology of human development', *American Psychologist*, vol 32, pp 513-31.

Bronfenbrenner, U. (1979) *The ecology of human development: Experiments by nature and design*, Cambridge, MA: Harvard University Press.

Browne, A. and Finkelhor, D. (1986) 'Impact of child sexual abuse: A review of the research', *Psychological Bulletin*, vol 99, pp 66-77.

Butler, J. (1988) 'Performative acts and gender constitution: An essay in phenomenology and feminist theory', *Theatre Journal*, vol 40, no 4, pp 519-31.

Butler, J. (1993) *Bodies that matter: On the discursive limits of sex*, New York: Routledge.

Buzzi, P. and Megele, C. (2011a) 'Cyber-communities and motherhood online – A reflection on transnational adoption', in M. Moravec (ed) *Motherhood online*, Cambridge: Cambridge Scholars Publishing, pp 232–41.

Buzzi, P. and Megele, C. (2011b) 'Reflections on the 21st century migrant: Impact of social networking and hyper-reality on the lived experience of global migration', in M. German and P. Banerjee (eds) *Migration, technology and transculturation: A global perspective*, St Charles, MO: The Center for International and Global Studies, Lindenwood University Press.

Calamaro, C., Mason, T. and Ratcliffe, S. (2009) 'Adolescents living the 24/7 lifestyle: Effects of caffeine and technology on sleep duration and daytime functioning', *Pediatrics*, vol 123, no 6, pp 1005-10.

Carskadon, M. (1999) 'When worlds collide: Adolescent need for sleep versus societal demands', *Phi Delta Kappan*, vol 80, pp 348-53.

Cash, S.J., Thelwall, M., Peck, S.N., Ferrell, J. and Bridge, J.A. (2013) 'Adolescent suicide statement on MySpace', *Cyberpsychology, Behavior and Social Networking*, vol 16, no 3, pp 166-74.

Chalfen, R. (2009) '"It's only a picture": Sexting, "smutty" snapshots and felony charges', *Visual Studies*, vol 24, no 3, pp 258-68.

Chief Coroner of England & Wales (2014) *Regulation 28: Prevention of future deaths report* (www.judiciary.gov.uk/wp-content/uploads/2014/08/Wilson-2014-0047.pdf).

Children's Commissioner (2017) *Growing up digital: A report of the Growing Up Digital Taskforce*, January (www.childrenscommissioner.gov.uk/sites/default/files/publications/Growing%20Up%20Digital%20Taskforce%20Report%20January%202017_0.pdf).

Children's Commissioner (November 2015) Protecting children from harm: A critical assessment of child sexual abuse in the family network in England and priorites for action. Available at: https://www.childrenscommissioner.gov.uk/sites/default/files/publications/Protecting%20children%20from%20harm%20-%20full%20report.pdf

Cilluffo, F., Saathoff, G., Lane, J., Cardash, S., Whitehead, A. and Magarik, J. (2007) *NETworked radicalization: A counter-strategy*, Washington, DC: George Washington.

Clark, A. (2003) *Natural-born cyborgs*, New York: Oxford University Press.

CNN (2017) 'How child predator was caught by tiny clue in photo he posted online (Game changing technology identifies child abusers)', 23 February (http://edition.cnn.com/2016/04/21/us/project-vic-child-abuse/index.html).

CNN (13 May 2017) Massive cyberattack targeting 99 countries causes sweeping havoc. Available at: money.cnn.com/2017/05/12/technology/ransomware-attack-nsa-microsoft/index.html

Cohen, A. (1955) *Delinquent boys*, New York: Free Press.

Cohen, L. and Felson, M. (1979) 'Social change and crime rate trends: A routine activity approach', *American Sociological Review*, vol 44, no 4, pp 588-608.

Coldwell, W. (2013) 'Why death is not the end of your social media life', *The Guardian*, 18 February (www.theguardian.com/media/shortcuts/2013/feb/18/death-social-media-liveson-deadsocial).

Cole, H. and Griffiths, M.D. (2007) 'Social interactions in massive multiplayer online role-playing gamers', *CyberPsychology & Behavior*, vol 10, pp 575-83. doi:10.1089/cpb.2007.9988.

Connell, R.W. (1987) *Gender and power*, Stanford, CA: Stanford University Press.

Conte, J.R., Wolf, S. and Smith, T. (1989) 'What sexual offenders tell us about prevention strategies', *Child Abuse & Neglect*, vol 13, no 2, pp 293-301. doi:10.1016/0145-2134(89)90016-1.

Corbett, A.T., Koedinger, K.R. and Hadley, V.V. (2001) 'Cognitive tutors: From the research classroom to all classrooms', in P.S. Goodman (ed) *Technology enhanced learning* (pp 235-63), Mahwah, NJ: Lawrence Erlbaum.

Corby, B. (1998) *Managing child sexual abuse cases*, London: Jessica Kingsley Publishers.

CPS (Crown Prosecution Service) (2013) *Guidelines on prosecuting cases involving communications sent via social media* (www.cps.gov.uk/legal/a_to_c/communications_sent_via_social_media/).

Dahl, R.E. (2004) 'Adolescent brain development: A period of vulnerabilities and opportunities', in R.E. Dahl and L.P. Spear (eds) *Adolescent brain development: Vulnerabilities and opportunities, Annals of New York Academy of Sciences*, vol 102, pp 1-22.

Dake, J., Price, A., Maziarz, L. and Ward, B. (2012) 'Prevalence and correlates of sexting behavior in adolescents', *American Journal of Sexuality Education*, vol 7, no 1, pp 1-15.

Daly, S. and Gerwehr, S. (2006) 'Al-Qaida: Terrorist selection and recruitment', in D. Kamien (ed) *McGraw-Hill homeland security handbook* (pp 73-89), New York: McGraw-Hill.

Davis, R.A. (2001) 'A cognitive-behavioral model of pathological internet use', *Computers in Human Behavior*, vol 17, pp 187-95.

DCMS (Department for Culture, Media and Sport) (2016) *Child safety online: A practical guide for providers of social media and interactive services*, London: DCMS (www.gov.uk/government/publications/child-safety-online-a-practical-guide-for-providers-of-social-media-and-interactive-services).

DCSF (Department for Children, Schools and Families) and Home Office (2010) *Safeguarding children and young people who may be affected by gang activity*, London: The Stationery Office (www.gov.uk/government/uploads/system/uploads/attachment_data/file/288804/Safeguarding_children_Gang_activity.pdf).

Department of Education (2014) *Guidance: Preventing Bullying. Guidance for schools on preventing and responding to bullying.* Available at: https://www.gov.uk/government/publications/preventing-and-tackling-bullying

Department for Education (2016) Keeping children safe in education. Available at: https://www.gov.uk/government/publications/keeping-children-safe-in-education--2

Downey, G., Dumit, J. and Williams, S. (1995) 'Cyborg anthropology', *Cultural Anthropology*, vol 10, no 2, pp 264-9.

Downs, C. (2008) 'The Facebook phenomenon: Social networking and gambling', Paper presented at the Gambling and Social Responsibility Forum Conference, Manchester Metropolitan University, Manchester, September.

Draucker, C.B. and Martsolf, D.S. (2010) 'The role of electronic communication technology in adolescent dating violence', *Journal of Child and Adolescent Psychiatric Nursing*, vol 23, pp 133-42.

Dreikurs, R. and Soltz, V. (1992 [1964]) *Children: The challenge*, New York: Hawthorn Books.

Duggan, M. (2014) *Online harassment*, Washington, DC: Pew Research Center.

Dunphy, R. (2000) *Sexual politics*, Edinburgh: Edinburgh University Press.

Eadington, W.R. (2004) 'The future of online gambling in the United States and elsewhere', *Journal of Public Policy & Marketing*, vol 23, pp 214-19.

Elliott, M., Browne, K. and Kilcoyne, J. (1995) 'Child sexual abuse prevention: What offenders tell us', *Child Abuse and Neglect*, vol 19, no 5, pp 579-94. doi:10.1016/0145-2134(95)00017-3.

EU Court of Justice (13 May 2014) Factsheet on the "Right to be Forgotten" ruling (C131/12). Available at: ec.europa.eu/justice/data-protection/files/factsheets/factsheet_data_protection_en.pdf

European Online Grooming Project (2012) *Final report* (http://natcen.ac.uk/media/22514/european-online-grooming-projectfinalreport.pdf).

Ferguson, C.J., Rueda, S., Cruz, A., Ferguson, D., Fritz, S. and Smith, S. (2008) 'Violent video games and aggression: Causal relationship or by product of family violence and intrinsic violence motivation?', *Criminal Justice and Behavior*, vol 35, pp 311-32.

Finkelhor, D., Mitchell, K.J. and Wolak, J. (2000) *Online victimisation: A report on the nation's youth* (www.unh.edu/ccrc/pdf/Victimization_Online_Survey.pdf).

Fischer, P., Kastenmüller, A. and Greitemeyer, T. (2010) 'Media violence and the self: The impact of personalized gaming characters in aggressive video games on aggressive behavior', *Journal of Experimental Social Psychology*, vol 46, pp 192-5. http://dx.doi.org/10.1016/j.jesp.2009.06.010.

Forbes (14 June 2016) Wearable For Kids With Autism May Help Predict, Avoid Meltdowns. Available at: https://www.forbes.com/sites/janetwburns/2016/06/14/wearable-for-kids-with-autism-may-help-predict-avoid-meltdowns/#2e57b4a14a8a

Forrest, D.K., McHale, I. and Parke, J. (2009) 'Appendix 5: Full report of statistical regression analysis', in Ipsos MORI, *British survey of children, the National Lottery and gambling 2008-09: Report of a quantitative survey*, London: National Lottery Commission.

Foucault, M. (1976/1998) *The will to knowledge: The history of sexuality*, Volume 1, London: Penguin Books.

Foucault, M. (1979) *Discipline and punish: The birth of the prison*, New York: Vintage Books.

Foucault, M. (1980) *Power/knowledge: Selected interviews and other writings 1972-1977*, New York: Pantheon Books.

Gentile, D.A. (2009) 'Pathological video game use among youth 8 to 18: A national study', *Psychological Science*, vol 20, pp 594-602.

Gentile, D.A. and Gentile, J.R. (2008) 'Violent video games as exemplary teachers: A conceptual analysis', *Journal of Youth and Adolescence*, vol 9, pp 127-41.

Gentile, D.A., Lynch, P.J., Linder, J.R. and Walsh, D.A. (2004) 'The effects of violent video game habits on adolescent aggressive attitudes and behaviors', *Journal of Adolescence*, vol 27, pp 5-22.

Giddens, A. (1991) *Modernity and self-identity: Self and society in the late modern age*, Cambridge: Polity Press.

Gilroy, P. (1997) 'Diaspora and the detours of identity', in K. Woodward (ed) *Identity and difference* (pp 299-343), London: Sage.

Goffman, E. (1956) 'Embarrassment and social organization', *American Journal of Sociology*, vol 62, pp 264-71.

Goffman, E. (1959) *The presentation of self in everyday life*, Garden City, NY: Doubleday.

Goffman, E. (1967) *Interaction ritual*, New York: Anchor.

Gomez, A.M. (2011) 'Testing the cycle of violence hypothesis: Child abuse and adolescent dating violence as predictors of intimate partner violence in young adulthood', *Youth & Society*, vol 43, pp 171–92.

Graham, J., Liyazheng, M.S. and Gonzalez, C. (2006) 'A cognitive approach to game usability and design: Mental model development in novice real-time strategy gamers', *CyberPsychology & Behavior*, vol 9, pp 361-6. doi:10.1089/cpb.2006.9.361.

Griffiths, M.D. (1995) 'Technological addictions', *Clinical Psychology Forum*, vol 76, pp 14-19.

Griffiths, M.D. (1996a) 'Internet addiction: An issue for clinical psychology?', *Clinical Psychology Forum*, vol 97, pp 32-6.

Griffiths, M.D. (1996b) 'Gambling on the internet: A brief note', *Journal of Gambling Studies*, vol 12, pp 471-4.

Griffiths, M.D. (1998) 'Internet addiction: Does it really exist?', in J. Gackenbach (ed) *Psychology and the internet: Intrapersonal, interpersonal and transpersonal applications* (pp 61-75), New York: Academic Press.

Griffiths, M.D. (2000) 'Internet addiction – Time to be taken seriously?', *Addiction Research*, vol 8, pp 413-18.

Griffiths, M.D. (2013) 'Adolescent gambling via social networking sites: A brief overview', *Education and Health*, vol 31, no 4, pp 84-7.

Griffiths, M.D. and Barnes, A. (2008) 'Internet gambling: An online empirical study among student gamblers', *International Journal of Mental Health and Addiction*, vol 6, pp 194-204.

Griffiths, M.D. and Parke, J. (2010) 'Adolescent gambling on the internet: A review', *International Journal of Adolescent Medicine and Health*, vol 22, no 1, pp 58-75.

Griffiths, M.D., Wardle, H., Orford, J., Sproston, K. and Erens, B. (2009) 'Sociodemographic correlates of internet gambling: Findings from the 2007 British Gambling Prevalence Survey', *CyberPsychology & Behavior*, vol 12, no 2, pp 199-202.

Gumbiner, J. (2003) *Adolescent assessment*, Hoboken, NJ: John Wiley & Sons.

Hall, S. (1996) 'Who needs identity?', in S. Hall and P. Du Gay (eds) *Questions of cultural identity* (pp 1-17), London: Sage.

Happ, C., Melzer, A. and Steffgen, G. (2013) 'Superman vs BAD man? The effects of empathy and game character in violent video games', *Cyberpsychology, Behavior and Social Networking*, vol 16, pp 774-8. http://dx.doi .org/10.1089/cyber.2012.0695.

Haraway, D. (1991) *Simians, cyborgs and women: The reinvention of nature*, New York: Routledge.

Hawkes, R. (4 May 2016) Whatever happened to Star Wars Kid? The sad but inspiring story behind of of the first victims of cyberbullying. The Telegraph. Available at: http://www.telegraph.co.uk/films/2016/05/04/whatever-happened-to-star-wars-kid-the-true-story-behind-one-of/

Heath-Kelly, C. (2012) 'Counter-terrorism and the counterfactual: Producing the "radicalisation" discourse and the UK PREVENT Strategy', *The British Journal of Politics & International Relations*, vol 15, no 3, pp 394-415.

Heidegger, M. (1962) *Being and time* (translated by J. Macquarrie and E. Robinson), New York: Harper & Row.

Heidegger, M. (1977) *Basic writings* (edited and translated by D. Farrell Krell), New York: HarperCollins Publishers.

Hinduja, S. and Patchin, J.W. (2013) 'Social influences on cyberbullying behaviours among middle and high school students', *Journal of Youth and Adolescence*, vol 42, pp 711-22.

Hiniker, A., Suh, H., Cao, S. and Kientz, J.A. (2016) 'Screen time tantrums: How families manage screen media experiences for toddlers and preschoolers', in *CHI'16. Proceedings of the 2016 CHI Conference on Human Factors in Computing Systems* (pp 648-60), 7-12 May, New York (http://dl.acm.org/citation.cfm?doid=2858036.2858278).

Hirsh-Pasek, K., Zosh, J.M., Golinkoff, R.M., Gray, J.H., Robb, M.B. and Kaufman, J. (2015) 'Putting education in "educational" apps: Lessons from the science of learning', *Psychological Science Public Interest*, vol 16, no 1, pp 3-34.

HM Government (2016) Revised Prevent Duty Guidance: for England and Wales. Available at: https://www.gov.uk/government/uploads/system/uploads/attachment_data/file/445977/3799_Revised_Prevent_Duty_Guidance__England_Wales_V2-Interactive.pdf

HM Government (2012) Channel: Vulnerability assessment framework. Available at: https://www.school-portal.co.uk/GroupDownloadFile.asp?GroupId=1247517&ResourceId=5068980

Home Office Task Force (2008) *Good practice guidance for the providers of social networking and other user interactive services 2008*, London: Home Office (www.manchesterscb.org.uk/docs/Home%20Office%20Task%20Force%20in%20CP%20on%20the%20Internet.pdf).

Horgan, J. (2008) 'From profiles to pathways and roots to routes: Perspectives from psychology on radicalization into terrorism', *The Annals of the American Academy of Political and Social Science*, vol 618, no 1, pp 80-94.

Huesmann, R. and Guerra, N. (1997) 'Children's normative beliefs about aggression and aggressive behavior', *Journal of Personality and Social Psychology*, vol 72, no 2, pp 408-19.

Huston, A.C. and Wright, J.C. (1994) 'Educating children with television: The forms of the medium', in D. Zillman, J. Bryant and A.C. Huston (eds) *Media, children, and the family: Social scientific, psychodynamic, and clinical perspectives* (pp 73-84), Hillsdale, NJ: Erlbaum.

Ipsos MORI (2016) *Young people and gambling 2016: A research study among 11–15 year olds in England and Wales*, Birmingham: Gambling Commission.

Jack, G. and Gill, O. (2003) *The missing side of the triangle: Assessing the importance of family and environmental factors in the lives of children*, Barkingside: Barnardo's.

Jack, S., Munn, C., Cheng, C. and MacMillan, H. (2006) *Child maltreatment in Canada: Overview paper*, Minister of Health. Available at: http://publications.gc.ca/Collection/HP10-10-2006E.pdf

Jacobsen, K. and Bauman, S. (2007) 'School counsellors' response to school bullying scenarios', *Professional School Counselling*, vol 11, pp 1-9.

Jenkins, H., Clinton, K., Purushotma, R., Robison, A. and Weigel, M. (2006) *Confronting the challenges of participatory culture: Media education for the 21st century*, Chicago, IL: MacArthur Foundation.

Jiang, J. (2009) 'Inside China's fight against internet addiction', *Time Magazine*, 28 January (http://content.time.com/time/world/article/0,8599,1874380,00.html).

Jones, S.E., Manstead, A.S.R. and Livingstone, A.G. (2011) 'Ganging up or sticking together? Group processes and children's responses to text-message bullying', *British Journal of Psychology*, vol 102, pp 71-96.

King, D.L. and Delfabbro, P. (2016) 'Adolescents' perceptions of parental influences on commercial and simulated gambling activities', *International Gambling Studies*, vol 16, no 3, pp 424-41. http://dx.doi.org/10.1080/14459795.2016.1220611.

King, D.L., Delfabbro, P. and Griffiths, M.D. (2010) 'The convergence of gambling and digital media: Implications for gambling in young people', *Journal of Gambling Studies*, vol 26, pp 175-87.

King, D.L., Delfabbro, P.H., Kaptsis, D. and Zwaans, T. (2014) 'Adolescent simulated gambling via digital and social media: An emerging problem', *Computers in Human Behaviour*, vol 31, pp 305-13.

King, D.L., Haagsma, M.C., Delfabbro, P.H., Gradisar, M.S. and Griffiths, M.D. (2013) 'Toward a consensus definition of pathological video-gaming: A systematic review of psychometric assessment tools', *Clinical Psychology Review*, vol 33, pp 331-42.

Kirwan, G. and Power, A. (2012) *The psychology of cybercrime: Concepts and principles*, Cambridge: Cambridge University Press.

Kolb, D.A. (1984) *Experiential learning: Experience as the source of learning and development*, Englewood Cliffs, NJ: Prentice Hall.

Kruglanski, A.W., Gelfand, M.J., Bélanger, J.J., Sheveland, A., Hetiarachchi, M. and Gunaratna, R. (2014) 'The psychology of radicalization and deradicalization: How significance quest impacts violent extremism', *Political Psychology*, vol 35, pp 69-93.

Laney, C., Heuer, F. and Reisberg, D. (2003) 'Thematically-induced arousal in naturally-occurring emotional memories', *Applied Cognitive Psychology*, vol 17, pp 995-1004. http://dx.doi.org/10.1002/acp.951.

Lanigan, R. L. (1992) The Human Science of Communicology: A Phenomenology of Discourse in Foucault and Merleau-Ponty. Pittsburgh: Duquesne University Press.

Lanning, K. (2010) *Child molesters: A behavioral analysis for professionals investigating the sexual exploitation of children* (5th edn), Alexandria, VA: National Center for Missing and Exploited Children (www.missingkids.com/en_US/publications/NC70.pdf).

Latané, B. and Darley, J.M. (1970) *The unresponsive bystander: Why doesn't he help?*, Englewood Cliffs, NJ: Prentice Hall.

Leaton Gray, S. and Phippen, A. (2017) Invisibly Blighted: The digital erosion of childhood. UCL IOE Press.

Leino, T., Torsheim, T., Blaszczynski, A., Griffiths, M., Mentzoni, R., Pallesen, S. and Molde, H. (2015) 'The relationship between structural game characteristics and gambling behavior: A population-level study', *Journal of Gambling Studies*, vol 31, pp 1297-315.

Lippman, J.R. and Campbell, S.W. (2014) 'Damned if you do, damned if you don't … if you're a girl: Relational and normative contexts of adolescent sexting in the United States', *Journal of Children and Media*, vol 8, no 4, pp 371-86.

Livingstone, S. and Haddon, L. (2009) 'Horizons: EU Kids Online', *Journal of Psychology*, vol 217, pp 233-9.

Livingstone, S., Bober, M. and Helsper, E.J. (2005) 'Active participation or just more information? Young people's take-up of opportunities to act and interact on the internet', *Information, Communication & Society*, vol 8, pp 287-314. http://dx.doi.org/10.1080/13691180500259103.

Livingstone, S., Haddon, L., Görzig, A. and Olafsson, K. (2011a) *Risks and safety on the internet. Perspective of European children. Full findings and policy implications from EU Kids Online survey of 9-16 year olds and their parents in 25 countries*, London: London School of Economics and Political Science (www.eukidsonline.net).

Livingstone, S., Haddon, L., Görzig, A. and Olafsson, K. (2011b) Risks and safety on the internet: the perspective of European children, *EU Kids Online*, London, UK (www.lse.ac.uk/media%40lse/research/EUKidsOnline/EU%20Kids%20II%20(2009-11)/EUKidsOnlineIIReports/D4FullFindings.pdf).

Livingstone S. (2012) Children, risk and safety on the internet: Research And Policy Challenges In Comparative Perspective. Bristol: Policy Press.

Lodge, J. and Frydenberg, E. (2005) 'The role of peer bystanders in school bullying: Positive steps toward promoting peaceful schools', *Theory Into Practice*, vol 44, pp 329-36.

Lorenz, K. (1963) *On aggression*, New York: Harcourt, Brace & World.

Lund, I. (2008) 'The population mean and the proportion of frequent gamblers: Is the theory of total consumption valid for gambling?', *Journal of Gambling Studies*, vol 24, pp 247-56.

Macleod, M. and Saraga, E. (1988) 'Challenging orthodoxy', *Feminist Review*, vol 28.

Mandel, D.R. (2008) 'Radicalization: What does it mean?', in T. Pick and A. Speckhard (eds) *Indigenous terrorism: Understanding and addressing the root causes of radicalization among groups with an immigrant heritage in Europe*, Amsterdam: IOS Press, pp 101–13.

Martin, D.C. (1995) 'The choices of identity', *Social Identities*, vol 1, no 1, pp 5-20.

Mason, K.L. (2008) 'Cyberbullying: A preliminary assessment for school personnel', *Psychology in the Schools*, vol 45, no 4, pp 323-48.

McFarlane, Lord Justice (2017) *Holding the risk: The balance between child protection and the right to family life*. Available at: https://www.judiciary.gov.uk/wp-content/uploads/2017/03/lecture-by-lj-mcfarlane-20160309.pdf

McLuhan, M. (1964) *Understanding media: The extensions of man*, Harmondsworth: Penguin Books.

Megele, C. (2014a) 'eABLE: Embedding social media in academic curriculum as a learning and assessment strategy to enhance students learning and e-professionalism', *Innovations in Education and Teaching International*, vol 52, no 4, pp 414-25.

Megele, C. (2014b) 'Theorizing Twitter chat', *Journal of Perspectives in Applied Academic Practice*, vol 2, no 2 (http://jpaap.napier.ac.uk/index.php/JPAAP/article/view/106/html).

Megele, C. (2015) *Psychosocial and relationship-based practice*, London: Critical Publishing.

Megele, C. and Buzzi, P. (2018a, forthcoming) 'ENABLE e-professionalism using a relational boundary scale', Peer reviewed article.

Megele, C. and Buzzi, P. (2018b, forthcoming) 'E-safeguarding children and young people: Classifying online risks and resilience from a systemic and child-centred perspective', Peer reviewed article.

Megele, C. and Buzzi, P. (2018c, forthcoming) *Learning through observation: A bio-psychosocial and developmental perspective*, Abingdon: Routledge.

Megele, C. and Buzzi, P. (2018d, forthcoming) *Parenting in a digital age*, e-book .

Megele, C. and Buzzi, P. (2018e, forthcoming) *Using social technologies in health and social care: Strategies for implementation and good practice*, London: Jessica Kingsley Publishers.

Megele, C. and Buzzi, P. (2018f, forthcoming) *Safeguarding adults online*, Bristol: Policy Press.

Mesch, G. and Talmud, I. (2010) *Wired youth: The social world of adolescence in the Information Age*, New York: Routledge.

Mims, C. (2017) 'For Generation Z, "live chilling" replaces hanging out in person', *Wall Street Journal*, 20 February (www.wsj.com/articles/for-generation-z-live-chilling-replaces-hanging-out-in-person-1487519134).

Minuchin, S. (1974) *Family and family therapy*, Cambridge, MA: Harvard University Press.

Mitchell, K.J., Finkelhor, D., Wolak, J. (2007). Youth Internet users at risk for the most serious online sexual solicitations. *American Journal of Preventive Medicine*, 32, 532–537.

Monks, C. and Smith, P.K. (2006) 'Definitions of "bullying": Age differences in understanding of the term, and the role of experience', *British Journal of Developmental Psychology*, vol 24, pp 801-21.

Mossberger, K., Tolbert, C.J. and McNeal, R.S. (2008) *Digital citizenship*, Cambridge, MA: The MIT Press.

Munro, E.R. (2011) *The protection of children online: A brief scoping review to identify vulnerable groups*, London: Childhood Wellbeing Research Centre, Thomas Coram Research Unit, Institute of Education.

Mynard, H., Joseph, S. and Alexander, J. (2000) 'Peer-victimisation and posttraumatic stress in adolescents', *Personality and Individual Differences*, vol 29, no 5, pp 815-21.

Nabi, R.L., Finnerty, K., Domschke, T. and Hull, S. (2006) 'Does misery love company? Exploring the therapeutic effects of TV viewing on regretted experiences', *Journal of Communication*, vol 56, pp 689-706.

Nansel, T., Overpeck, M., Pilla, R.S., Ruan, W.J., Simmons-Morton, B. and Schmidt, P. (2001) 'Bullying behaviors among US youth', *Journal of the American Medical Association*, vol 285, pp 2094-100.

National Gang Intelligence Center (2009) *National gang threat assessment*. Available at: https://rems.ed.gov/docs/FBI_NationalGangThreatAssessment2009.pdf

NBC News (28 April 2015) Teen Icon Bethany Mota's Inspiring Anti-Bullying Message. Available at: www.nbcnews.com/news/latino/teen-icon-bethany-motas-inspiring-anti-bullying-message-n349646

Nickerson, A., Aloe, A., Livingston, J. and Feeley, T.H. (2014) 'Measurement of the bystander intervention model for bullying and sexual harassment', *Journal of Adolescence*, vol 37, pp 391-400.

O'Connell, R. (2003) *Be somebody else but be yourself at all times: Degrees of identity deception in chatrooms*, Preston: University of Central Lancashire.

Ofcom (2015) *Children and parents: Media use and attitudes report* (www.ofcom.org.uk/__data/assets/pdf_file/0024/78513/childrens_parents_nov2015.pdf).

O'Leary, P., and Barber, J. (2008) 'Gender differences in silencing following childhood sexual abuse', *Journal of Child Sexual Abuse*, vol 17, no 2, pp 133–43.

Olson, C., Kutner, L. and Warner, D. (2008) 'The role of violent video game play in adolescent development: Boys' perspectives', *Journal of Adolescence Research*, vol 23, pp 55-75.

Olson, L.N., Daggs, J.L., Ellevold, B.L. and Rogers, T.K.K. (2007) 'Entrapping the innocent: Toward a theory of child sexual predators' luring communication', *Communication Theory*, vol 17, no 3, pp 231-51. doi:10.1111/ j.1468-2885.2007.00294.x.

Olweus, D. (1991) 'Bully/victim problems among schoolchildren: Basic facts and effects of a school based intervention program', in D. Pepler and K. Rubin (eds) *The development and treatment of childhood aggression* (pp 411-48), Hillsdale, NJ: Erlbaum.

Olweus, D. (1993) *Bullying at school: What we know and what we can do*, Oxford: Blackwell.

Olweus, D. (1999) 'Norway', in P.K. Smith, Y. Morita, J. Junger-Tas, D. Olweus, R. Catalano and P. Slee (eds) *The nature of school bullying: A cross-national perspective* (pp 28-48), London: Routledge,

O'Neill, J. (1989) The Communicative Body: Studies in Communicative Philosophy, Politics, and Sociology. Evanston: North Western University Press.

Pabian, S., Vandebosch, H., Poels, K., van Cleemput, K. and Bastiaensens, S. (2016) 'Exposure to cyberbullying as a bystander: An investigation of desensitization effects among early adolescents', *Computers in Human Behavior*, vol 62, pp 480-7.

Papachristos, A., Hureau, D. and Bragab, A. (2013) 'The corner and the crew: The influence of geography and social networks on gang violence', *American Sociological Review*, vol 78, no 3, pp 417-47.

Patchin, J. and Hinduja, S. (2006) 'Bullies move beyond the schoolyard: Preliminary look at cyberbullying', *Youth Violence and Juvenile Justice*, vol 4, no 2, pp 148-69.

Patton, D.U., Eschmann, R.D. and Butler, D.A. (2013) 'Internet banging: New trends in social media, gang violence, masculinity and hip hop', *Computers in Human Behavior*, vol 29, no 5, A54-A59.

Perren, S., Corcoran, L., Cowie, H., Dehue, F., Gracia, D.J., Guckin, C.M., Sevcikova, A., Tsatsou, P. and Vollink, T. (2012) *Coping with cyberbullying: A systematic literature review*, Final report of the COST IS Working Group 5, Zurich: University of Zurich.

Pew Research Center (2015) 'Gaming and gamers', 15 December (www.pewinternet.org/2015/12/15/gaming-and-gamers/).

Pratarelli, M.E. and Browne, B.L. (2002) 'Confirmatory factor analysis of internet use and addiction', *CyberPsychology & Behavior*, vol 5, no 1, pp 53-64.

Prensky, M. (2001) 'Digital natives, digital immigrants', *On the Horizon*, vol 9, pp 1-6.

Prevent (2015) *Prevent duty guidance*, HM Government. Available at: https://www.legislation.gov.uk/ukdsi/2015/9780111133309/pdfs/ukdsiod_9780111133309_en.pdf

Quayle, E., Jonsson, L. and Loof, L. (2012) *Online behaviour related to child sexual abuse: Interviews with affected young people*, Preliminary version, ROBERT Project (Risktaking Online Behaviour Empowerment Through Research and Training), European Union and Council of the Baltic Sea States.

RAN (Radicalisation Awareness Network) (2016) *The root causes of violent extremism*, Issue Paper, Radicalisation Awareness Network, European Commission.

Rice, E., Rhoades, H., Winetrobe, H., Sanchez, M., Montoya, J., Plant, A. and Kordic, T. (2012) 'Sexually explicit cell phone messaging associated with sexual risk among adolescents', *Pediatrics*, vol 130, no 4, pp 667-73.

Ricoeur, P. (1992) *Oneself as another* (translated from the French by Kathleen Blamey), Chicago, IL: University of Chicago Press.

Rigby, K. (2002) *New perspectives on bullying*, London: Jessica Kingsley Publishers.

Ringrose, J., Gill, R., Livingstone, S. and Harvey, L. (2012) *A qualitative study of children, young people and 'sexting': A report prepared for the NSPCC*, London: National Society for the Prevention of Cruelty to Children (NSPCC).

Rosser, I.C., Lynch, P.J., Cuddigy, L., Gentile, D.A., Klonsky, J. and Merrell, R. (2007) 'The impact of video games on training surgeons in the 21st century', *Archives of Surgery*, vol 142, pp 181-6.

Ruder, T.D., Hatch, G.M., Ampanozi, G., Thali, M.J. and Fischer, N. (2011) 'Suicide announcement on Facebook', *Crisis. The Journal of Crisis Intervention and Suicide Prevention*, vol 32, no 5, pp 280-2.

Rutter, M. (1987) 'Psychosocial resilience and protective mechanisms', *American Journal of Orthopsychiatry*, vol 57, pp 316-31.

Ryan, R., Rigby, C.S. and Przybylski, A. (2006) 'The motivational pull of video games: A self-determination theory approach', *Motivation and Emotion*, vol 30, pp 344-60.

Sageman, M. (2007) *Radicalization of global Islamist terrorists*, United States Senate Committee on Homeland Security and Government Affairs, 27 June (www.hsgac.senate.gov/download/062707sageman).

Salmivalli, C., Lagerspetz, K., Björkqvist, K., Österman, K. and Kaukiainen, A. (1996) 'Bullying as a group process: Participant roles and their relations to social status within the group', *Aggressive Behavior*, vol 22, pp 1-15. http://dx.doi.org/10.1002/(SICI)1098-2337(1996)22.

Sawicki, J. (1991) *Disciplining Foucault: Feminism, power, and the body*, New York: Routledge.

Schwarz, N. (2007) 'Attitude construction: Evaluation in context', *Social Cognition*, vol 25, pp 638-56. http://dx.doi.org/10.1521/soco.2007.25.5.638.

Selwyn, N. (2009) 'The digital native – Myth and reality', *Aslib Proceedings*, vol 61, pp 364-79.

Sexual Offences Act 2003, The National Archives (www.legislation.gov.uk/ukpga/2003/42/section/82).

Shapira, N., Goldsmith, T., Keck, P., Jr, Khosla, D. and McElroy, S. (2000) 'Psychiatric features of individuals with problematic internet use', *Journal of Affective Disorders*, vol 57, pp 267-72.

Sharif, I. and Sargent, J.D. (2006) 'Association between television, movie, and video game exposure and school performance', *Pediatrics*, vol 118, e1061-e1070.

Sherry, J. (2007) 'Violent video games and aggression: Why can't we find links?', in R. Preiss, B. Gayle, N. Burrell, M. Allen and J. Bryant (eds) *Mass media effects research: Advances through meta-analysis* (pp 231-48). Mahwah, NJ: Erlbaum.

Silver, K. and Karakurt, G. (2014) 'Therapy for childhood sexual abuse survivors using attachment and family systems theory orientations', *American Journal of Family Therapy*, vol 42, no 1, pp 79-91.

Skinner, B.F. (1953) *Science and human behavior*, New York: Macmillan.

Slate (2014) '*Looney Tunes* cartoons were more brutal than you may remember', 24 June (www.slate.com/blogs/browbeat/2014/06/24/looney_tunes_and_gun_violence_the_cartoons_had_a_lot_of_murder_and_suicide.html).

Smallbone, S., Marshall, M. and Wortley, R. (2008) *Preventing child sexual abuse: Evidence, policy and practice*, Cullompton: Willan.

Smart, C. (2000) 'Reconsidering the recent history of child sexual abuse, 1910-1960', *Journal of Social Policy*, vol 29, no 1, pp 55-71.

Smeaton, M. and Griffiths, M.D. (2004) 'Internet gambling and social responsibility: An exploratory study', *CyberPsychology & Behavior*, vol 7, pp 49-57.

Smith, E.R. and Semin, G.R. (2007) 'Situated social cognition', *Current Directions in Psychological Science*, vol 16, pp 132-5. http://dx.doi.org/ 10.1111/j.1467-8721.2007.00490.x.

Smith, P.K., Mahdavi, J., Carvalho, M., Fisher, S., Russell, S. and Tippett, N. (2008) 'Cyberbullying: Its nature and impact in secondary school pupils', *Journal of Child Psychology and Psychiatry*, vol 49, pp 376-85.

Staksrud, E. and Livingstone, S. (2009) 'Children and online risk: Powerless victims or resourceful participants?', *Information, Communication & Society*, vol 12, no 3, pp 364- 87.

Stanley, J. (2001) *Child abuse and the internet*, Melbourne, VIC: Australian Institute of Family Studies (https://aifs.gov.au/cfca/publications/child-abuse-and-internet).

Stanley, T. and Guru, S. (2015) 'Childhood radicalisation risk: An emerging practice issue', *Practice: Social Work in Action*, vol 27, no 5, pp 353-66.

Stith, S.M., Lui, T.L., Davies, C., Boykin, E.L., Alder, M.C., Harris, J.M. et al (2009) 'Risk factors in child maltreatment: A meta-analytic review of the literature', *Aggression and Violent Behavior*, vol 14, pp 13-29. http://dx.doi.org/10.1016/j.avb.2006.03.006.

Stockholm Declaration and Agenda for Action (1996) *First World Congress against commercial sexual exploitation of children*, Stockholm, Sweden.

Suler, J.R. (1999) 'To get what you need: Healthy and pathological internet use', *CyberPsychology & Behavior*, vol 2, pp 385-94.

Suler, J.R. (2004) 'The online disinhibition effect', *CyberPsychology & Behavior*, vol 7, no 3, pp 321-6.

Suseg, H., Skevik Grødem, A., Valset, K. and Mossige, S. (2008) *Seksuelle krenkelser via nettet – hvor stort er problemet?* [*Sexual harassment on the internet – How great is the problem?*], NOVA Rapport 16/2008, Oslo: Norsk institutt for forskning om oppvekst, velferd og aldring (NOVA) (www.nova.no/asset/3525/1/3525_1.pdf).

Taarnby, M. (2003) *Profiling Islamic suicide terrorists: A research report for the Danish Ministry of Justice*, Aarhus: University of Aarhus.

The Guardian (2016) '"This is awful": robot can keep children occupied for hours without supervision', 29 September. Available at: https://www.theguardian.com/technology/2016/sep/29/ipal-robot-childcare-robobusiness-san-jose

The Telegraph (2015) 'Parents discover children's Facebook photos on Russian paedophile website', 13 January. Available at: www.telegraph.co.uk/news/uknews/crime/11342175/Parents-discover-childrens-Facebook-photos-on-Russian-paedophile-website.html

Turkle, S. (1995) *Life on the screen: Identity in the age of the internet*, New York: Simon & Schuster.

Turner, V. (1979) *Process, performance and pilgrimage: A study in comparative symbology*, New Delhi: Concept.

Twemlow, S.W., Fonagy, P., Sacco, F.C., Otoole, M.E. and Vernberg, E. (2002) 'Premeditated mass shootings in schools: Threat assessment', *Journal of the American Academy of Child and Adolescent Psychiatry*, vol 41, no 4, pp 475-7.

Underwood, M.K. (2002) 'Sticks and stones and social exclusion: Aggression among girls and boys', in P.K. Smith and C.H. Hart (eds) *Blackwell handbook of childhood social development* (pp 533-48), Oxford: Blackwell.

University Homeland Security Policy Institute and University of Virginia Critical Incident Analysis Group (https://med.virginia.edu/ciag/).

Vagi, K.J., Olsen, E.O., Basile, K.C. and Vivolo-Kantor, A.M. (2015) 'Teen dating violence (physical and sexual) among US high school students: Findings from the 2013 National Youth Risk Behavior Survey', *JAMA Pediatrics*, vol 169, pp 474-82.

VanDeventer, S.S. (2002) 'Expert behavior in children's video game play', *Simulation & Gaming*, vol 33, pp 28-48. doi:10.1177/104 6878102033001002.

Van Duijenvoorde, A., Jansen, B., Visser, I. and Huizenga, H. (2010) 'Affective and cognitive decision-making in adolescents', *Developmental Neuropsychology*, vol 35, pp 539-54.

Victim Support (2007) *Hoodie or goodie? The link between violent victimisation and offending in young people.*

Vygotsky, L.S. (1978) 'Interaction between learning and development', in M. Cole, V.J. Steiner, S. Scribner and E. Souberman (eds) *Mind in society* (pp 79-91). Cambridge, MA: Harvard University Press.

Walther, J.B. (2007) 'Selective self-presentation in computer-mediated communication: Hyperpersonal dimensions of technology, language, and cognition', *Computers in Human Behavior*, vol 23, pp 2538-57.

Wartella, E. (2013) *Parenting in the age of digital technology*, Chicago, IL: Northwestern University Press.

Weithorn, L. and Campbell, S. (1982) 'The competency of children and adolescents to make informed treatment decisions', *Child Development*, vol 53, no 6, pp 1589-98.

Werner, N., Bumpus, M. and Rock, D. (2010) 'Involvement in internet aggression during early adolescence', *Journal of Youth and Adolescence*, vol 39, pp 607-19.

Whittaker, E. and Kowalski, R.M. (2015) 'Cyberbullying via social media', *Journal of School Violence*, vol 14, no 1, pp 11-29.

Winters, G. and Jeglic, E. (2016) 'Stages of sexual grooming: Recognizing potentially predatory behaviour of child molesters', *Deviant Behavior*, vol 38, no 6, pp 724-33. doi: 10.1080/01639625.2016.1197656.

Wolak, J., Finkelhor, D., Mitchell, K.J. and Ybarra, M.L. (2008) 'Online "predators" and their victims: Myths, realities and implications for prevention and treatment', *American Psychologist*, vol 63, pp 111-28.

World Bank (2016) Digital Divedends. World Bank Report, 102725. Available at: documents.worldbank.org/curated/en/896971468194972881/pdf/102725-PUB-Replacement-PUBLIC.pdf

Ybarra, M. and Mitchell, K. (2004) 'Youth engaging in online harassment: Associations with caregiver–child relationships, internet use, and personal characteristics', *Journal of Adolescence*, vol 27, pp 319-36.

YJB (Youth Justice Board) (2012) *Preventing religious radicalisation and violent extremism: A systematic review of the research evidence*, YJB for England and Wales (www.gov.uk/government/uploads/system/uploads/attachment_data/file/396030/preventing-violent-extremism-systematic-review.pdf).

Yoon, G. and Vargas, P.T. (2014) 'Know thy avatar: The unintended effect of virtual-self representation on behavior', *Psychological Science*, vol 25, pp 1043-5. http://dx.doi.org/10.1177/0956797613519271.

Yoon, J.S. and Kerber, K. (2003) 'Bullying: Elementary teachers' attitudes and intervention strategies', *Research in Education*, vol 69, pp 27-34.

Young, K. (1996) 'Psychology of computer use: XL. Addictive use of the internet: A case that breaks the stereotype', *Psychological Reports*, vol 79, pp 899-902.

Young, K. (1998) *Caught in the net*, New York: John Wiley.

Young, K. (1999) 'Internet addiction: Evaluation and treatment', *Student British Medical Journal*, vol 7, pp 351-2.

Zillman, D. (1988) 'Mood management through communication choices', *American Behavioral Scientist*, vol 31, pp 327-40.

Index

Note: Page numbers in *italics* refer to figures or tables.